DOING RESEARCH WITH REFUGEES

Issues and guidelines

Edited by Bogusia Temple and Rhetta Moran

First published in Great Britain in 2011 by

The Policy Press
University of Bristol
Fourth Floor
Beacon House
Queen's Road
Bristol BS8 1QU
UK

Tel +44 (0)117 331 4054
Fax +44 (0)117 331 4093
e-mail tpp-info@bristol.ac.uk
www.policypress.co.uk

North American office:
The Policy Press
c/o International Specialized Books Services (ISBS)
920 NE 58th Avenue, Suite 300
Portland, OR 97213-3786, USA
Tel +1 503 287 3093
Fax +1 503 280 8832
e-mail info@isbs.com

British Library Cataloguing in Publication Data
A catalogue record for this book is available from the British Library.

Library of Congress Cataloging-in-Publication Data
A catalog record for this book has been requested.

ISBN 978 1 84742 905 6 paperback

ISBN 978 1 86134 598 1 hardback

Cover design by Qube Design Associates, Bristol.
Front cover: image kindly supplied by www.thired-avenue.co.uk
Printed and bound in Great Britain by Marston Book Services, Oxford.

To everyone who has been, or considers themselves
to be, a refugee

Contents

List of figures and photographs

List of figures

List of photographs

Foreword

In what ways does research benefit from the involvement of refugees? Can research also be empowerment? These key questions are raised by this provocative collection of essays. Here is a book about refugee people, including those seeking asylum, as agents. Their participation in the research processes which inform the policies that shape their lives is seen as vital to the success both of the research and the ensuing social action.

The chapters in this book are the product of an initiative by RAPAR (Refugee and Asylum Seeker Participatory Action Research), which resulted in an ESRC Seminar Series. They are shot through with first-hand experience of the predicament of refugees. They demonstrate, through a series of case studies and theoretical contributions, that engagement with the methodological issue of giving 'voice' to refugees within the research process has benefits at various levels. It produces better research and it develops the skills and confidence of the refugees themselves.

These essays also show, sadly, that such empowerment is a threat to established ways of doing things. This is a pioneering collection that explores a new, and to some, disconcerting, direction in research. No one engaged in research with refugees can afford to ignore the questions it raises.

Nicholas Sagovsky
Canon Theologian at Westminster Abbey and Visiting Professor in
Theology and Public Life at Liverpool Hope University

Preface

The final stages of preparing this book for publication were completed against the backdrop of the bombings in London in July 2005 in an atmosphere of fear of difference, and an increase in racial harassment and abuse.

The media focus is on the extent to which people should be allowed to have different views and come from different backgrounds and still be entitled to be 'citizens'. Moreover, research interest in ethnicity continues to mushroom, with religion moving to centre stage. In the current climate it is more important than ever for researchers to be inclusive with whom they work. If we want to ensure that we do not, in effect, silence sections of society it is essential that we continue to have debates around the range of research approaches that can be applied and how views can be obtained in practice so that we can examine differences and similarities across groups of people.

The chapters in this book demonstrate the breadth and depth of research that is possible with refugee people seeking asylum. They show the benefits and challenges for policy developers and service providers when researchers, refugee people seeking asylum and practitioners discuss their different views.

Acknowledgements

The editors wish to thank all those who took part in the ESRC seminar series on which this book is based and particularly those contributors who wrote chapters for the book in their own time.

Notes on contributors

Rosalind Edwards is Professor in Social Policy and Director of the Families and Social Capital ESRC (Economic and Social Research Council) Research Group at London South Bank University. Her main expertise is in family policies and family lives, although she also has interests in methodology. Her recent publications include: *Children, home and school: Resistance, autonomy or connection?* (2002); *Analysing families: Morality and rationality in policy and practice* (with A. Carling and S. Duncan, 2002); *Making families: Moral tales of parenting and step-parenting* (with J.R. McCarthy and V. Gillies, 2002); *Caring and counting: The impact of mothers' employment on family relationships* (with T. Reynolds and C. Callender, 2003); and *Access to services with interpreters* (with C. Alexander and B. Temple, 2003).

Felicity Greenham SRN, HV cert, Dip PH & HP, MSc, has worked for 34 years within the NHS. This work has included developing policy and commissioning joint services in Merseyside, coordinating innovation approaches to HIV for the World Health Organization across 13 member cities, and latterly working within a Neighbourhood Renewal area to develop partnership approaches to the public health agenda and address health inequalities in Greater Manchester. Throughout her career, her work has been guided by the principle that service users should be central to both the operational and strategic planning and delivery of health and social care. In the past three years her doctoral studies have involved her researching self-management and collective efficacy at the Revans Institute, Salford University.

Jennifer Harris is Professor of Social Science at the University of Dundee, Scotland. Her research interests are the social model of disability and services for Deaf and disabled people in the UK. Her first book, *The cultural meaning of Deafness*, was published by Avebury Press (1995) and her second, *Deafness and the hearing*, by Venture Press (1997). She is an Editor of *Disability and Society* in which she has made contributions on housing issues for disabled people (1998, 1999), and Deaf people's access to services (2001). Current work includes a project for the Department of Health entitled Outcomes for Disabled Service Users, which aims to introduce a focus on outcomes to professional practice with disabled people in contact with social services.

Manawar Jan-Khan was born in Manningham, Bradford and now lives and works in Oxford but continues to provide support on a voluntary basis to the Manningham Residents'Association as an adviser and spokesperson. In Bradford, Manawar was active in the local community as vice-chair of the Toller Police Community Forum and then in setting up Foundation 2000, writing the first report, *Voices must be heard – a community response to the Manningham disturbances*, after the 1995 riots. He also supported the development of the Young People's Forum and the Westbourne Green campaign, and set up the Manningham Social Justice Foundation and Police Race Monitoring Group. In his professional life he now works in a partnership unit as a partnership project manager, focusing, among other things, on race and equality within the NHS and social care. In 2002, Manawar was one of the first Muslim councillors to be elected to Oxford City Council.

Priya Kissoon is a PhD candidate in the Geography Department at King's College, London. Her research is an exploration of the home/lessness experiences of refugees in London and Toronto. Her dissertation straddles issues of the meaning and sense of home, immigration, settlement and housing. Previous research includes a case study of the housing histories of homeless people in Toronto and the housing experiences of refugee women in Toronto.

Hermione Lovel is a public health scientist. She was a Senior Lecturer at the then World Health Organization (WHO) Collaborating Centre for Primary Care at the University of Manchester for 10 years, during which time she developed research with members of the Somali community. She has worked in international health for many years including 15 years based at the Centre for International Child Health, Institute of Child Health, University College, London. Her recent work has been in collaboration with Sudan, the Democratic Republic of Congo, Pakistan and Kuwait, as well as a multi-site study with the reproductive health research unit of WHO. She has undertaken numerous consultancies for WHO, UNICEF and others, particularly on child health, women's health and health services issues. Her ongoing research includes developing a prototype to address Somali linguistic and sociocultural problems around asthma in primary care settings. She is now working for the UK Department of Health.

Elizabeth Mestheneos is a UK-trained sociologist based in Greece whose work has focused primarily on refugees and on older people.

She is currently researching changes in policies towards older workers among selected Greek employers for the European Foundation, Dublin; and, in the context of the European Union-funded collaborative research project EuroFamCare, is completing research on family care and services that support families. She has recently finished a review of research in Greece on older women as well as a feasibility study on setting up a national organisation for older people (50 plus) in Greece.

Anna Maria Miwanda Bagenda is a journalist who has written about human rights abuses, politics and the ways in which governments can best include people in development. As a woman from Uganda who is separated from her children while she seeks asylum in the UK, Anna Maria brings enormous depth of experience to her role as a community development researcher. She is the Chair of Salford City's Social Inclusion Forum, the Vice Chair of Salford Community Network and an active member of a range of media and refugee and asylum seeker networks.

Zeinab Mohamed is a qualified midwife, who came to Britain from Somalia with her four children in 1989. During the past 10 years she has spearheaded community development with women from Somalia in Greater Manchester and has generated a range of research about Somali socioeconomic, cultural and health needs, the subject of her current MPhil studies. Zeinab has been involved in pioneering work with museums and art galleries and is currently a Research Associate at the University of Manchester.

Rhetta Moran has worked across the statutory, voluntary and academic sectors developing action research projects for 20 years. With the encouragement and support of the Revans Institute for Action Learning and Research at Salford University she initiated the development of an asylum seeker-led charity for research (RAPAR) in 2001. She represented the family of Israfil Shiri, a destitute man from Iran, at his inquest in 2003 when the coroner returned an open verdict on his death. She is most interested in applied research that explores the full range of sensuous human behaviours that can effect constructive change in the lives of vulnerable people.

M. Louise Pirouet was formerly Senior Lecturer in Religious Studies at Homerton College, University of Cambridge and Joint Coordinator for Charter '87 for Refugees between 1987 and 1997. She is a member of Cambridge Oakington Concern, which works for safeguards of

Oakington Immigration Reception Centre. She is also a trustee at the Refugee Legal Centre and author of *Whatever happened to asylum in Britain? A tale of two walls* (2001).

Keri Roberts has a PhD in geography and was formerly a Research Fellow at the Social Policy Research Unit, University of York. She has extensive experience of voluntary work with disabled people, and her research in York focused on families with disabled children, and disabled people in refugee and asylum seeker communities. She now works for the NHS as a genetics counsellor.

Kirsteen Tait has been a social entrepreneur for the past 15 years. She worked for seven years with Lord Young of Dartington at the Institute of Community Studies in Bethnal Green (now the Young Foundation), setting up a number of education and social welfare projects. She worked for seven years at the (then) Department for Education and Science in various roles, including that of Private Secretary to Shirley Williams as Minister of State. Most recently she set up and directed ICAR (the Information Centre about Asylum and Refugees) at Kings College, London. Her particular interest in refugees and asylum seekers developed over 20 years of living abroad, including in Iraq under Saddam Hussein, and several years at the Refugee Council. She has written chapters for books on subjects as diverse as the Youth Training Scheme and education for sick children.

Bogusia Temple is Professor of Health and Social Care Research at the University of Central Lancashire. She is interested in a wide range of research methods, particularly around cross-language research and research with minority ethnic communities. She has published extensively in this area, including in *Housing Studies*, *Sociology*, *International Journal of Qualitative Methods*, *Qualitative Health Research*, *International Journal of Social Research Methodology* and *Qualitative Research*. Her research involves work with a range of communities and service providers in health, housing and social care. She recently contributed to the 2004 Home Office National Integration Conference as well as a conference in Warsaw run under the patronage of the Office of the United Nations High Commissioner for Refugees.

ONE

Introduction

Bogusia Temple and Rhetta Moran

Our collection of chapters is drawn from a two-year Economic and Social Research Council (ESRC) seminar series, during which a range of statutory and voluntary organisations and refugees met to focus on methodological issues relating to research that sets out to elicit views of refugee people on service development and research. This book is not intended as a literature review of current research with refugees. Readers looking for this may be interested in the review by Castles et al (2002) and the website of the Information Centre about Asylum and Refugees (www.icar.org.uk). The value of involving refugees in research was taken as given in the seminar series and in writing the chapters for this book.

Rather than 'asylum seeker', we use the terms 'refugee' or 'refugee people seeking asylum' in their broadest senses in this chapter to make the point that, irrespective of where individual people may be in relation to their claims for asylum, they are all seeking refuge from persecution and, like everyone else, they have many other roles: they are mothers, sisters, fathers and brothers. We are not interested in how many people the government feels should be allowed to stay in the UK or in the different labels it uses to categorise people as deserving or otherwise. Where other contributors use different terms in their own chapters, we have kept these.

Some authors in this collection write about minority ethnic communities generally, which they see as including refugees. Refugees can become part of established minority ethnic communities. Some communities that are now defined as minority ethnic communities were originally refugees and sometimes still define themselves as such. The Polish communities in England are one such example. Researchers working with minority ethnic communities often include refugee people seeking asylum within their research, sometimes without realising they are refugees until the research is under way. We are not arguing that recent refugees seeking asylum have identical issues to longer-established groups or that all of them have established communities they can become involved with (Alexander et al, 2004). There may be tensions within communities, as well as additional sensitivities around legal status that may lead to access and trust (Hynes, 2003) issues for researchers. However, for researchers many of these issues apply to all communities in different degrees, whatever the labels attached to them.

Policy background

Both legislation (see Schuster, 2002 for historical overview of immigration legislation) and services relating to immigration and asylum have been ever shifting and heavily contested (Moran, 2003) since forced dispersal took effect in December 1999. People began to be moved out of areas such as Dover and London to areas with housing to spare. Previously, having entered the UK, people tended to gravitate to areas that they felt to be relatively hospitable: perhaps their language group was present, they had friends and family there, and they could access foodstuffs that were culturally familiar. Now, they would often find themselves isolated within very poor environments that had not been prepared in any way for their arrival and that had little recent history of multiculturalism (Gamaledin-Ashami et al, 2002).

Then, in April 2000, asylum in Britain became the responsibility of the National Asylum Support Service (NASS). NASS, working at arm's length from the Home Office but taking action under Home Office direction, was set up so that refugee people seeking asylum could support themselves in accommodation and/or through subsistence payments while waiting for decisions about their claims.

In early 2001, just after the British government declared that it was interested in overhauling the 1951 United Nations Convention on Human Rights to agree a clearer definition of 'genuine' refugees and economic migrants (UK Politics, 2001), a heavily contested European study found that intolerance of refugees and people seeking asylum was particularly acute in the UK (Council of Europe Racism Commission Report, 2003). Then, in July 2002 the government prohibited refugee people seeking asylum from working or undertaking vocational training until they are given a positive decision on their asylum application. This represented a further and very significant change. Previously, prohibition had lasted for only the first six months of any application. Thereafter, in practice, refugee people seeking asylum who had work permission, and those whose applications subsequently failed, still had the option of working legally, thereby earning money to live and being able to participate legally, as fellow workers, with people who were not refugee people seeking asylum.

By the end of 2002, just as the ESRC seminar series was beginning, the British Refugee Council was asserting, in the Home Affairs Committee for the 2002-03, session that poverty was the prevailing context for the asylum seeker community (Refugee Council, 2003, p 4).

ESRC seminar series and guidelines

The seminar series, funded by the ESRC, was founded on the now widely accepted premise, built into government policies, that involving service users in planning and implementing service provision is beneficial for all. The idea for the series was a response to the arrival of increasing numbers of people seeking asylum in the UK during the period immediately before the 9/11 terrorist attack on the US, and a growing awareness by the editors that this was impacting on practice and service development, especially where people began to be forcibly dispersed. In the course of our networking with people across the country involved in developing research on immigration and asylum issues, it had become evident that some people in this informal network were feeling constrained by the lack of resourced space and time to share and develop a more coherent understanding about the intersections between their research and development activities and the constantly changing policy landscape. Members of this network, and representatives from national organisations with whom we mooted the idea of a seminar series, were enthusiastic about creating regular opportunities for information sharing and dissemination about research practices.

Funding was awarded for the series to take place in collaboration with the newly formed charity Refugee and Asylum Seeker Participatory Action Research (RAPAR). RAPAR had begun to conduct small-scale, seed corn-funded, exploratory studies during 2001 in response to local practitioners' concerns about the emerging impact of the introduction of forced dispersal (Moran, 2003) on people newly arriving in, and those already living in, the city of Salford.

The seminar series ran from October 2002 to May 2004, and included a seminar held at the beginning of the war on Iraq. As such, participants came to the series with very contemporary questions, concerns and perspectives on the rapidly changing government legislation about whether, how and when refugee people seeking asylum should receive support and service from the state. For the most part, the participants were actively confronting these issues in their various practice environments: doing research in this field, being involved in policy and service delivery and development, and/or as refugees themselves. Asylum policy development has posed new challenges in the development and delivery of services and, in consequence, brought new issues for applied research in this area.

The series extended the principle of consultation to a forum comprising representatives of refugee groups, researchers, policy makers and practitioners whose remit was to discuss how to develop guidelines for eliciting refugees' views and participation in the future evolution of service delivery. Presentations were followed by group discussions out of which the participants drafted a set of guidelines for researchers working with refugees. At the final seminar the guidelines for involvement of refugees in research and service development were agreed (see Appendix). These are the first guidelines of their kind and were jointly developed between academics, voluntary organisations, service providers and refugee communities based on existing experiences of what works.

All the authors in this book, except for Louise Pirouet and Felicity Greenham, gave presentations at the seminar series. (Anna Maria Miwanda Bagenda presented a different paper to the one published in this book.) The chapter by Pirouet replaces the seminar contribution on religion and research, which could not be included here. There was also a presentation by a woman refugee on her experiences of working with other refugee women. She presented with a male interpreter and the session was interesting for the dynamics around interpreting (discussed in Chapter Three) as well as for its content. This speaker and the seminar participant who presented on developing forums with refugee people were also unable to write up their work for this book. Their contributions have been replaced by chapters from Anna Maria Miwanda Bagenda and Felicity Greenham.

The challenges we faced in securing written contributions from refugees are not purely technical concerns but also methodological ones. First, refugees' lives may be taken up with issues that many academic researchers do not have to face: deportation, the memories and effects of torture and even ongoing threats to friends and relatives. Publishing timetables are the least of their concerns. Second, writing can be daunting and writing for academic publishers is not the same as writing for a general audience. There is an academic language and way of arguing that takes time to learn. We have found that refugees, and service providers, in our seminars found it easier to speak about the issues than to reproduce them in writing for an academic audience.

Research has shown that merely choosing people from particular social categories, such as ethnicity or gender, to take part in research does not change exclusionary practice. For example, Schick (2002) has shown that power relations are manifest in differential access to material, interpretive and communicative resources. Moreover, it has also been shown that when English is not a first language – and, we would add, sometimes when it is a first language but has not been learned in England – conforming to standards of presentation of written texts based on the English language may be problematic (Spivak, 1992; Venuti, 1998). We acknowledge that these power relations existed within the seminar series, were evident when the chapters were being put together, and crystallised the tension between doing research within this intensely politically charged field of policy and practice, and making the time to publish from it.

Temple and Edwards address some of these issues in their research with interpreters when they attempt to move away from an English language baseline of understanding concepts and words that is solely that of the researcher (see Chapter Three). The centrality of language within the research process is also addressed through the theoretical framework of 'language creation from below' (Volosinov, 1986), which is developed in Chapter Four. The guidelines themselves were drawn up to reflect the importance of moving beyond the unproblematic use of language. They recognise that words and concepts have different meanings in different languages and that the languages used in research may affect findings. They encourage service development, audit and research that investigates language differences and does not base findings on one language framework, English.

Following the final seminar in May 2004, the guidelines were presented at the Home Office Integration Conference in London in June 2004 and sent out for final comments (Temple et al, 2004).

The guidelines were developed to describe the variety of ways in which refugees can be involved in research. They are not intended to be prescriptive in terms of methods used, since the speakers at the seminar series demonstrated that refugees could be involved in many different ways in both small- and large-scale quantitative and qualitative research. The way they are involved depends on the aims of the research. The guidelines are also pragmatic in that they recognise that issues of funding and time restraints are important influences on research, whatever the intention of the researchers. They were also drawn up with an understanding of the importance of ethical considerations. One of these is that it is better to admit constraints on what is feasible rather than lead people to believe that their involvement will change the immediate material circumstance of their lives when it will not.

In this introduction we draw the chapters in this collection together around three themes. In this way we hope the reader will be able to draw lessons from the individual projects the authors describe and begin to fit them into wider debates in social science research. The themes we have selected are the different ways of doing research 'with' refugees, the status of such research and the twinned issues of gatekeeping and representation.

Doing research 'with' refugees

There is now a huge literature on the 'involvement' and 'participation' of different groups in research (see, for example, Kretzmann and McKnight, 1993; Barnes and Walker, 1996; Wadsworth, 1998; Beresford, 2001; Schwabenland, 2002; McKnight, 2003). We do not want to rehearse in depth the advantages and disadvantages of participatory research in this introduction. As stated above, we assume that researchers have already decided to involve refugees in some way in the research. We focus on some of the issues brought up in individual chapters. The following benefits and disadvantages of these kinds of approach are intended as a brief overview and are drawn from the presentation at the Home Office Integration Conference in 2004 (Temple et al, 2004).

The benefits of participatory approaches are as follows:

- They maximise local participation so that proposed projects better fit the needs of local people. There is now a large literature that shows that people who speak little or no English do not access services because they see them as inappropriate (Robinson, 2002).
- They force researchers to employ rigorous processes of checking interpretation and exposing their own perspectives (see below).
- They can lead to a sense of ownership, responsibility and self-esteem.
- They recognise that people have skills and capacities rather than seeing sections of society as permanently needy (see below).
- They can release community development capacities (see below).

However, structural inequalities pervade society and not everyone is equal in research or service development.

The disadvantages of participatory approaches are that:

- They are highly resource and labour intensive (see below).

- People tend not to give up power willingly and so consensus may not be achieved.
- Participation tends to stay at the practice level, leaving academics and service deliverers to reassert their expertise at the policy level.
- They are sometimes seen as not real science and are therefore dismissed. The disadvantages of participation are related to concerns with qualitative research generally. The disadvantages surrounding traditional, completely researcher-led agendas using quantitative methods are less often spelt out.
- Communities are often seen as undifferentiated wholes and little time is given to engaging with different sections within communities (see below).
- Sometimes only formal community organisations are approached and issues of accountability and representation are often not addressed (see below).
- Users rarely have the resources, insider knowledge of the system or language used by service providers and academics to engage on an equal footing.

Readers interested in following these arguments may find Campbell (2002) and David (2002) useful as they provide in-depth debate on user participation in research and service development.

The guidelines developed via the seminar series reflect the different ways refugees can take part in service development and research generally. They advise researchers to state clearly the aims of the research from the outset. Researchers who consult with refugees and do not intend actively to encourage participation in shaping the research process or final report should make this clear.

To date, much research with minority ethnic communities is arguably not 'with' minority ethnic communities, including refugee communities, at all. Refugees are employed because they have particular skills, such as language abilities, and knowledge that can facilitate access. They are not invited to take part in other aspects of research, such as discussing concept differences across languages, looking at their perspectives on issues, setting the research questions, reviewing findings or writing the report. They cannot challenge the researchers' perspectives. For example, some research projects employ community researchers solely as interpreters (for examples of this see Karn et al, 1999; Steele, 1999; and Steele and Sodhi, 1999). They are given questions to translate or issues to cover in focus groups and their main role remains at the level of translation and interpretation. Issues of perspective, difference and relative power across languages are rarely taken on board in this kind of approach and the baseline remains that of the researcher who set up the project.

The benefits of community researchers in administering standard questionnaires are obvious in that, in many cases, without them a project could not involve anyone who is not a fluent English language speaker and/or writer. The chapters in this book demonstrate that the benefits involve much more than these obvious pay-offs and that there are issues involved in using community researchers to carry out service provider, English language-based research. All researchers on a project actively contribute to the production of the research findings and there may be differences in perspective between researchers and research participants. A community researcher can provide an avenue for opening up different ways of looking at the world, as demonstrated in Chapters Four and Eleven.

The research described in this book involves refugees in different ways and using different methods, including biographical methods (Chapter Two), focus groups and interviews using open and closed questions (Chapter Four), individual presentations to a community-based project that became action research case exemplars (Chapter Eleven) and rating scales and photographs (Chapter Five). The authors succeed in demonstrating that involvement of refugees need not be limited to one method or to small-scale research.

For example, Mestheneos (Chapter Two) describes a large-scale study across different languages and countries that employed refugees to carry out interviews. Researchers were keen to include the diversity of refugee experiences and worked to ensure, for example, that women were not excluded from research. Some of the techniques she used are also present in other smaller-scale studies in this book. For example, she discusses debriefing sessions with refugees that are similar to those adopted by Temple and Edwards in their research (Chapter Three) and arguably the approaches used are similar in that they both centre individual biographies within the research process. The authors acknowledge the limitations of their kind of engagement but aim to open up issues of perspective.

Other contributors do not engage refugees in the research process to such an extent. For example, Priya Kissoon in Chapter Five explains her research process in detail when she investigates definitions of home and soft indicators of integration. Her detailed exposition of her research process explores the decision about whom to involve and to what extent. She shows how the purpose of the research, resources and access influence how she decided to carry out the research.

Chapters Four, Seven and Eleven explore some of the potential of human agency on the part of both refugees and practitioners to effect changes during the life of individual research studies. These chapters adopt participatory action research methods and, in Chapters Seven and Eleven, the approaches are situated within an action learning framework (Revans, 1982) that seeks sustained changes in both community and practitioner capacities to take action through research and learn from it.

The position of the researcher

In this section we look at debates about the status of research carried out with refugees. We argue against the view that such research is in some way tainted as it falls short of the aim to make research objective and that this can be done only by researchers who are not part of the social world they are exploring. We argue this around two points. First, although involving refugees in research per se does not make the research 'good' by definition, making judgements about validity based on someone's status is fraught with dangers. There is no way to describe someone as a complete insider or an objective outsider in research. Communities may have internal divisions that mean there is no one view on an issue and people may form views based on allegiances to more than a single social categorisation such as race or ethnicity. Second, research does not exist in a vacuum outside of the social world (Gouldner, 1971; Delphy, 1984). There must be very few people in Britain who do not see immigration and asylum as a political issue. However, when 'people' become 'researchers' it is often assumed that their views can be removed from their research or that only particular categories of people should be carrying out research, as they are the only ones who can put their beliefs to one side.

Although the criteria for evaluating research are the subject of extensive debate, it is now generally accepted that, if the research is aiming to look at the needs of particular groups of people, they should have a say in how their needs are defined. We take two contrasting positions concerning the status of research with refugees in order to explore these issues. Most researchers fall somewhere between these two extremes, although their research may lean towards one or the other position. Advocates of the first position aim to be 'objective' and not to influence their research. Advocates of the second position argue that everyone, including academics, sees the social world from their own position within it (see, for example, discussions by Gouldner, 1971; Harding, 1987; Atkinson, 1990; Stanley and Wise, 1993;

Hammersley, 1995; Campbell, 2002; and David, 2002, for discussions relevant particularly for researchers seeking some measure of participant involvement). Subscribers to the first position may value the views of refugees but refugees are seen as 'subjects' of research rather than participants. The research process will be 'biased' if either the researcher or the refugee tries to influence the research. Supporters of the alternative view argue that we are all part of the world we research and cannot remain outside of it. We therefore all influence research, academics included.

Many researchers have demonstrated the value of 'insider' or lay knowledge (see, for example, Bie, 1996; Popay and Williams, 1996). They describe the drawbacks of a traditional view of research and service development in which researchers gather findings from those they research using an agenda drawn up almost entirely from the outsider's perspective, with any input from communities being minimal and tokenistic. Critics of traditional needs assessment (for example, Kretzmann and McKnight, 1993; Schwabenland, 2002; McKnight, 2003) see them in just this light and argue that they are based on a deficit model of community – communities' assets and capabilities are unrecognised. Such an approach, as discussed within the context of urban regeneration in Chapter Seven in this collection and Moran, Mohamed and Lovel's exploration of whether and how participatory research processes about health may enable people to move beyond the inherent passivity of 'subject' status (Chapter Four), does nothing in the long term to equip people to take hold of the situation and change things for themselves. An interesting example is the research by Forrest and Kearns (1999) that looked at social cohesion and neighbourhood regeneration in Teesside, London, Liverpool and Nottingham and noted that:

> There was also resentment that such (regeneration) professionals, 'the suits of regeneration', were making 'vast sums' out of the community's needs without allowing the community to define their own requirements and whilst expecting a significant voluntary input from the community (p 41).

The guidelines encourage service development and research that has capacity-building and capacity-releasing elements in it. This may take the form of help with the development of skills for creating and implementing action plans and/or with initiating research or advocacy. This kind of alternative community development model of research values the capabilities of people with different perspectives, as explored through Miwanda Bagenda's descriptions of how asylum seeking people became volunteer researchers, and at least goes some way towards building up and releasing skills bases in the future (Chapter Eleven).

However, there is another side to this issue. In contrast to the danger of assuming that the 'outsider' independent researcher always knows best, there is a tendency, when employing refugee people seeking asylum, and people from minority ethnic communities generally, as community researchers, to assume that, as 'insiders', their knowledge is superior. The argument that the insider always knows best has had much critical debate in many areas of social science research, for example, in relation to feminist research (see, for example, Stanley and Wise, 1990) and race research (Twine, 2000; Campbell, 2002; David, 2002; Schick, 2002).

Researchers have argued that the 'only the insider knows' perspective can lead to a hierarchy of knowledge according to ascribed hierarchies of oppression. For example, women's knowledge would be more valuable in terms of casting light on 'the truth' of oppression (Pollert, 1996, p 643), black women would be better than white, working class than middle class, and so on. As Schick (2002) argues, such a position oversimplifies the factors that shape identity and communication and define in advance what can be said by whom. Twine (2000) also points out that one of the limitations of racial 'matching' is that race is not the only relevant social characteristic in research. Extreme arguments, Twine posits, for or against racial matching "rest on an implicit model that characterizes all researchers as either absolutely inside or outside homogeneous sociocultural style" (p 9). Twine argues that insider status generates its own barriers and that difference may stimulate, rather than block, communication by focusing on understandings taken for granted. Insiders and outsiders, according to Twine, generate different kinds of knowledge rather than either one producing better knowledge (p 13).

Twine's arguments apply equally to arguments that only particular people can carry out research, or alternatively that they cannot. Researchers, for example, who argue that some people are politically motivated and biased, while they themselves are not, ignore the fact that all researchers are part of the social world they research and all have views that they bring to that research. Refugees who carry out research have views on immigration and asylum that influence their research, but so does everyone.

It is impossible to pick any criteria for deciding who is an insider in a community and who is not, as defining both 'community' and 'insider' is not straightforward and there is value in maintaining dialogue across difference. The guidelines recognise the diversity within refugee communities and urge researchers to specify whom they are working with. They also recognise that groups within communities may not agree on future policy and service development. All communities have knowledge bases that can be drawn on and views may differ within and across communities defined along class, gender, ethnicity and sexuality, for example. Even within the term 'refugee' there are differences that need to be taken into consideration. For example, there is increasing interest in the influence of religious belief on social life and on research and service development with refugees. Pirouet argues in Chapter Ten that in a secular society the value of religion for refugees is often underestimated and Moran, Mohamed and Lovel (Chapter Four) show the value of working with religious elders. However, Manawar Jan-Khan's concerns in Chapter Six about working solely with community representatives need to be considered (we return to this below).

Authors in this collection illustrate well the differences within communities. For example, Chapters Four and Eleven discuss the influence of gender on refugees' lives and on research. Chapter Four is an example of three women working together to explore health needs, one of whom is a refugee. In Chapter Eleven, Miwanda Bagenda describes her position in her research as a woman and as a refugee who is currently seeking asylum, writing of the experiences that have taught her to value her emotions. In Chapter Five, Kissoon discusses her concerns about research that can bring up traumatic memories and how she dealt with these in her interviews. Jennifer Harris and Keri Roberts discuss their research with disabled refugees in Chapter Nine. They point to the needs of disabled people within refugee communities and describe in detail the arrangements they had to make to ensure that disabled refugees could participate in their research. They cover many of the issues we have raised, including that of language difference, but also point out that work in this area can affect not only refugees but also researchers themselves. Here again, we move from the notion of objective researchers to researchers who affect, and are affected by, their research.

The different emotions brought into play when talking of traumatic events are part of the research and need to be acknowledged, discussed and engaged with in ethical ways, as much as the practical issues around how to do the research. Although some of the seminars included sexuality as an important influence on perspective, none of the chapters here directly addresses this issue and it is not one that features significantly on the agenda of either researchers or service providers. It is an area that needs further investigation, as sexuality has been shown by many researchers to be important to many people when looking at identity and needs.

In sum, it is not possible to divide researchers into those who are 'insiders' and cannot remain objective and those who are 'outsiders' and can produce valid, objective research. No researcher comes to a research project with a blank mind and no one is objective in this sense.

Issues of immigration and asylum have become heavily intertwined and, in the process, have moved up the political agenda to occupy a central position within national, political debate (IPPR, 2003, p 36; MORI, 2003). Chapters Six, Seven and Eleven in this collection make explicit the political nature of research in this field, whoever carries it out. Kissoon notes that refugees in her research felt that, for example, who funded the research influenced their decision about whether to participate and therefore the findings and outcomes. Jan-Khan warns researchers that limiting research to refugees accessed via 'community representatives' embroils the researcher in political divides within communities of which they may not be aware. Miwanda Bagenda points out in her chapter about action research that the researcher should stop pathologising refugees as needy *individuals* and start analysing their social circumstances. By definition, this is a political act because it involves making connections between current policies towards refugees and their position within society.

Gatekeepers

We have argued above that refugee communities are differentiated along many lines, as are all communities. The current trend towards employing one researcher from within a community to represent community views is therefore problematic from the outset. Community is often narrowly defined in research (Jewkes and Murcott, 1998) and generally encompasses only formal organisations, not reaching informal groups of people who equally view themselves as 'community'. Employing someone from a formal organisation or even an elected representative from a minority ethnic community does not automatically ensure access to 'the community'.

The focus on formal organisations that choose refugees as community researchers and find people to include in research may ease access issues to particular groups of people within communities but it has repercussions in terms of whose views are heard. For example, Bowes and Dar (2000) point out that organisations can act as gatekeepers to resources and that this may leave some people without support from generic services and from services designed for people from minority ethnic communities. Employing researchers from community groups to gain access to sections of communities does not mean that all sections of communities are represented.

There is a particular danger for researchers who rely on refugee community leaders to speak for 'their' communities. Many community researchers are chosen from community organisations, since this is the easiest way to recruit. Questions are increasingly being directed at the issue of representation, accountability and who drives the research agenda (Jan-Khan, 2003a and 2003b; Wilson and Wilde, 2003). The guidelines in the Appendix acknowledge the need to specify which sections of communities or groups are being involved and how. For example, research based on findings from self-appointed community leaders may differ from that based on findings from accountable elected leaders, and readers need this kind of information when looking at the research.

Many of the chapters in this book address this issue of gatekeeping and representation. It is the particular concern of Manawar Jan-Khan, who questions for whom community leaders speak when they tend to be older men and the views of younger members of the community, who have not selected them as their representatives, differ. Kirsteen Tait argues in Chapter Eight that the voluntary sector and local authorities can help with access but may skew the findings as not all refugees use such organisations, there are rivalries within them, and women tend not to be involved. Kissoon states that non-governmental organisations presented barriers to her research but that community-based refugee organisations were very helpful. She found snowball sampling useful – asking refugees for names of others whom she could approach – although she felt that this excluded those with no social networks.

It has been argued that representative sampling is a way of making research more objective. The issue of representative sampling is problematic in this area of research for two reasons. First, as Tait shows in Chapter Eight, there are no complete databases from which to sample. Government statistics are notoriously unreliable (Temple et al, 2005, p 19) and cannot be used to form a sampling frame that is the basis of any traditionally quantitative representative sampling (Esterhuizen, 2004). Second, many researchers do not wish to use quantitative definitions of representative samples and ask: representative of what? Jennifer Mason (1996, p 91) argues that much qualitative research uses a different analytic logic, for example, theoretical or purposive sampling. She states that representative sampling may not "facilitate the detailed exploration of social processes" and that commonly defined 'variables' such as age and gender may be "too static or cross-sectional and not sufficiently processual or conceptually rich". For example, if the research is concerned with the views of refugee people seeking asylum as defined in this chapter, it makes no analytic sense to use existing databases based on pre-existing government defined categories (see above). A similar case can be made for researchers looking at ethnicity. Using census categories has been shown to be problematic if the researcher is interested in people's own definitions, which are context-specific. This does not mean that representative sampling should not be used but that the sampling procedure should match the aim of the research.

As Taylor (2003) argues, policy developers and service providers, and we would add funders, find it problematic to deal with the many voices coming from within communities and they favour one voice. Choosing one person to represent an entire community may be an issue in that they can be accused of being unrepresentative by both sides. Taylor feels that researchers need to acknowledge who is representing whom. Part of the problem stems from tight deadlines and limited resources. Cross-language research is expensive, involving interpretation, translation and transcription costs. It is also increasingly being accepted that there is an obligation to ensure that there are no cost implications for refugees taking part in service development and research. This means covering the cost of time off work, transport, childcare, and food and venues when the participant's home is not an appropriate place for conducting the research. Not covering these costs means sections of refugee communities are excluded from the outset.

Consulting communities in a meaningful way is resource-intensive (Anastacio et al, 2000; Taylor, 2003). Some communities have few formal representative organisations and some people within communities have little contact with the organisations that have sprung up with the aim of helping them. There may be active informal groups of people with particular issues that are excluded from the focus on formal constitution due in part to constraints of time, money and knowledge about how to become constituted in the first place. For example, destitute refugees may not be in a position to even consider belonging to a formal organisation, but may feel able to present their views and seek to communicate as widely as possible about their experiences of government asylum policy (Moran, 2003).

Also, in our experience it is difficult to secure enough funding for time to enable refugees who have no prior academic research experience to carry out interviews, analyse data and help to write the report (Temple et al, 2005). Academic researchers are often contract researchers and are rarely paid for writing research proposals. When the approach they use involves the participation of refugees in drawing up a project proposal, this often means that both researchers and refugees have to give large amounts of their time, often with no result. If refugees are not involved in drawing up the project, it is harder to change things once it has started. This may leave refugees asking whether they really can influence the research process or service development.

However, it is easy to dismiss someone as not representative, particularly when their views are uncomfortable and challenging, or when questions are raised about differences within communities. There is no one single undifferentiated and fixed community for community researchers to work with. Jan-Khan's chapter shows that the concern should rather focus on how adequate the process of finding community representatives is, how accountable these representatives are and how they affect findings (see Jewkes and Murcott, 1998).

Even when the process of choosing a community representative is judged to be adequate, there are limits to the extent to which community researchers who are not academics (and sometimes also academics themselves) have been allowed to influence the final product. We advocate in the guidelines that researchers should specify their funding source. Then readers can judge for themselves the influences on the research, rather than having to take the researcher's word that they have remained 'objective'. Any restrictions on publication and dissemination should also be clear.

The issue of payment for refugees who carry out research and take part in it surfaced during the seminar series. Research with minority ethnic communities is often with unpaid volunteers from community organisations as researchers. When they are paid it is often a minimal amount with little recognition of the language or cultural brokerage skills, let alone the time, involved. Similarly, Forrest and Kearns (1999, p 41) note the scale of unpaid voluntary work in the regeneration field.

Researchers who work with refugee communities note the same phenomena. Both Kissoon and Mestheneos in this collection introduce the idea of paying a minimal amount for the time of refugees who take part in research.

The authors in this collection all agree that refugees have valuable knowledge bases from which to voice their views on service development and from which to participate in research. They offer a range of views about the benefits and drawbacks of different methods and provide practical examples of how they have dealt with some of them. The methods used include the collection of biographies on a small and large scale, interviews using open and closed questions, individual presentations to a community-based project that became action research case exemplars, reflections on personal experiences and the examination of the range of existing data sources. These chapters are all intended to open up debate on research with refugees, to expand what is counted as evidence in future research, and to foster the inclusion of perspectives of people whose experience it is, that is, refugees themselves.

References

Alexander, C., Edwards, R. and Temple, B. with Kanani, U., Liu, Z., Miah, M. and Sam, A. (2004) *Access to services with interpreters: User views*, York: Joseph Rowntree Foundation.

Anastacio, J., Gidley, B., Hart, L., Keith, M., Mayo, M. and Kowarzik, U. (2000) *Reflecting realities: Participants' perspectives on integrated communities and sustainable development*, Bristol: The Policy Press.

Atkinson, P. (1990) *The ethnographic imagination: Textual constructions of reality*, London: Routledge.

Barnes, M. and Walker, A. (1996) 'Consumerism versus empowerment: a principled approach to the involvement of older service users', *Policy and Politics*, vol 24, no 4, pp 375-93.

Beresford, P. (2001) 'Service users, social policy and the future of welfare', *Critical Social Policy*, vol 21, no 4, pp 494-512.

Bie, N. (1996) 'The lay perspective in health technology assessment', *International Journal of Technology Assessment in Health Care*, vol 12, no 3, pp 511-17.

Bowes, A. and Dar, N. (2000) 'Researching social care for minority ethnic older people: implications of some Scottish research', *British Journal of Social Work*, vol 30, pp 305-21.

Campbell, J. (2002) 'A critical appraisal of participatory methods in development research', *International Journal of Social Research Methodology*, vol 5, no 1, pp 19-29.

Castles, S., Korac, M., Vasta, E. and Vertovec, S. with Hansing, K., Moore, F., Newcombe, E., Rix, L. and Yu, S. (2002) *Integration: Mapping the field, Report of a project carried out by the University of Oxford Centre for Migration and Policy Research and Refugee Studies Centre contracted by the Home Office Immigration Research and Statistics Service*, Home Office Online Report 28/03 (www.homeoffice.gov.uk/rds/pdfs2/rdsolr2803.doc).

Council of Europe Racism Commission Report (2003) (www.news.bbc.co.uk/1/hi/uk/1257321.stm).

David, M. (2002) 'Problems of participation: the limits of action research', *International Journal of Social Research Methodology*, vol 5, no 1, pp 11-17.

Delphy, C. (1984) *A materialist analysis of women's oppression*, Amheerst, MA: University of Massachusetts.

Esterhuizen, L. (2004) *Doing case studies for the refugee sector: A DIY handbook for agencies and practitioners*, London: Information Centre about Asylum and Refugees in the UK.

Forrest, R. and Kearns, A. (1999) *Joined-up places? Social cohesion and neighbourhood regeneration*, York: Joseph Rowntree Foundation.

Gamaledin-Ashami, M., Cooper, L. and Knight, B. (2002) *Refugee settlement. Can communities cope?*, London: Charities Evaluation Services and Evelyn Oldfield Unit.

Gouldner, A. (1971) *The coming crisis of Western sociology*, London: Heinemann.

Hammersley, M. (1995) *The politics of social research*, London: Sage Publications.

Harding, S. (ed) (1987) *Feminism and methodology*, Milton Keynes: Open University Press.

Hynes, T. (2003) *The issue of 'trust' or 'mistrust' in research with refugees: Choices, caveats and considerations for researchers. New issues in research working paper no 98*, London: Evaluation and Policy Analysis Unit, United Nations High Commissioner for Refugees.

IPPR (Institute for Public Policy Research) (2003) *Asylum in the UK. An ippr fact file*, London: IPPR.

Jan-Khan, M. (2003a) 'The right to riot?', *Community Development Journal*, vol 38, no 1, pp 32-42.

Jan-Khan, M. (2003b) 'Community cohesion: myth or reality', Paper presented at the ESRC seminar series 'Eliciting the views of refugees and asylum seekers', Salford: University of Salford.

Jewkes, R. and Murcott, A. (1998) 'Community representatives: representing the "community"?', *Social Science and Medicine*, vol 46, no 7, pp 843-58.

Karn, V., Mian, S., Brown, M. and Dale, A. (1999) *Tradition, change and diversity: Understanding the housing needs of minority ethnic groups in Manchester*, London: Housing Corporation.

Kretzmann, J. and McKnight, J. (1993) *Building communities from the inside out: A path toward finding and mobilizing a community's assets*, Evanston: IL: Center for Urban Affairs and Policy Research, Northwestern University.

Mason, J. (1996) *Qualitative researching*, London: Sage Publications.

McKnight, J. (2003) 'De-clienting society – new directions in community building (lessons from the USA on asset-based community building)', Paper presented at the From Client to Citizen conference, London.

Moran, R.A. (2003) 'From dispersal to destitution: dialectical methods in participatory action research with people seeking asylum', Conference proceedings from Policy and Politics in a Globalising World, 24 July, University of Bristol (www.bristol.ac.uk/sps/p&pcomf/stream4.html).

MORI (2003) *Attitudes towards immigration and asylum*, Powerpoint presentation by Heather Crawley (www.mori.com).

Pollert, A. (1996) 'Gender and class revisited; or, the poverty of "patriarchy"', *Sociology*, vol 30, no 4, pp 639-59.

Popay, J. and Williams, G. (1996) 'Public health research and lay knowledge', *Social Science and Medicine*, vol 42, no 5, pp 759-68.

Refugee Council (2003) *Hungry and homeless: The impact of the withdrawal of state support on asylum seekers, refugee communities and the voluntary sector. Findings from research into the impact of section 55 of the Nationality, Immigration and Asylum Act 2002*, London: Refugee Council with funding from Oxfam.

Revans, R.W. (1982) *The origins and growth of action learning*, Bromley: Chartwell Bratt.

Robinson, M. (2002) *Communication and health in a multi-ethnic society*, Bristol: The Policy Press.

Schick, R. (2002) 'When the subject is difference: conditions of voice in policy-oriented qualitative research', *Qualitative Inquiry*, vol 8, no 5, pp 632-51.

Schuster, L. (2002) 'Asylum and the lessons of history', *Race and Class*, vol 44, no 2, pp 40-56.

Schwabenland, C. (2002) 'Towards a paradigm shift: lessons from anti-oppression movements', in J. Merrifield, R. Tandon, C. Flower and C. Schwabenland (eds) *Participation – north and south: New ideas in participatory development from India and the UK*, London: Elfida Society, pp 5-17.

Spivak, G. (1992) 'The politics of translation', in M. Barrett and A. Philips (eds) *Destabilising theory: Contemporary feminist debates*, Cambridge: The Polity Press, pp 177-200.

Stanley, L. and Wise, S. (1990) 'Method, methodology and epistemology in feminist research processes', in L. Stanley (ed) *Feminist praxis: Research, theory and epistemology in feminist sociology*, London: Routledge, pp 20-60.

Stanley, L. and Wise, S. (1993) *Breaking out again: Feminist ontology and epistemology*, London: Routledge.

Steele, A. (1999) *The housing and social care needs of Black and minority ethnic older people in Derby*, Salford: Salford Housing and Urban Studies Unit, University of Salford.

Steele, A. and Sodhi, D. (1999) *The housing and related needs of BME communities in Luton*, Luton: Luton Borough Council.

Taylor, M. (2003) *Communities at the heart? Approaches to inclusion in the UK*, Paper presented at the From Client to Citizen conference, London.

Temple, B. and Moran, R.A., with Fayas, N., Haboninana, S., McCabe, F., Mohamed, Z., Noori, A. and Rahman, N. (2005) *Learning to live together: Developing communities with dispersed refugee people seeking asylum*, York: Joseph Rowntree Foundation.

Temple, B., Moran, R.A., Ndjuimot, Ndluvo, E. (2004) 'Eliciting the views of refugee people seeking asylum', in E. Clery and N. Daniel (eds) *UK National Integration Conference: What Works Locally? Balancing National and Local Policies, London 29-30 June*, London: Immigration Research and Statistics Service, Home Office.

Twine, F. (2000) 'Racial ideologies and facial methodologies', in F. Twine and J. Warren (eds) *Racing research, researching race: Methodological dilemmas in critical race studies*, New York and London: New York University Press, pp 1-34.

UK Politics (2001) (www.news.bbc.co.uk/1/hi/uk_politics/1155120.stm).

Venuti, L. (1998) *The scandals of translation: Towards an ethics of difference*, London: Routledge.

Volosinov, V.N. (1986) *Marxism and the philosophy of language*, Translation of *Markism i filosofia iazyka* by L. Matejka and I.R. Titunik (1929) Cambridge, MA: Harvard University Press.

Wadsworth, Y. (1998) *What is participatory action research?* Action Research International, Paper 2 (www.scu.edu.au/schools/gcm/ar/ari/p-ywadsworth98.html).

Wilson, M. and Wilde, P. (2003) *Benchmarking community participation: Developing and implementing the Active Partners benchmarks*, York: Joseph Rowntree Foundation.

TWO

Refugees as researchers: experiences from the project 'Bridges and fences: paths to refugee integration in the EU'

Elizabeth Mestheneos

Background to the research

In 1997, the European Parliament decided to support actions to aid refugee integration in Europe. Between 1997 and 1999, the European Commission provided 63.5 million euros for 180 pilot actions within member states across the European Union (EU), as well as several EU-level projects. Pilot actions were aimed either at improving reception conditions for asylum seekers in individual member states, facilitating voluntary return, or supporting the integration of refugees given permission to settle.

With the aim of finding and disseminating good practice in the various member states with respect to refugee integration, one of the EU-level projects undertaken by the European Council on Refugees and Exiles[1] (ECRE, 1998, 1999) through the Task Force on Integration (later renamed the Networks for Integration)[2], lasted for three years. The first year concentrated on actions mainly by non-governmental organisations (NGOs), local authorities and governments, and these formed the basis for the six good practice guides on refugee integration produced by the Task Force (ECRE, 1998). The guides contained descriptions and assessments of projects and activities by NGOs, local authorities, government agencies and refugee community organisations that were practical solutions to the main integration themes initially identified – community and culture, housing, health, education, vocational training and employment. However, during the second year of operation, the seven participant organisations decided to focus on refugees' perceptions while involving as many refugees as possible in its overall actions and project work[3].

A decision was made to fund two pieces of research on refugee perceptions of integration. One was a qualitative study by Dr Maja Korac[4] of the Refugee Studies Centre, University of Oxford, comparing two contrasting 'models' of reception and integration and their effects on the socioeconomic situation of refugees from former Yugoslavia settled in Rome and Amsterdam. She focused on refugees as dynamic social actors who have to overcome structural and social barriers hindering their settlement. In these two very different country contexts, policies and provisions influence the development of refugee strategies for integration. Objective problems in the labour market and educational integration exist in both study sites, but refugees' social roles, personal satisfactions and perceptions of the receiving societies differ as well. Dr Korac's findings[5] agree in great part with the second piece of research – the refugee perceptions study (Mestheneos et al, 1999) described below, which was carried out in the 15 EU member states and is the focus of this chapter.

The Task Force study

The Task Force research project on perceptions by refugees of integration, designed to be completed very quickly, started in April 1999, with the results being announced in the report *Bridges and fences* (Mestheneos et al, 1999) at the third European Union Conference on Refugee Integration in Brussels in November 1999. The design of the research, the training of the interviewers, the analysis of the data and the writing of the report was undertaken by the Athens-based research team supported by Overlegcentrum voor Integratie von Vluchtelingen (OCIV) in Belgium[6]. The short time available, the desire to elicit refugees' perspectives, the very limited financial and time resources, as well as the research leaders' recent experience in using biographical interpretive methods[7] were critical factors in the decision to use an adapted qualitative methodology. The central focus and purpose of the research was to find out and understand refugees' own perspectives and experiences of integration in the member states[8], and thus aid agencies supporting refugees (government, NGOs, refugee community organisations, local authorities) to reflect on and rethink their policies and practice.

There were some interesting logistical problems involved in conducting the research:

- How could one cover a representative range of refugee perspectives in each of the member states? Refugees are distinctive in terms of their ages, gender, educational levels, family status, religions, cultures and languages as well as the length of time they have lived in the member state, and their legal status.
- How could one design a research instrument that could be used in every one of the 15 member states taking into consideration the very different levels of welfare and social provision for asylum seekers and refugees?
- How could one compare results? Many refugees have been over-interviewed, by social workers, agencies and authorities.
- What would help ensure that refugees did want to tell interviewers of their experiences?
- Could the research be done in a very limited time period and on a small budget and produce valuable results?

Fortunately, as members of the ECRE Task Force, the researchers had direct access to, and support from, then refugee agencies in each of the 15 member states. One agency in each country volunteered to select an interviewer and support him or her during the interviewing, for example, helping with transcriptions and translations and providing office space, while the limited budget was used to pay the interviewer.

The researchers requested that these refugee agencies would identify a refugee who could undertake the interviews, since it was felt that this might give the research greater credibility with the refugees being interviewed, would allow them to speak more openly, and would generate some paid work and experience for a few refugees. Since they had to attend a two-and-a-half-day training session in Brussels with the research team in English and then a debriefing session in June in Dalfsen, the Netherlands, one further requirement was that interviewers had to be able to speak and understand English, even if they needed translating help with interview material. Funding could not cover simultaneous translation during these sessions and those attending all managed in English and by using some French. The final composition of the team of interviewers was 12 refugees, two migrants and two EU nationals with experience of living in other countries[9].

The decision to use refugee interviewers had other results:

- A very committed set of interviewer-researchers who managed to finish the work within tight schedules.
- The use of refugees and migrants of 13 different nationalities, as well as varied religious, professional and political backgrounds.

- Access to a total of 28 different languages. Everyone spoke at least three languages and some could communicate adequately in as many as seven. All were fluent in either English or French and in the language of their host country, if this was different. Interviews were held in the most accessible language for the interviewee.
- Access to male and female refugees, since there were equal numbers of men and women interviewers[10].

Refugee interviewers were aged between 30 and 50 years and highly educated, with the norm being a university degree either from their home country or a second country[11]. Comments are made later on the influence this had on those interviewed as well as the reactions of interviewers to the interviewing experience. Overall, the quality of the interview material generated tended to depend on the competencies and commitment of the individual interviewer rather than their gender or (non-) refugee status.

Another important decision was to use a modified form of biographical interpretative method (Bertaux and Kohli, 1984; Kohli, 1986; Rosenthal, 1993; Fischer-Rosenthal, 1995; Breckner, 1998). This involved refugees being asked to tell their biographical story from the moment they arrived in the host country, emphasising their experiences of coming to live, adapt and integrate in the new host society and ending with their expectations about the future. They were told to take as much time as they needed and to talk about any issues they felt were relevant. They were thus able to construct their answers in any way they liked, to express their thoughts and feelings as well as experiences without any intervention or prompting from the interviewer. The answers were fully recorded and subsequently transcribed and, where necessary, translated into English or French.

The subsequent analysis by the Athens research team tried to discover and interpret what were the main structuring themes prioritised in the interviewee's presentation, the language used (description, argument, evaluation, report), the length of time dedicated to each subject, and any emotions expressed. A sociological interpretation of processes of integration and valuable information on the perspectives of refugees was thus derived, often in ways not necessarily intended by the interviewee (Rosenthal, 1993; Chamberlayne and Rustin, 1999).

What was important about the initial open question was that it did not define or ask for positive or negative aspects of integration, which would have oriented respondents to a particular mindset, but rather allowed them to define the issue of integration in any way they wished. The openness of this initial question was complemented by more direct open questions concerning the various aspects of integration with which the Task Force was concerned, including employment, education, vocational training, health, housing, culture and community. Additional questions were also asked about the respondents' experiences of NGOs, if they had not already discussed this issue in the opening question, and their plans for the future. If, in the answer to the opening question, the specific issues had been adequately covered, they were not repeated in the semi-structured questions.

The significant variations in refugee backgrounds and national contexts in which respondents experienced their refugee status might appear to make it difficult to come to strictly comparable results[12]. However, by taking the refugee as an active agent in the creation of his or her own life story (Rustin, 1998)[13], the methodology used went beyond reporting individual stories of refugee integration and adaptation to the host societies of Europe, to an attempt to understand the mechanisms of adaptation and integration.

In the analysis and report, comparisons between countries or cases were not made – there was no aggregating of results into numbers. Rather, each opening question in an interview was taken as an illustrative case of responses to experiences that may be found in many European countries. Common elements in refugee biographies, of living and adapting to a new society, did emerge. Additionally, certain critical themes and issues emerged in various national and personal situations, which indicated their relative importance to refugees' subsequent lives. Among these were:

- conditions and length of reception
- racism and ignorance
- social class effects and assumptions
- cultural differences
- problems in accessing proper employment
- welfare state dependency or inadequacies
- problems of accessing information
- the age and personalities of the refugees.

The decision to provide a common training that was undergone by all interviewers, as well as the common debriefing session, undoubtedly had important repercussions for the validity and usefulness of the research. Training was essential, since qualitative interviewing requires research skills that are not part of normal communication. Emphasis was given to the importance of interviewers not commenting, overtly sympathising, rejecting or expressing their feelings about the answers they heard.

Given that refugees come from varied political and religious backgrounds with different values, it was critical that interviewers kept their influence on answers to a minimum. They were also taught how to select refugees to interview, how to present themselves as interviewers, how to conduct the interview, and how to transcribe and summarise the results. An important training issue was the emphasis on the importance of anonymity. Refugees, with good reason, may be worried about exposing their details to public authorities, whether of their home country or the country of asylum. Interviewees were given the opportunity to use a pseudonym, used throughout the interview. Interviewers were requested to tape the interview, since they had to be transcribed subsequently to ensure accurate and full details from the interview. It was recognised that since refugees and interviewers would be working in various languages and that subsequently these would need to be translated in part or completely, the research data would rarely be available in their original form (except for English, Greek and French). The researcher-analysts would not be able to have full access to the emotions expressed, the setting of the interview, and the comments and reactions once the tape recorder was switched off. For this reason, interviewers were asked to comment on these issues and they were discussed at the debriefing session.

The debriefing session allowed interviewers to relate their experiences of carrying out the interviews, highlight difficulties encountered, explain the circumstances in which they had interviewed people and provide other background information to the tapes and transcripts they had sent for analysis. The Athens research team recorded this information.

Sample interviewed

A total of 144 interviews were completed[14]; each interviewer had to interview a varied sample of 10 refugees with legal status[15], between the ages of 18 and 65[16], living in the member state from two to 10 years following recognition as a refugee, taking into consideration gender, national origins[17], varying levels of education, and whether they were single or married, with or without children. The work of interviewing was completed over two months.

From the 10 interviews, the interviewers fully transcribed two interviews[18], summarising the remaining eight interviews under the various integration topics, including the material in the opening question. They were also asked to include in these summaries any quotations (transcribed and translated) from the refugees interviewed that they felt were particularly illuminating or typical of either the individual's opinions or situation, or more generally of the situation of refugees in that particular member state.

Clearly, in transcribing and translating between so many languages, there may have been a loss of meaning in the words used. Where the interview or selected quotations had to be translated into English, it was of considerable help that translators tended to be drawn from the refugee NGOs and were thus sensitive to terminology and issues, and could work closely with the interviewer to ensure that there was as little loss of meaning and fewer inaccuracies as possible.

All tapes were sent to the research team in Athens. Full use was made of the transcriptions and as far as possible very little intervention was made with the English used except when it aided clarity. Thus, despite sometimes having been translated twice from the original language of the interview, for example, from Arabic to Italian to English, the characters and styles of speech of some individuals still emerged.

Findings

Not all interviews were insightful, since some tended to reproduce the same types of materials and comments, while in other cases the quality of interviews varied with the skills of the interviewer or the willingness of the interviewee to talk freely. The reproduction of the same issues simply confirmed the presence of the issue for many refugees. An interesting dimension, rarely available to the qualitative researcher, is that the relatively large number of interviews permitted extensive and substantive analysis within the framework of the qualitative method used[19].

In a project of this magnitude across so many countries, cultures and social circumstances, it was fascinating to be able to develop an understanding of the social processes, personal strategies and attitudes that emerged in refugees' life stories that often cut across the objective situations in member states. Not surprisingly, the way in which refugees responded to the initial opening question was affected by personal characteristics such as social, religious, cultural and educational background, personality, gender, age; by the length of time in the member state; and by the concerns of the individual at the time of the interview (for example, divorce, unemployment, illness, housing). Refugees living in southern member states were generally preoccupied with meeting their material needs, whereas in countries where these needs are normally met and comprehensive programmes exist for refugees, the predominant concerns were frustrations and disappointment with employment, the quality of language teaching or the suitability and location of the social housing provided.

Since the research was aimed at eliciting a refugee perspective on integration, it is worth underlining a few of the findings:

- Integration is affected by experiences of the past and expectations of the future with respect to the situation in the home country – is the end of exile in sight?
- Age is an important intervening variable, with younger people adapting to a new country more easily.
- Social class affects integration; the disproportionate representation of the middle class and educated among refugees in most member states affects their expectations of integration, since few are willing to start a new life from the bottom. In contrast, many Europeans dealing with refugees (for example, as officials, neighbours, services staff, and so on) generally perceive refugees as belonging to the lower classes and being socially deprived. This is partly the result of the fact that most refugees are dependent on social benefits and support at least initially. Additionally, they are often unable to communicate with the locals at their class and educational level.
- The above-mentioned attitudes are further compounded by the prevailing ignorance and racism of many Europeans described in interviews. Some refugees, by virtue of their personalities and experiences, are more able to confront and overcome racism and institutional barriers. Personal strategies by refugees to gain acceptance in the European host societies appear to be particularly significant in the integration process. Changing attitudes is a matter of political and social action by both local and refugee groups and individuals. But racism is a difficult issue to confront.
- In countries where refugees have to live in public housing or low rent areas they are often in neighbourhoods or settlements where marginal and socially excluded local people live, enforcing their identification with the socially deprived. In these circumstances, making friends and having social relationships with people who share the same world outlook and experiences is difficult. Making friends from the host country is an important social resource and strategy in every member state.
- The most significant problem is the lack of access to permanent employment in work commensurate with refugees' abilities and training. Qualifications and prior service are rarely recognised, while

private and public employers tend to prefer local people. Racism (not only based on colour) and ignorance, as well as considerable arrogance among sections of European society exclude refugees from equal opportunities in the labour market. The enforcement of equal rights legislation in the EU may help alter this.

• The presence of a refugee's family or kin as well as a wider community of fellow nationals who can provide support and solidarity inevitably affects integration; this varies for each individual and the country in which she or he lives.

• The role of self-help refugee community organisations in the integration of refugees constitutes another difference in EU national contexts, with the Netherlands and the UK making refugee community organisations an intrinsic and funded part of support for integration.

• There are different national criteria for gaining nationality and citizenship; stricter and negative policies to the granting of citizenship did not aid refugee integration.

• The welfare states of some countries are so bureaucratic and inflexible, and occasionally overgenerous, that they can inhibit initiatives by refugees to become independent. On the other hand, the lack or very limited nature of support by the public authorities in southern Europe leads to tremendous problems, especially in the early reception period. Those refugees who survive this have had to be particularly active in the local society, legally and illegally. Although they have developed personal integration strategies in the local societies, they cannot easily be included in the labour market at the level of their education and professional qualifications.

• There appear to be social, cultural and political differences within member states in terms of willingness to accept refugees. Belgium and Luxembourg stand out from the research findings as countries that appear to be more likely to make refugees feel socially accepted and able to adjust and integrate at different levels; though there are still difficulties in adequate and appropriate labour market integration.

• Many refugees knew it would be difficult to ever go back home to live; yet not all were able to develop integration strategies. The individual personality of the refugee, their personal reactions to the loss of their country, family and social status, and how these personal traits were encouraged or discouraged in the national social structural context in which they found themselves living were critical. Thus, those with strong political and social commitments to live in and change the host country, or to be involved in the world as artists and creative cosmopolitans, had adopted positive life strategies that worked for them. Others could not adapt, since going home was the only dream, or else they postponed adaptation and integration as a goal for their children, rather than themselves. Others were still trapped in nightmares of the past, depression and inadequate and difficult current circumstances.

Positive benefits from using refugee interviewers

The overwhelming response by the interviewers was that meeting and having to really listen to the life stories of people from other cultures and backgrounds had enriched their own lives. Many made friends, and for some interviewers it made them realise that others had experienced isolation and frustration in the process of integrating into the host society. As one of the interviewers said, "After I heard all these stories I realised I was more fortunate than many of them, while at the beginning I thought I was in the worst and most miserable situation".

Refugee interviewers were overwhelmingly drawn from professional backgrounds, yet most were finding it difficult to find commensurate employment and obtain professional recognition in their host country. They reported finding their participation in the research a valuable professional experience and a significant boost to their self-esteem. It was also fun for all involved in the research, with satisfaction reported from working on an innovative research project that could help influence policy and practice.

Research problems in interviewing refugees

The experiences of the 16 interviewers suggested a number of interesting points about interviewing refugees that are relevant to any research undertaken with this group. Identifying refugees willing to be interviewed took time and patience, especially given the necessity of recording the interviews on tape. Refugees often did not have telephones, and thus could be hard to contact. Even finding a suitable place to conduct the interview was sometimes difficult; for example, interviewees often had no private space of their own, and interviews in noisy cafes could make it difficult to use the tape recorder. In addition, even with the assurance of anonymity, many refugees were reluctant to be interviewed and taped; some still feared persecution in their country of origin and others were reluctant to voice negative thoughts about the host society for fear of being seen to criticise those who had given them refuge. Some refugees were willing to talk and provided interesting comments, but refused to be taped. In these few cases, extensive notes were kept. For others, the tape recorder was inhibiting and they said some important things when it was switched off. This information was written down. Some refugees were unwilling to provide identifying details of their country of origin.

Some national groups were less willing to be interviewed; at the time of this research, Somali refugees were particularly reluctant because of bad press they had received as a group in their host countries (Denmark and Germany, in particular) in the months prior to the research. Some interviewers also had difficulties in reaching women and particularly uneducated women in the home. During training, women interviewers were encouraged to interview more people of their own sex as a way of ensuring an adequate representation of refugee women's voices, but overall there were difficulties in identifying and getting uneducated refugee women to speak. Even when willing, their husbands were sometimes present for some of the interview. Married women sometimes requested that their husband was not told about the interview.

Men seemed to be more likely to provide generalised responses, while women tended to tell their personal stories. Similarly, educated refugees tended to respond globally rather than personally about their experiences. Some took the interview as an opportunity to criticise, as a way of getting their voices heard by the authorities, though after the interview they were far more positive. Some clearly thought it was an opportunity to get their opinions heard at the European level. Thus consideration must be given to the fact that the political and ideological context of any research influences answers. Less educated refugees were not always willing to talk to the educated interviewers or else did not understand the purposes or value of the research. However, most of the refugees liked being interviewed: they expressed satisfaction in having an (uninterrupted) opportunity to talk to someone about their experiences. But not all refugees were interested in expressing their opinions; though polite, they responded in a very formal and uninvolved way. Some refugees remained doubtful or cynical about the usefulness of the research and others rejected the term integration, since for them it was synonymous with assimilation.

Although the interviewer offered the interviewee a small fee for out-of-pocket expenses at the end of the interview, this was often refused and even offended some. However, one refugee woman in Denmark was delighted, since it was the first money entirely 'earned' by her. She immediately spent it on treating the interviewer to a coffee in a cafe.

The behaviours and emotions encountered were highly varied. Sometimes this was the result of cultural difference; one African woman interviewer had her handshake refused by an African man, since "men don't shake hands with women". A male interviewer reported that a woman refugee cried throughout the interview and another laughed throughout. Interviewers had to confront their own emotions; one interviewer reported having cried through every one of her interviews with women refugees, who were also crying.

The fact that the refugee interviewer was often known to the interviewee clearly did influence responses; for example, a refugee doctor interviewing about health, whose professional background was known, received more elaborate answers about health services and personnel than did a non-medical interviewer. The way in which refugees were recruited for interviewing also affected responses; the interviewers were sometimes known to have come from a specific agency. As a result, in some countries there are far more elaborate responses to some subjects, for example, on education in the UK and on NGOs and refugee involvement in the Netherlands, because the interviewers in the UK had a background in education and those in the Netherlands were involved in NGOs and refugee organisations and the interviewees had been chosen via contacts in these fields. However, this should be seen as a positive contribution rather than a negative one.

The link between the research and policy

The report *Bridges and fences* was part of a more general attempt within the framework of the EU-supported ECRE Task Force/Networks on Refugee Integration to change the perceptions and practices of institutions, governments and agencies. For some of the latter it was not easy to adjust to the idea that, with the necessary support, refugees could help themselves, form their own advocacy bodies, and be actively involved in policy planning, the design, operation and organisation of services and the running of NGOs. Some of the quotations used from the *Bridges and fences* research report in conferences and meetings undoubtedly made decision makers and service organisers rethink their practices. Overall, there appeared to be some shift in a number of member states so that they did increasingly involve refugees in service planning and provision. This was evident in the greater frequency in which refugees appeared in international meetings for the project and NGOs reported employing refugees to a greater extent[20]. Research findings can be important tools for altering ideas and policies if used and promoted appropriately. Research for policy must also have its advocates and end users.

Notes

[1] The European Council on Refugees and Exiles is a cooperating body of 70 NGOs in 40 European countries.

[2] The ECRE Task Force on Integration was a consortium of seven NGOs with responsibility for different areas of integration. OCIV – the Flemish Refugee Council – was the Coordinating Secretariat (see www.refugeenet.org). In 1999, the consortium became the ECRE Networks for Integration.

[3] While there were many refugee representatives from the different member states at the second European-level meeting in Antwerp on refugee integration, in addition to representatives of the NGOs and public bodies supporting refugees, in other meetings (for example, those in Dalfsen (the Netherlands), Madrid, Nuremberg, Paris and Brussels), refugees formed the majority of participants.

[4] She was a senior research officer, and also a refugee.

[5] Reported at the Metropolitan Conference in Rotterdam in November 2001.

[6] Dr Elizabeth Mestheneos and Dr Elisabeth Ioannidi from the Sextant Group worked with Sara Gaunt from OCIV, Belgium (Mestheneos et al, 1999).

[7] Descriptions of the methodology as well as selected biographies and analyses based on the EU research-funded project SOSTRIS (Social Strategies in Risk Societies) are to be found in Chamberlayne et al (2002).

[8] The 15 Member States prior to 2004.

[9] There were 16 interviewers in total, as two interviewers carried out the work in France.

[10] In fact, there were fewer difficulties with male refugee interviewers accessing women refugees than anticipated.

[11] The original professions of the 12 refugee interviewers included architecture, civil engineering, medicine, journalism, sociology, economics, and accountancy. Their biographies illustrated the difficulties refugees experience in being able to continue in their existing professions or further develop their careers in the host country: only one of the refugees was working in his original profession, while two more had been able to continue working in their professions only in a voluntary or unofficial capacity. The employment experiences in the host country of the remaining refugee interviewers included working in construction and catering, working (often in a voluntary and/or unskilled capacity) for refugee-assisting NGOs, teaching the language of the host country to other refugees, working as interpreters/advisers to newly arrived asylum seekers, and creating their own employment through running refugee community organisations. Three of the non-refugee interviewers currently work for refugee assisting NGOs and had trained as social/political scientists.

[12] Being highly diverse in terms of their histories, economies, welfare and social infrastructure and state welfare systems, the 15 EU member states constitute important parameters in helping refugee integration. Thus the situation of refugees in the southern member states where only piecemeal and low levels of support are available compared with more northern member states. These different national contexts are compounded by the divergent socioeconomic, cultural and political backgrounds of refugees, including their gender, family and kinship ties.

[13] A more theoretically grounded and elaborate analysis of the rich material gathered from the refugee interviews and specifically the responses to the opening question is needed, but there are no resources for this.

[14] In one country, the interviewer did not complete the interview schedule.

[15] Permitting them to stay legally in the host country. Terms vary among EU countries but include those with Convention status, humanitarian status and exceptional leave to remain.

[16] Almost no refugees arrive in the member states after 55 years of age.

[17] They were asked to interview more refugees from the majority groups in the host country and from any group to which they had access, for example a Bosnian refugee interviewer had more Bosnian interviews, an Iranian with good Arabic and Farsi had access to Arab speakers and Afghans.

[18] The speed with which the research had to be conducted led to the first interview being sent to the researchers, thus enabling any comments to be made to ensure adherence to the research protocol for the remaining nine interviews. Subsequently, the interviewer was requested to transcribe the 'best' interview as described by the research team. The criteria set for this included the interviewer's sense that the interview did give a full description of a refugee's experiences in the host country, that the opening question was rich in material and that it covered many of the substantial themes relating to integration.

[19] However, the limited funding meant that the analysis of the responses to the initial open question could not be done using the biographical-interpretive method systematically, except in one case, since it requires considerable resources that were and are not available to the research team. Researchers have their own agendas; while it would have been wonderful to have the time and resources to make a full analysis and write up the results in the more permanent form of a book, in reality the research achieved its ends of helping to provide evidence for policy and practice changes to benefit refugees (Mestheneos and Ioannidi, 2002).

[20] Known examples include the Greek and Finnish Ministries running training programmes on refugee empowerment, and the Greek Council of Refugees supporting the training of one or two refugees to become social workers.

References
Bertaux, D. and Kohli, M. (1984) 'The life story approach: a continental view', *Annual Review of Sociology*, vol 10, pp 215-37.

Breckner, R. (1998) 'The biographical-interpretative method – principles and procedures', in *SOSTRIS Working Paper No 2*, London: University of East London, pp 91-105

Chamberlayne, P. and Rustin, M. (1999) *Social strategies in risk societies: From biography to social policy. Final report of the SOSTRIS Project*, Targeted Socio-Economic Research (TSER) SOE1-CT95-3010, London and Brussels: Centre for Biography in Social Policy, University of East London and European Commission.

Chamberlayne, P., Rustin, M. and Wengraf, T. (eds) (2002) *Biography and social exclusion in Europe: Experiences and life journeys*, Cambridge: The Polity Press.

ECRE (European Council on Refugees and Exiles) (1998) *Good practice guides to integration of refugees in the European Union*, (www.refugeenet.org) and (www.ecre.org).

ECRE (1999) 'Position on the integration of refugees in Europe', September, ECRE Secretariat, Policy paper, London.

Fischer-Rosenthal, W. (1995) 'The problem with identity: biography as solution to some (post)-modernist dilemmas', *Comenius,* vol 15, pp 250-65.

Kohli, M. (1986) 'Social organisation and subjective construction of the life course', in A.B. Sorenson, F.E. Weiner and L.R. Sherrod (eds) *Human development and the life course*, Hillsdale, NJ: Lawrence Erlbaum, pp 271-92.

Mestheneos, E. and Ioannidi, E. (2002) 'Obstacles to refugee integration in the European Union Member States', *Journal of Refugee Studies*, vol 15, pp 304-20.

Mestheneos, E., Ioannidi, E. and Gaunt, S. (1999) *Bridges and fences: Refugee perceptions of integration in the European Union*, Belgium: OCIV (www.refugeenet.org).

Rosenthal, G. (1993) 'Reconstruction of life stories. Principles of selection in generating stories for narrative biographical interviews', in R. Josselson and A. Lieblich (eds) *The narrative study of lives, vol 1*, Thousand Oaks, CA: Sage Publications, pp 59-91.

Rustin, M. (1998) 'From individual life histories to sociological understanding', in *SOSTRIS Working Paper No 3, Annexe I*, London: Centre for Biography in Social Policy, University of East London.

THREE

Limited exchanges: approaches to involving people who do not speak English in research and service development[1]

Bogusia Temple and Rosalind Edwards

Introduction

It has been estimated that there are nearly two million adults in Britain whose first language is not English, about a third of whom speak little or no English. Particular areas of the country have greater concentrations and ranges of minority ethnic groups and languages than others (Baker et al, 1991; OPCS, 1993; Edwards, 1995; Dorsett, 1998). The world of people who speak little or no English, in Britain, is significantly constrained, and there are links between English language disadvantage and social exclusion and deprivation. Those who most need to register with, and draw on, the services of health and welfare professionals and officials may be least able to do this because of language difficulties (see, for example, Kalantzis et al, 1989; Baker et al, 1991; London Research Centre, 1992; Edwards, 1993; Stills et al, 1995; Yu, 2000). Furthermore, English language competence is not equally distributed within minority ethnic groups for whom it is not their first language, reflecting variable socioeconomic background and education both in countries of origin and in Britain, and also relating to age and gender (Alexander et al, 2004).

Researchers, service providers and policy makers are aiming to involve people from minority ethnic communities, including refugee people seeking asylum, in improving services and in general needs assessments. The extent of their involvement and the methods used to achieve it vary. At one end of the spectrum are postal surveys to the general population that include people who come from minority ethnic communities and can read and write English. Judgements are then made about the likely extent of any 'bias' (NHS Executive, 1998). Other methods include formal membership of committees or boards, and employment of link workers, key workers or bilingual workers or of researchers selected from within particular communities (Temple, 2002).

There is little written about involvement in research interviews and even less written about language difference in focus group research with people who do not speak English (see Esposito, 2001 for an exception). There is some work on the role of interpreters and translators in relation to best practice and models of provision – for example, the relative merits of professional services, bilingual providers, community interpreters, interpreter advocates, or informal interpreters. In this vein, Thomson et al (1999) review bilingual support services in the North of England and provide a thorough analysis of the relative merits of employing bilingual workers in different roles. There is also a body of literature aimed at English-speaking health and social welfare professionals, giving them advice on how to work with interpreters (see Karseras and Hopkins, 1987; Freed, 1988; Fuller and Toon, 1988; Phelan and Parkman, 1995; and also Edwards, 1995, 1998, and Alexander et al, 2004, for discussion of this advice).

Beyond issues of 'value-free' technique (for example, Jentsch, 1998), however, there is very little reflection on the implications of language difference and the use of third parties in communication across languages (see Edwards, 1995, 1998; Temple, 1997; Birbili, 2000). Interpreters and translators seem to be excluded from such calls to investigate different perspectives. There are many useful lessons that can be learnt from the translation literature, which suggests that there is no one correct translation and that the translator is like Aladdin in the enchanted vaults: spoilt for choice (Bassnet, 1994). Rather than there being an exact match, word for word, in different languages, the translator is faced with a dazzling array of possible word combinations that could be used to convey meaning. Issues concerning translation and interpretation are not always the same, not least because the latter usually involves face-to-face interaction rather than working with written texts. Nevertheless, in this chapter we draw on some of the lessons that can be learned from a reflexive examination of the literature on issues in translation in order to explore working with people who do not speak English. We use the term interpretation to include both written and oral communications across languages, as we focus here on similarities between them.

Although we focus in this chapter on interpreters, the issues raised are also relevant for others working with community researchers and bilingual, link or key workers to address the needs of people who speak little or no English. Very few of these projects spell out the extent of involvement deemed appropriate or how funders have overcome the issue of communicating with their wider non-English-speaking populations. The use of an interpreter to assess an individual's need or a link worker to assess general need does not automatically overcome concerns about perspective (Temple, 2002). Such people are often treated as conveyers of messages in an unproblematic way. Their unproblematic use has consequences. When examined from a language framework, what looks like involvement at the level of method may be a one-dimensional framing of relevance and meaning chosen exclusively by the English language speaker. This chapter is concerned with how to involve people who do not speak English in such a way that acknowledges that there are baseline language issues whatever level and method of involvement is chosen.

We begin with a description of our conceptual base. As illustrative empirical material, we refer to two research projects that we have conducted and in which we worked with interpreters/translators. We consider the way in which we separately came to the same conclusion: that to meaningfully engage with people who speak little or no English, English-speaking researchers need to talk to the interpreters and translators they are working with about their perspectives on the issues being discussed. Finally, we draw out the advantages of our perspective on working with interpreters.

Conceptual base

There is now a large and complex literature on different perspectives in relation to research generally and qualitative research specifically (see, for example, Stanley and Wise, 1983, 1993; Harding, 1987; Hammersley, 1995). We will only engage in this debate to illustrate the implications of adopting a perspective that acknowledges differences in the way the social world is seen. Theorists and researchers have elaborated a range of ways of understanding people as social actors, including interpretative or social constructionist views (see, for example, the influential work by Berger and Luckmann, 1991). Researchers who see the social world in these terms do not subscribe to the view that there is only one correct way in which to describe it. They argue that the researcher and the research participant are both producers of accounts. Their social location in the world influences how they come to experience and describe it. People have particular histories and occupy social positions, which means that they do not see the world from another's standpoint – although they may understand each other across difference through dialogue (Young, 1997).

The strengths of qualitative research lie in its attempt to carry out this dialogue, and to record and reconcile complexity, detail and context. A critical appraisal of this can be the integration of reflexivity – the ability of researchers to take stock of their actions and role in the research process, and to interrogate systematically research relations (see Steier, 1991; Hertz, 1997). Even within qualitative frameworks that are open to the influences of social location, however, it appears that qualitative researchers have not discussed the influence of translators and interpreters on their research, where they have been part of their work.

Much of the translation literature points to the impossibility of a literal movement of meaning from one language to another (see contributions to Hantrais and Mangen, 1999; Wilson and Revauger, 2001) and would therefore sit comfortably within social constructionist views of the world. If there is no one meaning to be gleaned from experiences of the social world, then there can be no one translation, and it may be necessary to convey meaning using words that were not spoken by research participants.

The theoretically informed, rather than technically focused, literature on translation demonstrates that communication across languages involves more than just a literal transfer of information (Spivak, 1992; Bhabha, 1994; Simon, 1996; Temple, 1997). Simon (1996) shows that the translator is involved in discussing concepts rather than just words, and that context, assumptions and inference are all-important in deciding equivalence or difference in meaning. It is not a case of finding the meaning of a text from a culture. Simon describes the problems with such an approach:

> The difficulty with such statements is that they seem to presume a unified cultural field which the term inhibits; the translator must simply track down the precise location of the term within it and then investigate the corresponding cultural field for corresponding realities. What this image does not convey is the very difficulty of determining 'cultural meaning'. This meaning is not located within the culture itself but in the process of negotiation which is part of its continual reactivation. The solutions to many of the translator's dilemmas are not to be found in dictionaries, but rather in an understanding of the way language is tied to local realities, to literary forms and to changing identities.

> Translators must constantly make decisions about the cultural meanings which language carries, and evaluate the degree to which the two different worlds they inhibit are 'the same'. These are not technical difficulties, they are not the domain of specialists in obscure or quaint vocabularies. They demand the exercise of a wide range of intelligences. In fact the process of meaning transfer has less to do with *finding* the cultural inscription of a term than in reconstructing its value. (1996, pp 137-8)

Language is an important part of conceptualisation, incorporating values and beliefs, not just a tool or technical label for conveying concepts. It carries accumulated and particular cultural, social and political meanings that cannot simply be read off through the process of translation, and organises and prepares the experience of its speakers. It speaks of a particular social reality that may not necessarily have a conceptual equivalence in the language into which it is to be translated (Bassnet, 1994). Language can define difference and commonality, exclude or include others; it is not a neutral medium. The same words can mean different things in different cultures and the words we choose matter. For example, Temple (1999) argues that 'the Polish diaspora' in England has been defined in research to date in a way that excludes people who do not belong to formal organisations led almost exclusively by the male intelligentsia.

Overing (1987) argues that we should not be over-anxious about the loss of ability to translate words literally but we should be concerned about the scope that then opens up for the use of perspectives that are alien to the people who actually used the words. She states (1987, p 76) that "It is not the 'word' about which we should be anxious, we should be concerned, instead, about an 'alien' framework of thought which is based upon an 'alien' set of universal principles about the world". Applying our own set of views about the world to other people who may hold alternative beliefs sets up an overarching and supreme framework for understanding. Language is the medium for promoting claims to a dominant and correct perspective. The interaction between languages is part of the establishment and maintenance of hierarchical relations (Kalantzis et al, 1989; Corson, 1990) with English often, usually by default, used as the yardstick for meaning in societies where it is the language of state and public participation – a situation that has become institutionalised in citizenship practices in the UK (Alexander et al, 2004).

The translator, and by extending these arguments, the interpreter, is pivotal to the final research product. Without talking to people who are communicating directly to others for us, how can we even begin to know if we are imposing our framework of understanding? Some researchers have begun to look at ways in which we could investigate perspectives in cross-language research (Temple, 1997; Edwards, 1998). The use of a particular language or form of language can be an important element of identity, and aspects of identity, such as gender, ethnicity, religion and sexuality, as well as moral status, are constructed and ascribed in the process of using language. 'Speaking for' others is a political issue (Alcoff, 1991; Back and Solomos, 1993; Wilkinson and Kitzinger, 1996). Spivak establishes links between language and identity in a way that does not fix or privilege either when she states (1992, p 178) that: "Language is not everything. It is only a vital clue to where the self loses its boundaries. The ways in which rhetoric or figuration disrupt logic themselves point to the possibility of random contingency, beside language, around language".

We now go on to discuss the advantages of actively working with translators and interpreters and other key workers employed as links to non-English-speaking communities and the ways in which we have tried to put this into practice.

Our research bases

In order to explore some of the issues raised by recognising that interpreters or translators involved in research are constructing and producing accounts for themselves and others, we draw on two projects – one conducted by each of us. The focus here is on our reflexive consideration of working with interpreters in the research process, so we do not address other aspects of the studies (interested readers may follow these up through the references provided).

The first project concerned an in-depth evaluation of services aiming to facilitate homeless families' use of child health services and other facilities, carried out by Rosalind Edwards (Edwards, 1993). As well as indigenous and English-speaking families, a substantial proportion of homeless families are immigrants or refugees who speak little or no English. Of the 20 people Rosalind interviewed for the study, nine could not communicate fully in English and she could not speak their languages: four mothers from Bangladesh, two from Somalia, two from Eritrea and one from Nepal. Rosalind thus worked with three interpreters in order to carry out repeated semi-structured interviews with these women. Two of the interpreters were paid staff members, and the other an unpaid volunteer, in local voluntary agency projects working with the relevant minority ethnic groups. This method of accessing interviewees' accounts of their lives made Rosalind very aware of the way in which her own, her interpreters' and her interviewees' identities were invested in and constructed by the particular research process.

The second 'project' started life as research for Bogusia Temple's PhD thesis (Temple, 1993) and has continued for more than 10 years. It is unfunded and grew out of an interest in white ethnicity and Polish communities in particular. It has been the focal point of Bogusia's intellectual journey over the length of the research. Bogusia has now carried out in-depth interviews with over 40 people who sometimes describe themselves as Polish. Some people have been interviewed two or three times, with interviews across 'families' (see Temple, 2001 for an example of this work). The interviews have covered a range of issues, including identity, ethnicity, gender and family. Polish communities include people who have been labelled in different ways at different times. This is in part related to the period when they left Poland and to changing world circumstances. They can include refugee people seeking asylum (post-Second World War and more recently Polish Roma), people who came to marry during Soviet rule and economic migrants. People come for more than one reason and describe their ethnicity in flexible and changing ways.

Some Polish-born people do not speak English even after they have lived in England for a number of years. At one point Bogusia decided to employ an interpreter/translator, as cross-language interviews are very time-consuming to transcribe. The transcription involved both interpretation and translation: listening to the taped interview and then providing a written English version. The transcription of the interview threw into sharp relief the differences between their perspectives on what a woman interviewee speaking on tape was saying.

We conducted these projects separately, and were not aware of each other's work at the time of first thinking about the issues involved in working with interpreters as employees or researchers. When we did eventually make contact and discuss our experiences, however, we found that we had both come to question the dominant model of working with interpreters and developed an alternative. This was because both of us were steeped in feminist understandings of reflexive research practice.

Key informants and intellectual journeys

The implicit model behind the consensus of advice about working with interpreters is a version of the traditional, supposedly detached and value-free. Presentations in this vein write the researcher out of the research, ignoring their role in collecting data (or seeking to minimise it at least) in an attempt to eliminate 'bias' and maintain 'objectivity'. The aim is for interviews to take place 'through', rather than with, the interpreter. The interpreter is posed as a neutral mouthpiece, faithfully and passively translating back and forth between languages: "The interpreter is a conduit linking the interviewer with the interviewee and ideally is a neutral party who should not add or subtract from what the primary parties communicate to each other" (Freed, 1988, p 316).

This traditional, value-free representation of the research process has been criticised by those following what has been termed the 'reflexive turn' in social research (for example, van Maanen, 1988; Stanley and Wise, 1983, 1993; Atkinson, 1990; Holstein and Gubrium, 1995). While methodological reflexivity is not necessarily uniquely feminist, our own concerns in addressing issues around interpreters in social research were informed by this perspective.

Both our approaches were rooted in feminist and other critiques of textbook 'recipes' for interviewing as a one-way process in which the interviewer attempts to disappear, and in an accompanying questioning of the exercise of power and control in research (for example, Oakley, 1981; Hammersley and Atkinson, 1989; DeVault, 1990; Holstein and Gubrium, 1995). Rather, such critiques regard social involvement on the part of the interviewer as integral to the qualitative research process. They argue that researchers should acknowledge that they are part of the social world that they study and part of its production through research accounts. Moreover, it is possible for researchers to seek to implement more democratic, reciprocal, non-hierarchical and cooperative processes while still acknowledging responsibility. Thus, in this view, in order to be as rigorous as possible, researchers need to reflect on the ways in which they, as individuals with social identities and particular perspectives, impact upon the interpersonal relations of fieldwork. They need to place these perspectives and relations in their wider historical, political, economic, social and intellectual context, and consider the consequences for the production of research accounts. For example, Edwards (1990) has explored the ways that institutional and structurally-based divisions between researcher and researched on the basis of 'race' infuse themselves into the research process and the interview situation in particular.

This intellectual, methodological, critique and perspective led Rosalind to feel that she should work towards giving the interpreters she was working with personhood and visibility in her research and to consider their impact on the research process and the data collected from interviewees. Bogusia came to the same conclusion through realising that, although she had accepted the influence of researcher and research participant on her research, she had not initially extended the same consideration to the influence of the interpreter. Only when she felt the transcript she received was not what she had heard in the interview did she come to realise that she had done what many cross-language researchers do: assumed the interpreter was not a part of the production of the research account and that their involvement consisted of no more than changing words into another language. Like researchers, interpreters bring their own assumptions and concerns to the interview and the research process. The research thus becomes subject to 'triple subjectivity' (the interactions between research participant, researcher and interpreter), and this needs to be made explicit. Rigorous reflexivity in research where researchers are working with interpreters requires an exploration of the social location of the interpreter.

The reflexive model Rosalind developed for working with interpreters treated them as a form of 'key informant'. Key informants have been written about and utilised in qualitative research in varying ways, notably with researchers relying on professional and/or lay informants to provide a source of introduction to, and information and discussion on, the social world under investigation (see Whyte, 1955; Becker, 1970; Bulmer, 1984). Rosalind's use of the term 'key informant' encompassed a reflexive evaluation of the interpreters' social location, their values and beliefs, and their understanding of their relationship to the researcher and the interviewee. This involved Rosalind interviewing the interpreters she worked with, asking them about aspects of their own life experiences, their relationship to the ethnic groups they worked with, and what issues they regarded as important in relation to the topics being addressed in the interviews and the subject of the research project. This did not mean that interpreters became, as a consequence, experts whose insights were necessarily privileged over those of the interviewees (or indeed the researcher). Rather, the key informant interviews were part of the process of making interpreters visible, and to some extent 'accountable', in the same way as researchers may seek to be explicit about their own social and political position, and seek to explore this for research participants as part of the study they are undertaking.

Bogusia has used Stanley's (1990) concept of 'intellectual autobiography' as a way to describe and analyse her research. Stanley argues that research accounts are products of both the autobiographies of researchers and the biographies of research participants. She describes intellectual autobiography as "an analytic (not just descriptive) concern with the specifics of how we come to understand what we do, by locating acts of understanding in an explication of the grounded contexts these are located in and arise from" (1990, p 62). Stanley argues that the labour process involved in producing accounts of lives is often ignored, and that both the subject of an account and the writer work at constructing texts. The perspectives of both are woven into this labour process. This concept is similar to that of the key informant used by Rosalind in that it acknowledges the active participation of all involved in research.

Difference, perspective and identity are implicitly acknowledged in the literature on working with interpreters, but as a technical rather than reflexive matter. The interpreter–interviewee match in terms of social characteristics is regarded as an important factor, with several writers providing a hierarchy of suitability (Karseras and Hopkins, 1987; Freed, 1988; Fuller and Toon, 1988). Particular stress is laid on interpreter and interviewee being of the same sex, but culture, religion and age are also seen as important within the hierarchy of suitability. Within these characteristics, trained interpreters or professionals are generally felt to be most suitable. This matching of characteristics is with the aim of producing 'accurate' and 'truthful' data – both on the part of the interviewee to the interpreter, and on the part of the interpreter to the researcher. A more reflexive approach reveals the narrowness and implausibility of assumptions that communication and interpretation are necessarily and unvaryingly 'better' on the basis of social characteristic correspondence.

Extending dialogue in practice

Rosalind's research provides a good illustration of the point that difference may be 'reduced' according to one characteristic, but issues of perspective and identity remain. For example, Rosalind's Bengali/Sylheti interpreter's class positioning and her professional affiliations acted as a division between her and the interviewees just as much as their shared identity around gender and ethnicity. In addition, ethnicity acted as a division between her and Rosalind (as researcher) just as much as their shared gender, class and professional status. In the following extract from her 'key informant' interview, we can see how this interpreter constructed one particular border between her own identity and the identity of the research participants in relation to each other:

> "My background is, I come from an educated home. I come from a well-to-do middle-class family.... I know Bangladesh is a very underdeveloped country, but because I … went to an English school, my father … is the top man [for an insurance company] there in Bangladesh. You know, when I started working here at [the community centre] there was another class – you know, families who were deprived of all these things … people who would be uneducated … parents being unemployed, living in deplorable conditions with no money and too many children.... Because they don't speak the language, you see, they don't know how the [education, health and social welfare] system works."

As this interpreter performed the activity of translating the words of the interviewees to Rosalind and vice versa, she also performed the activity of constructing her own identity and those of the research participants. The very act of interpreting itself (her ability to do so) placed the interpreter as an educated, English-language proficient woman who can deal with public and private sector apparatus. Further, as she interpreted the interviewees' accounts of their difficulties and traumas in accessing and using child health services and other facilities, and chose the words best suited to convey their meaning to Rosalind, she constructed their social location in opposition to her own in significant ways. Her words also implicitly drew Rosalind into her constructions, as someone who was similarly 'educated' and placed alongside her in relation to the 'uneducated' interviewee group.

At other times, however, this interpreter constructed herself as rooted inside the culture of, and alongside the research participants. For example, one interviewee described how her mother-in-law loaded all the household tasks onto her, and how her husband would not allow her to confront her mother-in-law about this. During this account, the interpreter conveyed her empathetic understanding of the situation both in her body language and her interpretation, as well as her understanding of the recourses that were available to the interviewee. Indeed, she acted 'independently' (of Rosalind) within the interview to suggest a course of action, reporting as part of her ongoing interpretation: "... So I said, 'Can't you go back to Nepal, to your family, just for a holiday?' ...". In instances such as this, at the same time as she constructed a shared identity with the interviewee, the interpreter implicitly positioned Rosalind as an 'outsider' who lacked the cultural knowledge to be consulted, and included within, a discussion of what to do.

This example from Rosalind's research shows the key informant interviews as crucial in understanding, with significant implications for knowledge production. These implications become more explicit in the example from Bogusia's work.

In Bogusia's research, similar issues about where to locate researchers and interpreters in relation to research arise but are played out along different dimensions. Bogusia speaks Polish and this has undoubtedly been an advantage in terms of access. Research participants often assume a shared knowledge of history and cultural traditions and a certain sympathy with Polish perspectives on these. Many of these assumptions centre round the idea of what constitutes a 'Polish' way of life, and having been to a Polish Saturday School and attended a Polish Catholic church and club, certain shared values are often assumed. Bogusia has found that interviews are often a process of establishing the extent of this shared background and understanding. Comments such as 'you know' were common in the interviews. This process of positioning, however, is fluid and contextual and never final. More importantly, there are dangers in either assuming 'insider' or 'outsider' status as the example below illustrates.

Although there were many axes of similarity between research participants and Bogusia, there were also differences that are important to remember when considering Bogusia's interpretations and translations. For example, none of the women interviewed described themselves as feminist and most followed a way of life that Bogusia had in part rejected. She does not attend any church, has not taught her son Polish and is not a member of any formal organisation of Polish people. This was an issue with some of the people Bogusia interviewed and she sometimes felt an outsider. For others, however, it proved an advantage, as they did not follow these traditions either.

There are also other divisions in Polish communities, such as the time of settlement in Britain, that make ascriptions of belonging or being an outsider problematic. Many people who came from Poland after the Second World War still describe themselves as 'refugees' rather than 'migrants', a term reserved for more recent arrivals looking for work. However, few service providers see them in this way with consequences in terms of resources (Bowling, 1995). Bogusia's interpreter was a recent arrival from Poland. When they discussed the differences in their views of what a woman interviewee had meant when she said women 'must' behave in certain ways, Bogusia's interpreter told her: "You don't understand about Poland. You haven't lived there". Bogusia felt that the interviewee was saying 'must' because that was the way society had been structured and that the lack of choice was produced in society. The interpreter felt that 'must' had meant that there were biological imperatives underpinning why women had come to take their present roles in society. The interpreter went on to justify her version by describing Bogusia's Polish as "upper-class textbook stuff". The Polish taught to generations in England was, in her view, out of date and came from a particular class of people who had instilled very rigid views of language and culture into Polish communities in Britain. She may be right, but there were many people in Bogusia's research who were brought up with language and culture of a sort she described as "frozen in time". It is also interesting here that people from Poland sometimes take Bogusia's Polish as being from a particular region of Poland. The possible dimensions of difference and similarity are therefore many and fluid, and whether they matter or not depends on the context.

The significance of the examples that we have given is their illustration that, although discussing the influence of social location and identity is important, it is not sufficient. Perspective cannot be read off from your social location. Knowledge claims are thus contested and contingent.

Coming together

Rosalind and Bogusia have both come to the view that there is no one-to-one relationship between words and concepts across languages and that perspective comes in part from social location, of which culture and language are important aspects. Why does this matter for people working across languages to involve non-English speakers in research and service development? It matters because it means that it is not possible to choose one person to represent a particular language group and then assume that words and concepts move across languages in a neutral way. To assume this involves a form of language imperialism (Lauret, 1999). Rosalind and Bogusia have learnt to work across languages in a way that actively involves themselves and the interpreters they work with to carry out research, as well as the subjects of the research. Seeing interpreters as active key informants with intellectual autobiographies of their own enables us to position both ourselves and them in relation to research participants' views and to compare perspectives. This is a more active involvement with difference than assuming interpreters are mouthpieces either for other cultures or for us.

Simon (1996) discusses the concept of borders in her work and describes translation and writing as "forms of 'border writing' in the 'contact zone'. This is the place where cultures, previously separated, come together and establish ongoing relations" (1996, p 161). As we have argued earlier, debate on perspective is crucial in cross-language research. The examples above, however, also demonstrate that there is no single axis of similarity or difference on which to make decisions about who is representing whose views in interpreting words. The influence of particular social characteristics and points of view may be important, or not, according to context – as is the case in all qualitative research. As Simon asserts (1996, p 165), "rather than reconfirming the borders which separate nations, cultures, languages or subjectivities, translation shows them to be blurred. It is the very economy of translation as a system of regulating differences which has become problematic".

This problematising of translation has useful lessons for researchers working with interpreters. How interpreters produce borders between cultures and identities in qualitative research should become the focus of the kind of scrutiny that such issues have received in translation studies. Without this, we cannot justify claims that qualitative research can shed light on different perspectives, since we may have shut out one person who could enrich and challenge our understandings.

In this chapter we have attempted to show that applying some of the concepts developed in translation studies to research and service development with interpreters has many advantages. First, it extends debates over perspective in research to interpreters. As argued previously, to exclude them from debates on reflexivity and context is inconsistent. Second, when interpreters are included in such debates, valuable insights into the politics of location and identity can be reaped. Language can be a significant barrier to research with people who are not like the researcher in various ways. To assume that there is no problem in interpreting concepts across languages is to assume that there is only one baseline, and that is the researcher's own. Third, trying to make the interpreter as well as the researcher visible highlights the tensions in asking anyone to represent other people's views. That the researcher is positioned along multiple axes of belonging and not belonging during research, and that these border locations are not fixed, has been well recognised in qualitative research (see, for example, Song and Parker, 1995). Extending these insights to the choice of interpreter highlights the problematic nature of existing debates limited to the technical role of the interpreter and their language proficiency. Finally, using existing developments in cross-language research with translators provides a way of linking social context to individual situations, and situating debate of concepts, without assuming any view is linked unproblematically to social location.

Note

[1] The authors would like to thank the *International Journal of Qualitative Methods* for permission to reproduce a version of the paper from Temple and Edwards (2002).

References

Alcoff, L. (1991) 'The problem of speaking for others', *Cultural Critique*, vol 20, pp 5-32.

Alexander, C., Edwards, R. and Temple, B. with Kanani, U., Liu, Z., Miah, M. and Sam, A. (2004) *Access to services with interpreters: User views*, York: York Publishing Services/Joseph Rowntree Foundation.

Atkinson, P. (1990) *The ethnographic imagination: Textual constructions of reality*, London: Routledge.

Back, L. and Solomos, J. (1993) 'Doing research, writing politics: the dilemmas of political intervention in research on racism', *Economy and Society*, vol 22, no 2, pp 179-99.

Baker, P. with Hussain, Z. and Saunders, J. (1991) *Interpreters in public services: policy and training*, London: Venture Press.

Bassnet, S. (1994) *Translation studies*, London: Routledge.

Becker, H. (1970) 'Practitioners of vice and crime', in R.W. Habenstein (ed) *Pathways to data*, Chicago, IL: Aldine.

Berger, P. and Luckmann, T. (1991) *The social construction of reality: A treatise in the sociology of knowledge*, Harmondsworth: Penguin (original work published 1966).

Bhabha, H.K. (1994) *The location of culture*, London: Routledge.

Birbili, M. (2000) 'Translating from one language to another', *Social Research Update*, vol 31, pp 1-7.

Bowling, B. (1995) *Elderly people from ethnic minorities: A report on four projects*, London: Age Concern Institute of Gerontology.

Bulmer, M. (1984) *The Chicago school of sociology: Institutionalisation, diversity and the rise of sociological research*, Chicago, IL: Chicago University Press.

Corson, D. (1990) *Language policy across the curriculum*, Clevedon: Multilingual Matters.

DeVault, M. (1990) 'Talking and listening from a women's standpoint: feminist strategies for interviewing and analysis', *Social Problems*, vol 37, no 1, pp 96-116.

Dorsett, R. (1998) *Ethnic minorities in the inner city*, Bristol: The Policy Press.

Edwards, R. (1990) 'Connecting method and epistemology: a white woman interviewing black women', *Women's Studies International Forum*, vol 13, no 5, pp 477-90.

Edwards, R. (1993) *Evaluation of the Department of Health's new under fives initiative homeless families projects*, Report for the National Children's Bureau, London: South Bank University.

Edwards, R. (1995) 'Working with interpreters: access of services and to user views', in G. Wilson (ed) *Community care: Asking the users*, London: Chapman & Hall, pp 54-68.

Edwards, R. (1998) 'A critical examination of the use of interpreters in the qualitative research process', *Journal of Ethnic and Migration Studies*, vol 24, no 2, pp 197-208.

Esposito, N. (2001) 'From meaning to meaning: the influence of translation techniques on non-English focus group research', *Qualitative Health Research*, vol 11, no 4, pp. 568-79.

Freed, A.O. (1988) 'Interviewing through an interpreter', *Social Work*, July/August, pp 315-19.

Fuller, J.H.S. and Toon, P.D. (1988) *Medical practice in a multicultural society*, Oxford: Heinemann Medical.

Hammersley, M. (1995) *The politics of social research*, London: Sage Publications.

Hammersley, M. and Atkinson, P. (1989) *Ethnography: Principles in practice*, London: Routledge.

Hantrais, L. and Mangen, S. (eds) (1999) 'Special issue on cross-national research', *International Journal of Social Research Methodology: Theory and Practice*, vol 2, no 2, pp 91-189.

Harding, S. (ed) (1987) *Feminism and methodology*, Milton Keynes: Open University Press.

Hertz, R. (ed) (1997) *Reflexivity and voice*, London: Sage Publications.

Holstein, J.A. and Gubrium, J.F. (1995) *The active interview*, Qualitative Research Methods Series 37, London: Sage Publications.

Jentsch, B. (1998) 'The 'interpreter effect': rendering interpreters visible in cross-cultural research methodology', *Journal of European Social Policy*, vol 8, no 4, pp 275-89.

Kalantzis, M., Cope, B. and Slade, D. (1989) *Minority languages and dominant culture: Issues of education, assessment and social equality*, London: Falmer Press.

Karseras, P. and Hopkins, E. (1987) *British Asians' health in the community*, Chichester: John Wiley & Sons.

Lauret, M. (1999) 'The approval of headquarters': race and ethnicity in English Studies', in M. Bulmer and J. Solomos (eds) *Ethnic and racial studies today*, London: Routledge, pp 124–35.

London Research Centre (1992) *Housing Information Supplement No. 4: Refugees and asylum seekers accepted as homeless by London local authorities*, London: London Research Centre.

NHS Executive (1998) *National Surveys of NHS patients: General Practice 1998*, London: Department of Health.

Oakley, A. (1981) 'Interviewing women: a contradiction in terms', in H. Roberts (ed) *Doing feminist research*, London: Routledge & Kegan Paul, pp 30-61.

OPCS (Office for Population Censuses and Surveys) (1993) *1991 Census: County report*, London: OPCS.

Overing, J. (1987) 'Translation as a creative process: the power of the name', in L. Holly (ed) *Comparative anthropology*, Oxford: Basil Blackwell, pp 70-87.

Phelan, M. and Parkman, S. (1995) 'Work with an interpreter', *British Medical Journal*, vol 311, pp 555-7.

Simon, S. (1996) *Gender in translation: Cultural identity and the politics of transmission*, London: Routledge.

Song, M. and Parker, D. (1995) 'Cultural identity: disclosing commonality and difference in in-depth interviewing', *Sociology*, vol 29, no 2, pp 241-56.

Spivak, G.C. (1992) 'The politics of translation', in M. Barrett and A. Phillips (eds) *Destabilising theory: Contemporary feminist debates*, Cambridge: The Polity Press, pp 177-200.

Stanley, L. (1990) 'Moments of writing: is there a feminist auto/biography?', *Gender and History*, vol 2, pp 58-67.

Stanley, L. and Wise, S. (1983) *Breaking out: Feminist consciousness and feminist research*, London: Routledge & Kegan Paul.

Stanley, L. and Wise, S. (1993) *Breaking out again: Feminist ontology and epistemology*, London: Routledge.

Steier, F. (ed) (1991) *Research and reflexivity*, London: Sage Publications.

Stills, A., Sawhney, S. and Desai, P. (1995) *The communication needs of non-English speaking residents*, London: Newham Council.

Temple, B. (1993) 'Household strategies and types: the construction of social phenomena', unpublished PhD Thesis, University of Manchester.

Temple, B. (1997) 'Issues in translation and cross-cultural research', *Sociology*, vol 31, no 3, pp 607-18.

Temple, B. (1999) 'Diaspora, diaspora space and Polish women', *Women's Studies International Forum*, vol 22, no 1, pp 17-24.

Temple, B. (2001) 'Polish families: a narrative approach', *Journal of Family Issues*, vol 22, no 3, pp 386-99.

Temple, B. (2002) 'Crossed wires: interpreters, translators, and bilingual workers in cross-language research', *Qualitative Health Research*, vol 12, no 6, pp 844-54.

Temple, B. and Edwards, R. (2002) 'Interpreters/translators and cross language research: reflexivity and border crossings', *International Journal of Qualitative Methods*, vol 1, no 2, Article 1 (www.ualberta.ca/~ijqm).

Thomson, A.M., Rogers, A., Honey, S. and King, L. (1999) *'If the interpreter doesn't come there is no communication', A study of bilingual support services in the North West of England*, Manchester: School of Nursing, Midwifery and Health Visiting, University of Manchester.

van Maanen, J. (1988) *Tales of the field: On writing ethnography*, Chicago, IL: Chicago University Press.

Whyte, W.F. (1955) *Street corner society*, Chicago, IL: Chicago University Press.

Wilkinson, S. and Kitzinger, S. (eds) (1996) *Representing the other*, London: Sage Publications.

Wilson, G. and Revauger, J.P. (eds) (2001) 'Special issue on translation of words and concepts in social policy', *International Journal of Social Research Methodology, Theory and Practice*, vol 4, no 4, pp 259-338.

Young, I.M. (1997) *Intersecting voices: Dilemmas of gender, political philosophy and policy*, Princeton, NJ: Princeton University Press.

Yu, W.K. (2000) *Older Chinese people: A need for social inclusion in two communities*, Bristol: The Policy Press.

FOUR

Breaking the silence: participatory research processes about health with Somali refugee people seeking asylum

Rhetta Moran, Zeinab Mohamed and Hermione Lovel

Introduction

This chapter draws on the authors' experiences during the period 1998-2001 (Moran et al, 2002) when they developed a participatory research project (Nichter, 1984; Maguire, 1987; Whyte, 1991; Burkey, 1993; Chambers et al, 1996; Nieuwenhuys, 1997; Smith et al, 1997) in Manchester, England with people from Somalia recently arrived as refugees fleeing war. It begins by setting out a brief historical background to the situation in Somalia, then describes how members of Manchester's Somali community and academic researchers together developed their methods for finding out about – and improving – health (De Koning and Martin, 1996) among Somalis in Manchester.

After drawing some connections between a theory about 'language creation from below' (Volosinov, 1986) and community participation research processes where lay and researcher knowledge are respected as different and equal (Moran and Butler, 2001), the chapter describes and explains the process of evidence base development that began deep inside the Somali community with religious elders before moving out into the wider Somali community. It presents and discusses an early empirical example from the study that demonstrates how women from Somalia who are living in Britain are experiencing – and overcoming – barriers to their health needs within the primary care system, through creative interactions with healthcare practitioners. With the agency that is represented by one of the Somali women mentioned above as its starting point, the chapter analyses how our research approach has created a qualitative and quantitative dataset that is being incorporated into contemporary participatory action research protocol. It concludes by discussing the potential within this research approach for experiencing equality between academic and community-based researchers and community members.

Coming from Somalia

Somalia is on the east coast of Africa. It has a very low population density and is an extremely poor country with an average life expectancy at birth of 48 years compared with 78 in the UK; its infant mortality rate is 133/1,000, compared with 5/1,000 in the UK; its under-five mortality rate is 225/1,000, compared with 6/1,000 in the UK; only 29% of the population are using improved water sources; and only 25% are using adequate sanitation (Bellamy, 2004). It has a predominantly rural economy and the main religion is Sunni Muslim. In 1988, following a protracted war with Ethiopia, civil war broke out in Somalia. From 1989, Somali people began to arrive in refugee camps in Ethiopia and Kenya (Kibreab, 1993). The official, UN-backed, Arta Faction government was imposed without any meaningful consultation and, in October 2002, a Somali reconciliation process began where different parties signed a peace agreement to end hostilities and set up an all-inclusive federal system of government. To date, no national government operates in Somalia.

People from Somalia in the UK: past and present

Groups of Somali people have been living in the UK since the 1930s. On the basis that Somalia had been a British Protectorate, the UK government provided the international leadership to help the Somali people when the Somalian civil war peaked in 1990, resulting in the expulsion of Said Barre from the country in 1995. People then began to arrive in numbers in the UK from Somalia and, from 2000 onwards, Somalis came to the UK from refugee camps in Ethiopia, Kenya and elsewhere. They were often family members who had been separated in Somalia during the war; later, they were people whose entry into Britain had been delayed because of the political climate surrounding the twinned issues of immigration and asylum (Harris, 2004).

Soon after arriving, religious elders and mature women from the Somali community in Manchester became actively involved in a range of initiatives to address some of the community's basic social, educational and health needs. These included:

- becoming involved in a city-wide refugee group convened by the city council in the early 1990s to address the needs of refugee communities in the city;
- the formation of HAWEEN, a woman's organisation, in late 1993;
- cooperation with a survey (802 returns) of Somali people in Manchester conducted by the Planning Studies Group of the Planning and Environmental Health Department of the city council in 1994.

Background to the study

The three authors first met when Mohamed (delegated from her community group HAWEEN) opened up dialogue with Moran (then based at the Manchester Healthy City Project) and Lovel (then based at the University of Manchester) about working together to find out about the Female Genital Mutilation (FGM)-related health needs among Somali people in Manchester. Hosted by the Manchester Healthy City Project, a series of inter-agency meetings towards developing a city-wide approach to FGM were held between September 1997 and January 1998. They involved the three authors, representatives from HAWEEN, Manchester Health Authority's Primary Care Directorate, Central Manchester Healthcare NHS Trust, the Education, Social Services and Chief Executive Departments of Manchester City Council, Refugee Action and the national office of FORWARD UK, an international non-governmental organisation (NGO) dedicated to improving the health and well-being of African women and girls wherever they reside.

This pre-study exploration of purpose, conducted through dialogue between academics, people from the Somali community and a range of agency representatives, was the first and essential step towards developing an intrinsically participatory approach that was underpinned by a theory of 'language creation from below' (Volosinov, 1986), and formed the first phase of the process.

Theoretical model

All research aims, methods, results and analyses are communicated and interpreted through some combination of language based text, diagrams, pictures and numbers. The importance of language in the research process – its impact upon the formation of research questions, the methods adopted, the resultant findings and their analyses and dissemination – is rarely recognised or explored. (Moran and Butler, 2001, p 61)

Volosinov's theory of 'language creation from below' forms the backbone of the research approach that has developed in this study. The following interpretation (Moran and Butler, 2001) of Volosinov sets out his key points:

- the critical purpose of language is to communicate;
- it is through language that the reality that people experience is communicated;
- this 'reality' is both objective (that is, it exists independently of what people may or may not say about it), and intersubjective (that is, it is defined *between people through the communication of language*);
- intersubjective reality is fundamentally affected by the socioeconomic position (and inside of this, differences in gender, race, age, culture, able-bodiedness and citizenship status) of those who experience it;
- there are competing views of reality at any one point in time, held by different population groups. There is a continual process of struggle over, or 'contest' about, what the dominant meaning of reality is, and also over the means of communicating different versions of reality;
- what comes to prominence within any society as the dominant meaning of any particular reality is the result of that contest and is a refraction, rather than a direct reflection, of reality.

Taken together, these points explain the connections that exist between the meanings developed and communicated through language and the socioeconomic context of those who are producing and using that language. Figure 4.1 shows how this theoretical framework helps to advance the participatory approach that was adopted in this study. The figure has been specifically adapted to relate to this study about health and asylum.

Within any given urban locality, our physical context is composed of social, economic, cultural and political entities that are situated (Wright Mills, 1963) in time and place (background to the concentric circles).

In material terms, this context is a combination of buildings, for private and public accommodation, work, education, and shopping/consumer activities; the governmental system connected to regional

Figure 4.1: Social–economic–cultural–political–built environment

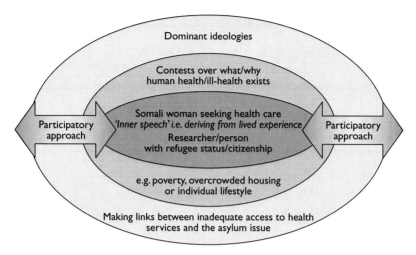

For example, quantitative data, both spatial and statistical: comparative statistics on how many refugee people seeking asylum have been detected across Europe.

Source: Moran (2002)

and national political and civil service networks; the business and community sector networks in the area; and the people who may have a wide range of different social networks within the locality, who work, live or visit in the area. This is the urban context within which any research study operates.

Within this context, dominant views circulate via a range of public arenas – newspapers, television, radio and the internet – about how public access to health resources is connected to asylum issues (outer circle of Figure 4.1). These views interrelate with peoples' own ideas about why health/ill health exists and their own experiences of asylum issues. These personal ideas are communicated between refugee people seeking asylum and the people around them as they use dialogue to work out what meanings they share and how and why their meanings may differ (middle circle of Figure 4.1). In turn, this dialogical or communicative act interrelates with their internal speech, the words that they form in their own heads that make up their ideas about the meanings of seeking asylum and seeking healthcare that are derived from their personal experiences (inner circle of Figure 4.1). However, the person seeking asylum will often speak a mother tongue that is other than the language of the dominant ideology; their 'inner speech' is in a different language from that which enables them to communicate with most members of the host community. This linguistic isolation –

and the powerlessness associated with it – adds to the physical isolation they experience when they are dispersed to a new and completely unknown locality (Moran, 2003).

Through our research, we aimed to encourage and enable individuals to share the meanings of their inner world by inviting them to talk, in their mother tongue, about issues they defined as important; thus the "culture of silence" (Freire, 1975, p 16) would be broken by "naming the world" (p 28) in dialogue *with*, not in monologue *to*, *for* or *at*, the oppressed (Wadsworth, 2002). Further, by agreeing from the outset that the data created would be analysed by the research team in partnership (represented by the arrow passing through all the circles) with members of the targeted community, the power dynamics between academic and community-based researchers are altered. As they reach agreement about the meanings of the data and communicate them beyond the community base, they begin to contest the dominant ideologies about how refugee people seeking asylum perceive and experience health systems in the UK.

The decision to attempt to develop a participatory research approach arose out of the desire, shared by both the community members and the researchers, to achieve an equal – but different – partnership in the study. However, during the course of the early meetings, three key, but potentially conflicting, issues emerged that compromised the ability of the group to work cohesively:

- In an effort to defuse distrust and the perception that positive aspects of the Somali culture may be threatened through this inter-agency working, the community representatives were keen to involve men alongside women and to stress an educational over a punitive approach towards addressing FGM.
- Under their statutory obligations, the education and social services personnel involved were bound to take legal steps on any information suggesting that female children may be at risk of FGM. This inhibited the possibilities for full and free formal information exchange between the community and these representatives.
- While remaining committed in principle to being involved in developing the appropriate health service dimensions, insufficient staffing levels led the health authority's Primary Care Directorate to withdraw from the meetings at the end of November 1997. Alongside weakening the inter-agency identity of the initiative, this contradicted the move towards repositioning primary health care services within the NHS and the developing public health agenda that sought both to locate health needs within their wider

socioeconomic context and to centralise self-involvement in improving health outcomes (Secretary of State for Health, 1997, 1998).

In January 1998 the inter-agency meetings ceased. However, the authors continued to develop the process when Somali religious elders asked Mohamed for sustained help with their concerns and, in so doing, the project moved into its second phase.

Developing the methodology

In the spring of 1998, Mohamed and Lovel met twice more with four Somali religious leaders. The meetings, conducted bilingually (in Somali and English), were tape recorded, simultaneously translated and transcribed by Mohamed, preliminarily analysed by Mohamed and Moran and presented back to the originators of the data (ie the religious leaders). The authors observed that the transcripts raised a number of pressing and current concerns, identified below, within the community and, flowing from this, the perception that FGM was an issue that could and should be addressed in tandem with a range of other health issues.

Lack of social nexus ... and all that flows from that

Notwithstanding their efforts to engage with the city's statutory agencies, the Somali communities had no community base of their own. They were sharing the Pakistani mosque but were unable to use it whenever there were visiting religious leaders and/or sessions in Urdu. It was the overwhelming view of the religious elders that acquiring a collective physical space, over which the community had control, was the cornerstone from which it would become possible to begin to address the complex interrelation of health, social, educational, housing and employment problems confronting the community. The lack of collective space inhibited the development of Somali community identity and shared culture:

> "... we have a large community which has no place at all whatsoever, no place, no community centre, no crèche for the kids, no place for the women ... so without the base there is no community ... where the people get together and develop their culture." (Religious elder, focus group)

Despite this, community members created temporary, but nevertheless inadequate, environments that enabled sporadic social interaction between children in the community but left the adults' needs to one side. However, these sorts of events were the exception rather than the rule. Considering the needs of pre-school children in particular, having no community space, little or no English language and being separated from fathers who had either remained in or returned to Somalia had resulted in acute social isolation and its attendant health problems:

> "The most problems, if I identified some of them ... those infants. Children who have not reached age of school ... it is possible that some mothers have three children under five ... and they have no place to take (them) to make break for the children, a community centre for example, or a place where they care the children, like crèche, or anywhere else, they haven't got it.... Most of the children then, as a result of that, that they are not going outside of the atmosphere, that they are not taking the climate outside, as a result they got further problems, relating particularly to the Somali women and children." (Religious elder, focus group)

In their role as spiritual carers in the community, the religious elders had acquired a grounded knowledge of the range of health problems that currently affect large numbers of the Somali population. One of the most pressing concerns, which they believed to be associated with the poor standard of some housing (Cole and Robinson, 2003) as well as the lack of opportunities to leave the home for social gatherings, was the number of young Somali children who were developing asthma:

> "Most of the Somali children are living with asthma. Every house you go there is an asthmatic case. Every house, almost every house ...condition of the house and the pollution in this area." (Religious elder, focus group)

In the first instance, a community space would begin to break down the social isolation that many experience:

> *First speaker:* There is a problem. Some of the community, they are already in depression, by the loneliness, haven't managed themselves.

Second speaker: Well, because they come in the war where they had a problem. So they go some area, they don't see their families, and ...

First speaker: They don't speak the languages, they can't communicate with other people.

Third speaker: And they are locked in all the time inside the house, they don't go anywhere else. (Religious elders, focus group)

However, in relation to mental health needs within the Somali community (MAAN Somali Mental Health Project, 2001), engagement with health services had sometimes been found to compound problems. In addition, young Somalis, newly arrived in this country and without employment or opportunities to learn English (Community Development and Empowerment Unit et al, 1996; Lawlor, 1999) were felt to be especially vulnerable. The elders felt that regular opportunities and secure spaces to meet would give young Somalis the opportunity to retain their cultural identity, including their religious identity (see Chapter Ten), and nurture their motivation to learn the language to enable them to undertake training and increase their employment opportunities:

First speaker: The religion is part of the culture. The religion and the culture go together.... Once they adopt their culture, they will have adopted their religion.

Second speaker: Well the religious side is to stop our community to befall in this bad thing which is running in the Western streets, to be honest. Which is what we all think about ... everybody is fighting with this. Because most of the children, no matter what they are, what religion they are, when they come to this Western society, there are some people who are drug dealers, spoiling all the youths. (Religious elders, focus group)

These physical obstacles to the maintenance of cultural education in general and the preservation of Somali language in particular were demonstrated through the example of a child, who used to speak Somali with ease, and who now struggled with their mother tongue:

> *First speaker:* Yesterday I went to a family, the house, I went to see the father of the family, and his daughter spoke to me and said 'Father is … what's the word?', she said.
>
> *Second speaker:* It was the language, they lost the language.
>
> *First speaker:* Now, we shouldn't lose our language, it's expensive … and it's unique language, we have to protect it. (Religious elders, focus group)

This range of social, medical, educational and cultural needs (Ibrahim, 2004), how people within the Somali community believe that the issue of FGM should be approached in the context of these needs, and the impetus from within the community to find meaningful ways and places to express their ideas and strategies for change were paramount. Contrary to dominant Western assumptions, and fully conscious of the extent to which the Somali culture was under pressure, the religious elders opposed the practice of FGM:

> *First speaker:* It's a very bad culture. It came from the Arab, the Arab. That's where it comes from. And it went throughout the Arab world and Africa. And I think UK or Europe used to do it.
>
> *Second speaker:* I heard, the Islamic leaders, the religious leaders what they do. They tour telling people.
>
> *First speaker:* Giving lectures …
>
> *Second speaker:* Lectures, saying what's wrong and what's right. And, at the moment, in the mosques, in back home, I remember they say this shouldn't happen. (Religious elders, focus group)

These elders made clear distinctions between the role of culture that misinforms about FGM and the role of religion that does not support the practice:

> "Every man must take responsibility. Because it's Islamic. And what Islamic is stop it. We must stop it. We must stop it.…What is useful and what is useless." (Religious elder, focus group)

For them, tackling the practice of FGM begins from the fundamental understanding that it is perceived as one way of preserving a cultural identity in an otherwise highly inhospitable cultural environment. This understanding was twinned with the recognition that, in order to draw down resources that could begin to engage with the full range of Somali perceptions and experiences of health needs, including those associated with FGM, there was a need for a robust evidence base that could be used to acquire a generic community base:

> *First speaker:* I think we need all Somalis to come together and have a survey from the local authorities, for the health centres, from the education, the housing, social services. With the Somalis we will work together and make a planned project.

> *Second speaker:* First of all, unless we work together and understand the problems and are determined to work, we will not reach our targets. (Religious elders, focus group)

Developing tools

These meetings grounded the third phase of the process, where women and men, elders and young people were brought together with Mohamed and Moran to explore practical methods for documenting the current health status of the Somali community and evolve FGM Type III training materials to help practitioners to learn what to do when confronted with this very severe type of FGM.

Working within the social networks that already existed between the community-based researcher and community members who had been involved in defining the areas of study, the research group created a snowball sample (see Chapter Five for further discussion about this method). Organised along gender and age lines, five focus group discussions involving 42 people were held in local health and community centres or private Somali homes. Facilitated by Mohamed and conducted in both Somali and English, the tape-recorded focus groups explored the key issues that had emerged so far. The groups were comprised of mothers over 50 ($n=10$); married women aged between 26 and 46 ($n=9$); young women aged between 17 and 23 ($n=7$), one of whom was married and had two children under three; religious elder males ($n=10$), all aged over 48, all married and fathers; and young men ($n=6$) aged between 18 and 22, two of whom were married and one who had a single child.

All the transcripts were simultaneously translated into English where necessary and transcribed into English by Mohamed. Out of reading and re-reading these transcripts, the research team identified a broader and deeper set of themes about self-identified health needs that were evident across all the discussion groups. The themes were concentrated in the areas of housing, education, social needs, young people, the family and FGM, and included the following case study that emerged from the focus group with married women.

Case study

> "When I made *Wuduu* [washing for prayer which includes washing between the legs after toileting and before prayer] I used to go out (quickly without drying myself properly), but then I had an itching below under, there was no one with me, who am (I) going to tell? I just scratched and scratched." (Somali woman, married women's focus group)

The interaction between this woman and the health authorities begins with the 'patient' deciding to actively break the barriers to receiving healthcare. She made an appointment at the local health centre and when she was called for the consultation, she overcame the language barrier between her and the doctor by showing him her problem:

> "The next day I went to the doctor, but I didn't know how to tell him that I had this problem, so I went straight in to [the] small bed [in] the GP room and jumped on [to] the bed, took all my clothes off and spread my legs apart so that he could look at the problem." (Somali woman, married women's focus group)

This action immediately, and unwittingly, placed the male doctor in a compromised position that he could not explain to the patient and so "the doctor then ran out of the room and called a nurse who took me to the [nurses' room] clinic".

Having examined and diagnosed her condition, the nurse:

> "… checked me and gave me a tablet but who's going to tell me how to take it? The nurse became frustrated with me when should couldn't make me understand. She [the nurse] gave a cream tube [and] show[ed] me how to use it by putting a bit [on] her thigh. I went home, I dried myself

[after washing] and used it at night." (Somali woman, married women's focus group)

Just as the language communication barrier forced the woman to physically show her problem without any accompanying verbal explanation of what she thought caused it (not drying properly after washing before prayer) and what her symptoms were ("I just scratched and scratched"), the practitioner had to physically demonstrate how to treat the condition. However, while this creative communicative process between the Somali woman, the doctor and the nurse overcame the immediate barrier to accessing diagnosis and treatments:

"I did not get any more itching [but it may return] and the medicine had finished, so how am [I] going to tell the doctor that I have finished the cream? I took the cover [from the box of the medicine] and went to the clinic and I saw the person [the nurse] who gave me the last cream. She wrote something on a paper but I couldn't understand her again. She took me and ask[ed] me to sit down. Then she phoned [a] Somali lady who explained [over the phone] to me [I should] come back the next day for another prescription." (Somali woman, married women's focus group)

This example has been chosen for three key reasons. First, it highlights the agency of the individual who is usually allocated the position of research 'subject' within traditional paradigms, with all the inherent passivity of that label: working out how to nurture, validate, amplify and augment this individual agency lies at the heart of our participatory approach. Second, it illuminates that, in practice, interaction between the individual agency on the part of refugee people seeking asylum that stimulates reactions by health service practitioners, and reactions to those reactions by witnesses and later listeners, creates alternative forms of health service delivery. Third, it captures this woman's 'conscientisation' (Freire, 1970, p 16) as she recognises, works with and then, with us, articulates the dialectic of the human interaction that communicates refugee health needs.

Taking ownership of and control over the means of research production

The themes identified by the researchers were shared with the community members supporting the study when Mohamed organised a further meeting between herself, Moran and 11 members of the community including some of the involved elders, members of HAWEEN and a small number of female and male youths. At this meeting it was agreed that Mohamed and Moran would create a first draft version of a health needs questionnaire to include the following sections: purpose of questionnaire; individual signifiers; health and housing; health and education; health and social needs; health and young people; health and the family: children and reproduction; female circumcision. Those present agreed to invite other people from within the community to attend a three-hour session at a local neighbourhood centre where they would work in groups to develop each section of the questionnaire.

Mohamed opened the session in Somali by explaining the purpose as being to develop tools for creating an evidence base of what the Somali community defines as its health needs.

After extending a welcome in Somali, Moran, with Mohamed interpreting, circulated the opening section of the draft questionnaire. She stressed that ownership of and control over the questionnaire content lay with the community so that if amendments were deemed necessary, they would be positively welcomed; indeed they would be one way of measuring the extent to which the process was enabling the community to participate.

A brief, open discussion followed, during which male members of the community who were present questioned Moran on the value of involving men in a questionnaire about health, given that health issues were of specific importance to women and children, and how this questionnaire related to their desire for the creation of a Somali community base. Drawing on the information previously gathered with the elders about the connections between having a community space and improving health within the community, Moran's responses to these questions appeared to satisfy the concerns that the research should advance the attainment of a community space.

From the outset, this openness to criticism of the draft material was an important demonstration of the researcher's respect for – and confidence in – the abilities of the group, and confirmation that an equal working partnership model was being sought in practice, not in theory.

The group then considered the first section of the questionnaire. Clarification was sought on the meaning of the aim of enabling health workers to learn about and look after Somali people better. Moran emphasised that this aim described the process as being directed towards the physical production of training materials that could guide and inform health carers when Somali people presented for services. This response met with strong signs of approval from the questioner who then suggested that the group move forward to consider each section of the questionnaire.

The community members were invited to divide themselves into discrete groups along gender and age lines, and each was given a section of the questionnaire to discuss among themselves. This meant that, at this stage, only the group working on a particular area had sight of that part of the questionnaire.

During the discussions, members of the groups asked the facilitators for clarification and challenged various points in the questionnaire. This interaction consolidated the feelings of equality between researcher and community member and reminded them that neither could produce what they intended to produce without the other.

Each group selected a spokesperson to present the key points from their section of the questionnaire using a flip chart. Thus, the fulcrum of control over the physical space and the content of the meeting shifted further towards the community members, who gradually built up a complete representation of all the views being expressed.

With the exception of the Health and Young People group, where two people made a concurrent bilingual presentation, each group spokesperson elected to speak first in English and then to repeat the findings in Somali. All groups expressed satisfaction with the questionnaire as it stood. The Health and the Family group did not wish to make any amendments, but during the individual group sessions, one member of this group had stated: "We've looked at it, it's fine. We don't want to change anything. It is very painful for us, talking about FGM."

At the end of the meeting, a female elder voiced her support for the approach as a whole and encouraged those present to remain involved and to secure the involvement of more people in the next phase of the process. As a result, Mohamed and Moran decided to incorporate the suggested amendments and then hold a longer session with more community members to finalise the questionnaire.

Seventy people completed the final questionnaires: 40 women and 30 men aged between 16 and 70.

Discussion

The burgeoning literature about participation and consultation demonstrates that valuing difference and respecting different perspectives are not in themselves indicators that equality exists between the members of research partnerships. Even when such values are present, the academic is invariably still the one who is writing the bids, controlling the resources, using academic language to write the final report and writing future bids.

In our work there are, however, a number of indications that the research process has moved beyond developing ways of securing the inclusion of refugees towards a transparent, and therefore contestable, set of developmental stages that continuously seek to reaffirm the assertion that equality within the researching partnership is the aim.

The initial impetus for the research came not from academic researchers but from members of the community with strong opinions about what issues needed to be explored. This is a reversal of the usual dynamic whereby researchers define the areas of enquiry and then go in search of a sample. The decision to broaden the process of data collection beyond those occupying positions of relative power within the Somali community, that is, the religious leaders, circumvented the notion that one group can adequately represent all views (see Chapters Five and Six). By agreeing from the outset (represented by the arrow passing through all the circles of Figure 4.1) that any preliminary data created must be analysed by the research team in partnership with members of the targeted community, and that any tools developed out of that analysis would remain in the ownership of the community group for it to decide when, where and how to apply them, the power dynamics between academic and community-based researchers were altered. This is best illustrated by the process of questionnaire development, whereby the fulcrum of control over both the physical space and the research content of the community-based meeting that developed the tool shifted towards the community members, who gradually built up a complete representation of all the views being expressed before suggesting amendments to the questionnaire.

This process was made possible through: a mutual preparedness to listen to each other; sharing our respective knowledge bases and social networks in order to advance the research process; maintaining a constant awareness that ownership and control over the questionnaire content lay with the community; and testing the consistency of that awareness about ownership and control through open discussions about suggested amendments.

In sum, we know that this constantly evolving participatory approach can offer a theoretical framework and practical guidance about how to move towards equality within researching processes between academic researchers and refugees who have been forced to flee war, because we have experienced and been a part of the approach to the extent that we can articulate key features of what this equality involves.

When we developed this research, we were all very optimistic about its possibilities. We presented regularly about this research process and its emergent findings and there was a heightened awareness, both within the Somali community and within the systems of the city, about what we were doing and about the issues that concerned the Somali community. The work formed the bedrock for progressing the perspectives of Somali people within the city.

However, in the main, the situation has remained static – or has even degenerated – for the following reasons:

• There are more Somali people, many with acute health needs, constantly being dispersed, and there are very few initiatives available to help them.
• The problems that existed within the community that participated in our research have worsened since the research process began.
• There is an enormous amount of rhetoric on equality, social inclusion and improved health outcomes and very little in the way of either mainstream or project-funded action. However, as local authorities are required to show how they are involving socially excluded groups and how they are addressing inequalities, a specific action plan developed with the Somali community that builds on our research could be developed, implemented and assessed.
• While there have been a number of positive, but very small, outcomes from our work, there is still no community centre for members of the Somali population in Manchester.

Further, without the political will and power to draw down resources to change things, the theorised and tested research process and the robust evidence base that has been developed out of that process remain stranded within the knowledges and experiences of the Somali communities and their academic research partners.

Our hope is that, in the process of making it possible for the inner voice (Volosinov, 1986) to join up with other, similar, voices and by continuing to engage with the challenge of 'conscientisation' (Freire, 1970, p 16) whereby people – whether they be academic researchers, community researchers and/or community members – connect their lived experiences to developing theory into practical action, the dominant sets of ideas become contested so that people transform how they think and act about the health issues of refugee people seeking asylum.

Photograph 4.1: Participatory action research with refugee people from Somalia in Manchester

References

Bellamy, C. (2004) *Childhood under threat. The state of the world's children 2005*, Geneva: UNICEF (www.unicef.org/sowc05/English).

Burkey, S. (1993) *People first, a guide to participatory self development*, London: Zed Books.

Chambers, R., Blackburn, J. and Barnard, G. (1996) *Power of participation: PRAIDS Policy Briefing no 7 and Policy Issue*, Brighton: Institute of Development Studies.

Cole, I. and Robinson, D. (2003) *Somali housing experiences in England*, Sheffield: Centre for Regional Economic and Social Research, Sheffield Hallam University.

Community Development and Empowerment Unit, Central Policy Unit, Liverpool 8 Educational Opportunities Initiative, Race Equality Management Team and the Youth and Community Service Education Directorate (1996) *The development needs of Somali young people in Liverpool*, Liverpool: Liverpool City Council.

De Koning, K. and Martin, M. (1996) *Participatory research in health: Issues and experiences*, London: Zed Books.

Freire, P. (1970) *Pedagogy of the oppressed*, New York, NY: Herder and Herder.

Harris, H. (2004) *The Somali community in the UK: What we know and how we know it*, London: Information Centre about Asylum and Refugees in the UK.

Ibrahim, M.M. (2004) 'Somalis suffer in Britain', *Eastern Africa Magazine*, no 16, p 13.

Kibreab, G. (1993) 'The myth of dependency among camp refugees in Somalia 1979-1989', *Journal of Refugee Studies*, vol 6, no 4, pp 321-49.

Lawlor, F. (1999) 'The social and educational problems of Somali children between 11-16 years old in the Liverpool 8 area', Thesis, Liverpool: University of Liverpool.

MAAN Somali Mental Health Project (2001) *Khat and mental health. Conference report*, Sheffield: Somali Mental Health Project.

Maguire, P. (1987) *Doing participatory action research: A feminist approach*, Cambridge, MA: Centre of International Education, University of Massachusetts.

Moran, R.A. (2003) *From dispersal to destitution: Dialectical methods in participatory action research with people seeking asylum*, Paper presented at Policy and Politics in a Globalising World conference, University of Bristol, (www.bristol.ac.uk/sps/papers/sream4/moran.doc).

Moran, R.A. and Butler, D.S. (2001) 'Whose health profile?', *Critical Public Health*, vol 11, no 1, pp 59-74.

Moran, R.A., Mohamed, Z. and Lovel, H. (2002) *Breaking the silence: Participatory action research with refugees in Britain*, Paper presented at XV World Congress of Sociology, Brisbane.

Nichter, M. (1984) 'Project community diagnosis: participatory research as a first step towards community involvement in primary health care', *Social Science and Medicine*, vol 19, no 3, pp 237-52.

Nieuwenhuys, O. (1997) 'Spaces for the children of the urban poor: experiences with participatory action research (PAR)', *Environment and Urbanization*, vol 9, no 1, pp 233-49.

Secretary of State for Health (1997) *The new NHS: Modern, dependable*, London: The Stationery Office.

Secretary of State for Health (1998) *A first class service: Quality in the New NHS*, London: The Stationery Office.

Smith, S.E., Wiliams, D.G. and Johnson, N.A. (1997) *Nurtured by knowledge, learning to do participatory action and research*, Ottowa: International Development Research Centre.

Volosinov, V.N. (1986) *Marxism and the philosophy of language*, Translation of *Markism i filosofia iazyka* (1929) by L. Matejka and I.R. Titunik, Cambridge, MA: Harvard University Press.

Wadsworth, Y. (2002) *Gouldner's child? Some critical reflections on sociology and participatory action research. Continuing work in progress*, Paper presented at XV World Congress of Sociology, Brisbane.

Whyte, W.F. (ed) (1991) *Participatory action research*, Newbury Park, CA: Sage Publications.

Wright Mills, C. (1963) 'Situated actions and vocabularies of motive', in I.L. Horowitz (ed) *Power, politics and people: Collected essays*, Oxford: Oxford University Press, pp 438-52.

FIVE

Home/lessness as an indicator of integration: interviewing refugees about the meaning of home and accommodation[1]

Priya Kissoon

Introduction

Although many Western nations are sites of asylum for refugees, their fulfilment of this humanitarian obligation has become increasingly begrudging and a matter of intense political debate. Different national and political attitudes, and different immigration and resettlement policies affect refugees' social and material trajectories (van der Veer, 1992; Renaud and Gingras, 1998), and can be prime determinants of their reconstructions of 'home' and belonging in the country of asylum (Black, 1994, 2002; Bloch, 2002; Korac, 2003). Research indicates that early stable housing trajectories beget security and autonomy and facilitate functional and social integration (Zetter and Pearl, 1999; Carey-Wood et al, 1995; Carey-Wood, 1997; Murdie and Teixeira, 2000; Garvie, 2001; Foley and Beer, 2003). Some research suggests that the terms 'social integration' and 'functional integration' are synonyms measured by socioeconomic or 'instrumental' indicators (Ray, 2002). However, more frequently a qualitative distinction is made between functional and social integration, where socioeconomic 'instrumental' indicators describe the former, and 'affective' indicators the latter. Functional integration is commonly measured in terms of language proficiency, labour market participation, civic and political participation, educational performance, and accommodation in adequate housing (Home Office, 2000; Ray, 2002) and social integration is inferred from issues of identity, belonging, and the quality and strength of social links (Korac, 2002; Zetter et al, 2002). Research has demonstrated that 'affective' indicators are profoundly significant to integration (Ryan and Woodill, 2000; Bloch, 2002; Korac, 2002; Zetter et al, 2002), and are knowable through in-depth interviews and a research process that creates room for participants to voice their evaluation of their circumstances and their personal satisfaction, and to reflect on their current situations in the context of the whole of their refugee experiences, including displacement, flight, asylum seeking and settlement.

Although governments pay lip-service to the rapid integration of newcomers, systemic and structural obstacles act to frustrate assertions of individual agency or upward mobility. Programmatic integration strategies that are based on involving, enabling and empowering refugees through actualising and validating their agency contribute to meeting their tangible and material, and 'fundamental needs'. 'Fundamental needs' include dignity, security, social connectedness and identity (Stenström, 2003, p 30), and are important not only because they buttress functional integration, but because they are essential to human welfare and a sense of home.

Yu and Liu (1986) suggest that the hegemony of economic self-sufficiency as the chief indicator of 'refugee adjustment' in research conducted by academics and federal agencies is related to methodological and conceptual difficulties of cultural and social adjustment, rather than indicators' worth or importance to society (1986, p 496). This chapter is based on doctoral research that attempts to redress this imbalance in refugee adjustment by interrogating the idea of home as a 'soft' indicator of integration that straddles issues of emotional and material well-being. Each person has an idea of home that merges place and personality, that goes beyond having four walls and a roof, and that indicates a positive feeling that derives from security, belonging, attachment or familiarity, among other things. The scale at which individuals interpret this place of home may vary greatly, ranging from the metaphysical and global, national, and regional to the local, neighbourhood, dwelling and even embodiment by specific people in one's life, such as a parent, spouse or child. The home may be more than mappable localities, and exist among institutions that reflect one's ideals, concerns or endeavours, and it may exist as feelings of permanence, agency, autonomy, dialogue and participation.

The home is important to integration as a foundation from which other trajectories are embarked upon and as a site of regeneration and rehabilitation, but additionally it is an assessment of well-being and satisfaction. As a place of "peace, of shelter from terror, doubt, and division, a geography of relative self-determination and sanctity" (Goldberg, 1993, p 199), people are attached to home just as they are attached to families and friends, and when these attachments converge, they produce "... the most tenacious cement possible for human society" (Mumford, 1961, p 287). This sense of home, therefore, is requisite for a healthy society and, according to Dummett (2001), it is the "destiny of nations" to create or facilitate this identity from the disparate inhabitants entitled to live in that country and be its citizens (Dummett, 2001, p 21).

The research on which this chapter is based employs the dialectic of home and homelessness (Porteous and Smith, 2001) to explore housing and settlement issues among refugees in Toronto, Canada and London, England. Only the interviews in England will be discussed in this chapter. It elicits refugees' own definitions, identities and locations of home/lessness and examines these in relation to their housing experiences in the countries of asylum and their senses of belonging and exclusion. The research relies on in-depth, semi-structured interviews with 60 participants (ie 30 in Canada and 30 in London), and explores three main questions: "How is home conceived, located and reconstructed in the asylum and settlement process?", "How do national and residential dynamics affect refugee participants' sense of home or homelessness?" and "In what ways can refugee participants' sense of home or homelessness serve as a marker of integration?".

Although homelessness is often used as a synonym for 'houselessness', the term originally described the lack of 'familial moorings' of drifters living in single room occupancy motels or improvised shelters that catered to transient single men (Daly, 1996). FEANTSA (the European Federation of National Organisations Working with the Homeless) considers 'home' to have three domains: having an adequate dwelling (or space) over which a person and his/her family can exercise exclusive possession (physical domain); being able to maintain privacy and enjoy relations (social domain); and having legal title to occupation (legal domain). FEANTSA defines 'homelessness', however, along the continuum of rooflessness, houselessness, insecure housing, inadequate housing and unaffordable housing.

This research moves beyond the traditional conceptions of home and homelessness to understand refugees' layered experiences. The research investigates the housing trajectories of refugees in the country of asylum, but then asks refugees to reflect on their personal definitions of home to gauge the extent to which their housing circumstances, their neighbourhood, their city of abode, their country of origin and country of persecution correspond with their definition and have changed over time and experience. Furthermore, this research was designed to focus on the settlement phase, rather than flight and persecution; however, it provides room for participants to locate feelings of home/lessness within all phases of the asylum process, past, present and future, and to reflect on the characteristics and site(s) of home/lessness.

There has been a lack of nuanced discussion of how people who have sought and achieved asylum resolve experiences of loss and how housing conditions affect their sense of well-being and belonging. This study responds to this gap, which is flanked by research presuming vulnerability, powerlessness and the subjection of asylum seekers to a psychosocial or 'post-colonial' homelessness beginning with forced migration. Such research often foregoes home as a process and presents it as precisely located, synonymous with the country of origin at one scale and the residential dwelling at another. This is most evident in accommodation studies that refer to refugees as homeless on arrival to the country of asylum (for example, Quilgars, 1993; Ryan and Woodill, 2000), and experiencing a 'double homelessness' in "... the loss of both a home and a homeland" (Garvie, 2001, p 6). The lack of critical reflection in the use of the terms home and homeless in relation to refugees is problematic in at least two ways: it assumes de facto homelessness for forced migrants or 'double homelessness' for poorly accommodated refugees, which simultaneously diminishes and normalises the homelessness experiences of citizens; and it presumes ties to, and a relationship with, the country of origin, which may reflect a Western image of 'the refugee' rather than a refugee's experiences.

Neither the country of origin nor the place of dwelling can be presumed to have been a home in any respect, and the imposition of this emotionally laden term on spaces that may have included persecution, destitution and fear constitutes sentimentalised concepts of both national and domestic spaces. Similarly, situations and experiences that researchers presume to be characterised by loss, remorse, stress, and insecurity may satisfy more pressing individual needs; for example, some asylum seekers may value proximity to family or social networks to the detriment of their material living conditions, rather than undergo dispersal. This is not meant to mitigate the hurdles that asylum seekers face in the asylum process, nor their effects, but to emphasise that the geographies of home and exclusion must originate from the individual and accommodate scale, time and space. What defines integration and how we measure integration cannot ignore the lived experiences, voices and perceptions of refugees themselves (see Chapter Eight).

Qualitative methods are essential for exploring complex, mutually constituting or contradictory ideas such as home and homelessness, belonging and exile, citizenship and asylum. This chapter looks at how qualitative methods can be used to investigate the processual notion of integration with the slippery notion of home in order to understand how refugees interpret their flight and settlement. It provides a brief background to forced resettlement and previous research in the field before going on to give a detailed account of the research process: inception, design, negotiating with gatekeepers, finding participants, and interviewing from the perspective of a research student, with all the advantages and limitations that implies. The research process is presented to explore the ways in which methodological considerations construct a project that responds to a gap in refugee and integration studies and the geographies of asylum and home. In particular, the chapter focuses on: how and why certain questions were chosen, including the issue of sensitive topics; the use of scales and photography; the issue of gatekeepers and key informants; the question of payment; the use of non-probability purposive rather than statistical sampling; and the influence of language on the research.

Background

Research has documented the importance of housing as one of the cornerstones of reception and successful resettlement for refugees and asylum seekers (van der Veer, 1992; Carey-Wood et al, 1995; Carey-Wood, 1997; Zetter and Pearl, 1999; Murdie and Teixeira, 2000; Garvie, 2001; Foley and Beer, 2003; Edgar et al, 2004). Housing is extremely important for refugees as a place of safety, autonomy and respite from the asylum process, the struggle for recognition and status, and the effort of integration or adaptation (Renaud and Gringas, 1998). More than filling a basic physical need for immigrant newcomers, it constitutes an important resource in re-establishing social structures such as the family and linkages to the wider community, and minimising dependency on welfare support (Zetter and Pearl, 2000). However, evidence of systemic under-housing among asylum-seeker and refugee households in London has been well documented (Quilgars, 1993; Zetter and Pearl 1999; Garvie, 2001; Palmer, 2001; Pearl and Zetter, 2002; Anderson, 2003).

Twenty-nine per cent (2.1 million) of London's population belong to a minority ethnic group, including 250,000 to 350,000 refugees who have settled in London since 1983 (Bardsley and Storkey, 2000; Edgar et al, 2004), or 56,000 between 1996 and 2000 (www.statistics.gov.uk). The shortage of local authority housing forces people with low or no incomes into the private rental sector where the majority of refugees begin their housing trajectories (Sales, 2002), facing low standards, widespread exclusion and marginality, virtually no housing rights, "… no choice in where they are housed, no security of tenure and no financial means to find alternative accommodation" (Garvie, 2001, p 54), making it very difficult for them to adjust to the UK. Among disadvantaged groups, asylum seekers and undocumented migrants are particularly vulnerable to homelessness and housing exclusion (Anderson, 2003; Edgar et al, 2004) because they are displaced from their countries of origin, often under traumatic circumstances, forced into statelessness and status-lessness, and have little chance of establishing, at least in the short term, full rights of citizenship (Pearl and Zetter, 2002). The 'problem' of asylum seekers was highlighted by housing pressures in London and the South East, which led to dispersal from 2000 under the 1999 Immigration and Asylum Act.

Dispersal was implemented across the UK on a no-choice basis and asylum seekers were transported to 'cluster areas' that reflected asylum seekers' ethno-cultural origins and the availability of social housing. However, these were also areas of high unemployment and poverty (Pearl and Zetter, 2002, p 238), and so the dispersal system exacerbated the experience of forced resettlement for vulnerable asylum seekers to communities that were already marginalised (Edgar et al, 2004). The National Asylum and Support System (NASS) was created under the 1999 Act as a separate benefit system that would manage housing and support for asylum seekers during the determination process. However, the system produced the greatest risk of homelessness on receipt of the asylum decision, which, even if positive, consisted of a 14-day eviction notice from NASS accommodation, doubled to 28 days in later legislation (Edgar et al, 2004).

The research process

Access and sampling issues

Chambon et al (1998) identified a number of important starting points for research with refugees, which were considered in planning and developing this study. Although this research was not conducted with a partnered agency, Chambon's work was used to consider whether certain agencies were appropriate for collaboration in formulating the research, selecting interviewees, and sharing a timeline for the research process that fitted the research capability:

- research projects at the agency should be participatory and flexible to adapt to the ways of functioning of the agency;
- research projects should benefit clients and contribute to their well-being;
- participants should be respected as persons, and their experiences, opinions and choices should be given weight;
- research procedures should not be disruptive to client–staff relations;
- research should not result in refugees becoming traumatised by reliving experiences from their past; and
- participation in research should be guided by the principle of informed consent without direct or indirect pressure (Chambon et al, 1998).

In order to ensure that the research conducted would reflect the needs of asylum seekers, I began an exploration of UK media coverage while still in Canada, contacted a number of refugee organisations in the UK about my research interests, and inquired after their most pressing concerns and possibilities for collaboration or cooperation. This served as an introduction and an expression of my interest in making the research relevant, and therefore important. I spent the next few months visiting refugee community organisations (RCOs) and non-governmental organisations (NGOs), and volunteering at the British Refugee Council's Brixton Day Centre and the Holy Cross Centre Trust B&B Project for Asylum Seekers and Refugees. During this time, I was able to finalise the interview schedule.

Several months elapsed between my first day as an observer-volunteer and permission to advertise the research on the premises and mention it to clients. In part, this can be attributed to inflammatory media reports and politically motivated anti-asylum rhetoric, as well as RCOs' and NGOs' protection of their vulnerable clientele. Organisations demanded assurance that the research was actually being conducted towards a PhD at the University of London, that I was the PhD candidate, primary researcher and interviewer, and that the research questions would be limited to those that were printed in the interview schedule. In effect, they acted as gatekeepers to refugees. They were critical intermediaries to refugees who were interested in speaking about their housing experiences and the meaning of home (Bloch, 1999).

I was able to gain their confidence by volunteering with two RCOs situated at different institutional scales, and conducting key-informant interviews with organisation staff prior to requesting interviews with clients or former clients and requesting to post flyers in their offices.

In a research climate fuelled by suspicion where some NGOs accused me of being a media correspondent posing as a student, establishing trust was not an easy task, but such organisations were the most valuable point of contact for refugee interviews. Their value came not from the numbers of prospective participants that had contact with the organisations, but from referral to one or two clients who found the interview process interesting or rewarding and contacted family, friends, classmates, or members of their ethno-cultural group in London who otherwise would not have been identified or informed about the research.

I conducted key-informant interviews with gatekeepers prior to requests for referrals to refugee clients, and so made space for organisations and staff to discuss their capacity building, best practices, and generally their contributions toward refugee settlement and integration, which they then were willing to strengthen through their clients' voices.

Before proceeding to contact participants, I conducted a small pilot study with three refugee volunteers from different RCOs as a way of assessing the actual length of the interviews, the level of difficulty of the questions, and the ability to communicate ideas with people for whom English was a second language, often recently acquired. It was as a result of this pilot phase that the use of photographs was considered as a complementary method (discussed below). The benefits of conducting a pilot were manifold: it offered the opportunity to experiment with the order and style of the questions; to hear responses that forced clarification, rewording, or follow-on questions; to pinpoint areas of confusion, hesitation, suspicion and sensitivity, for reconsideration; and ultimately to narrow and focus the interview schedule (van Teijlingen and Hundley, 2001).

The duration of the pilot interviews also prompted interviewees to suggest that future participants be interviewed in their residence. I had not anticipated the stories that would be evoked from what I thought were simple closed-response questions, and while I respected people's openness and expressiveness, I was concerned that people would tire early on and be unable to complete the interview. Subtly, therefore, I indicated the questions I was asking so that participants could gauge their response according to the amount of the space given to the questions in the interview schedule. This helped to manage time without cutting people short, although in a few cases a second meeting with the interviewee was necessary.

The average length of the interviews was two hours. Although it was outside the means of this research to offer true remuneration for refugees' expertise and time spent, a token of appreciation seemed appropriate. The use of remuneration in ethnographic research argues that it can minimise bias by including people who otherwise decline because they place a greater value on their time, energy and expertise (Thompson, 1996); and it provides some incentive to disadvantaged or over-researched groups (Patton, 2002). Offering participants some money in this case seemed the right thing to do; however, the amount needed to be small enough that it could not be seen as a bribe for participants who might feel financial pressure to 'sell' their experiences, and organisations were concerned that participation in the research should not jeopardise people's benefit income with a sum above the reportable limit (Dench, 2004). After the interview, fifteen pounds was given to each interviewee in an envelope with 'For you, with thanks!' handwritten on the front. This amount was discussed with pilot interviewees and organisation staff, who considered it adequate or generous.

Prior to the pilot, I had not anticipated that the funding source of the research would be important to interviewees, but it was. People were wary of research funded by the Home Office, and were very keen to understand the nature of the academic funding. Asserting my personal investment in the research from scholarships was reassuring to participants who would otherwise have declined to be interviewed (see Robinson and Segrott, 2002, p 9).

I designed flyers on A4 sheets appealing for refugees with indefinite leave to remain, or exceptional leave to remain, to contact me if they were interested in speaking about their housing and the meaning of home for a comparative study of conditions for newcomers in Canada and the UK. The posters were placed on NGO and RCO noticeboards and distributed to counsellors. In addition, I thought about other ways to contact refugees who might not attend formal organisations, to overcome some of the disadvantages of a sampling strategy that was skewed towards people chosen through gatekeepers (see Chapter Six). Posting notices with homeless and settlement services, and also in libraries, grocery stores, universities and refugee education and assessment services, through the refugee education list-serve, and by email to refugee organisations, widely disseminated the call for interviewees and allowed for the probability of interviewee self-selection.

Posting notices was intended to shift some of the burden of solicitation away from busy frontline staff, over-dependence on one network and interviewing people with similar experiences (Bloch, 1999, p 372), to preclude interview burnout, and to notify people who may not access formal services for various reasons, such as clan-based differences or relative success. While the posters did not elicit many responses on their own, those posted within organisations that I had contacted earlier did generate interested enquiries to staff, who were then able to refer people or, depending on their circumstances and vulnerability, dissuade them from participating (for a detailed discussion of the role of gatekeepers in refugee research, see Hynes, 2003).

Informal networks were crucial to the success of the study. Many interviewees were referrals from family, friends or acquaintances, and participated in the research with the self-confidence that came from knowing the types of questions in advance and how to answer them. This did not appear to change what people said and what they shared, but increased the self-possession with which they responded to questions and described experiences.

Ultimately, 30 interviews were conducted in London by instigating purposive sampling (to be discussed later) directly or indirectly through gatekeepers, who were conscientious about encouraging varied participants. Referral and self-referral were also employed, and in London, people from 13 different refugee origins participated. Interviews were conducted across the city in over 10 different local authorities, and in accommodation that ranged from homeless shelters to privately rented flats. Informed consent was sought from each participant, and confidentiality and anonymity were guaranteed. Interviews were tape recorded, and the recorder remained in the possession of the interviewee during the interview. Interviewees were shown how to operate the recorder, and encouraged to pause taping whenever they wanted.

The researcher can also be a gatekeeper to interviewees, and there were restrictions, deliberate and incidental, that excluded some participants. The number of interviewees was capped at 30 in each city due to limits in the research budget and time. Purposive sampling (Mason, 2002) was used to maximise the information collected and explore the heterogeneity of experiences rather than facilitate generalisation. The selection and background of the interviewees was diversified to maximise points of view and uncover multiple realities of home/lessness and housing among refugees.

Only people with leave to remain (exceptional or indefinite) were sought as participants, rather than asylum seekers waiting for decisions on their claim. Leave to remain entitles people to integration services as "full and equal citizens" (Home Office, 2000) and, therefore, the UK as a prospective home. Interviewees were selected from a pool of arrivals who made their claims in the UK between 1996 and 2001, to ensure that people's experiences as asylum seekers were relatively recent and that they had been resident for at least a year.

As well as sampling concerns around how to access people without a comprehensive database, there was a sampling issue around the language abilities of people involved in the research. Limitations to available resources, such as time and money, presented a barrier to extensive interviewing with language facilitators or interpreters. Instead, a sampling strategy was employed that favoured people who felt their English was adequate to discussing ideas of home, housing and migration. This was largely filtered through RCOs and NGOs that identified clients they deemed appropriate for the study, and whose stories they believed illustrated recurring, or unique, experiences (see also Bloch, 1999); it was also filtered by the posted flyers, which were written in English only.

Sometimes the organisations involved offered volunteer interpreters and space to conduct interviews, and at other times they encouraged a non-English speaker to participate with interpretation by a friend or relative. Overall, however, most of the interviews were conducted in English, with the attendant possibility that subtleties of meaning were lost and that an English language baseline for understanding remained unchallenged (Temple, 2005). Also lost through restricting the use of language, and therefore participation, were older people, people who may have been illiterate, women non-heads of households, and people who found themselves unable to maintain attendance in English language classes.

The interviews were long without interpreters and doubled in length with interpreters. The use of interpreters sometimes meant that people were interviewed at the offices of the organisations involved rather than a location more convenient to them, such as their residences. Interviews with interpreters were more staccato and not as nuanced as those where the dialogue, probing, and prompts came from the researcher. Despite the shortened responses that characterised interviews conducted with interpreters, the use of interpreters allowed the participation of people who might otherwise not be heard.

One example of an RCO providing access to its clients, who otherwise could not have participated, was the Arab Women's Group in London. I was invited to interview elderly Arab women on a specific weekday when elderly clients would gather to socialise. However, after two interviews the interpreter gave up, despite the growing interest among women in the centre to be interviewed. As a result, one interviewee recruited her granddaughter to act as interpreter; however, the child's inability to interpret some questions, tendency to answer questions for her grandmother, and to misinterpret refugee process-specific language led to her grandmother's frustration and termination of the interview.

Other participants scheduled their interviews according to their friends' availability to act as interpreters so they could participate from their homes with an interpreter they knew and trusted. Interviewees would also sometimes participate with their families as a strategy to pool the language resources of the household. Previous research has shown that people who do not speak English may experience a degree of comfort among friends or family when they act as interpreters, compared with trained members of the ethno-cultural linguistic group or indeed trained interpreters (Alexander et al, 2004). Alexander et al (2004) demonstrate that preferences are likely to be context-specific and include factors such as migration histories of national groups and personal social networks, making no particular choice of interpreter automatically more preferable.

Interview schedule

The interview schedule was influenced by the format and content of three studies: the Housing New Canadians Project (www.hnc.utoronto.ca), which focuses on the rental housing experience of low-income immigrants and refugees, paying particular attention to the role of housing-related discrimination; the best-practice research by former Romero House volunteers Ryan and Woodill (2000), which evaluates the success of the Romero House model as a refugee shelter providing bundled assistance to asylum seekers in the form of settlement advice, longer-term accommodation, and ongoing membership to the Romero community of former residents and volunteers; and the comprehensive interview schedule published by Carey-Wood et al (1995) investigating the settlement of refugees in Britain.

The interview schedule consisted of five sections: flight and arrival; making the claim and finding support; housing and accommodation experiences since arriving; the location(s) and necessary constituents of home as defined by interviewees; and background information.

Sometimes quantitative forms of collecting qualitative information were used, such as rating residential satisfaction on a scale of 1 to 10, rather than the typically used Likert scale that can obfuscate the relativity and subjectivity of responses in ratings that range from 'very dissatisfied' to 'extremely satisfied'. For example, a consistent rating of 'extremely satisfied' may, on a scale of 1 to 10, over the course of three residences consist of a 9 in the first accommodation, 8.5 in the second and 8 in the third. Awareness of the slight slippages, wavers, increases, stability and instability then leads to discussion of *why* the changes occurred, what variables produced the changes, and what feelings and characteristics were associated with the best and worst housing experiences since arrival. All of this information was captured in the detailed retrospective chronology of the 'housing résumé', organised in tabular form and consisting of closed and open-response questions (following Murdie and Teixeira, 2000). The housing résumé sets out individual residential histories according to well-defined characteristics, including location, duration of residence, unit type, tenure and size, affordability, income source, dwelling and neighbourhood satisfaction, and reasons for leaving as well as resources used in locating a new place. This information provides a snapshot of their dwelling circumstances and housing trajectory since arriving in the UK.

Two types of open-response questions were employed in the interview schedule: interpretation of personal experiences and, somewhat controversially, abstract philosophical questions. Although the former are common and useful in eliciting the views of refugees, the latter might only be applicable to a few respondents who would both understand the question and feel capable of considering and answering it in English. Asking abstract questions risked alienating or embarrassing interviewees who might feel inadequate in their inability to respond. However, I believed it was important not to presume that respondents would be unable to answer.

Since the characteristics and location of shelter can inspire a range of emotions, it was essential to compose questions that could capture the intricacies of the practical and symbolic meanings of housing as shelter, home, and source of feelings of homelessness, and the meanings of home as relational and structural at the scales of the individual, one's accommodation, community and neighbourhood, nation, ancestry, family and culture. Since the meanings of home and homelessness may not necessarily be associated with shelter, the definition of home was the first question posed to interviewees, and ultimately both home and homelessness were individually defined in their broadest senses. Scale, rather than being an obstacle, became a means for participants to clarify and explore their ideas and make sense of complicated feelings about home and homelessness.

To assist in understanding and responding to such questions, a series of diagrams was pre-produced and attached to the interview schedule. For instance, a diagram of nested orbs was used in asking for a multi-scalar conception of home. Integral to including abstract or theoretical questions is the sensitivity and skill of the interviewer in probing for meaning and in validating participants' efforts in answering. For example, if a participant repeatedly attributes safety and security as the necessary variables to feeling at home at each scale, it is incumbent on the interviewer to probe for the constituents and meaning of safety and security at each level. Once the meaning of safety and security are disaggregated according to scale, it is then possible to ask how these were experienced in the country of origin and the country of asylum. This produces an in-depth understanding of how home in the country of asylum compares to the country of origin and the participant's ideal or basic elements of home at the different levels. Despite reservations about asking theoretical or abstract questions, they were appreciated by most participants, many of whom were intrinsically compelled by issues of home as a preoccupation of their flight and settlement experiences.

Some open-response questions, which were designed to give interviewees a space to express themselves, were answered in point form. On the other hand, a few closed-response questions might be over-simplifications of extremely important experiences and stories. The interview was not designed to limit the self-expression of the interviewees, but to structure and organise a complex idea and series of events. It was therefore essential to permit unanticipated responses to questions, document all relevant spontaneous stories, and allow participants the space to express themselves, even in ways not directly relevant to the research. This was most evident when participants, though expressly told they would not be asked about persecution in their country of origin, wanted to share details of their trauma with someone with whom they felt comfortable and who had committed to respect their confidentiality. Listening to everything interviewees wanted to say, after making sure people understood they were not obligated to share any personal and sensitive information, was a principle of the research design.

Avoidances and sensitive issues

The interview schedule avoided asking questions about the nature of the persecution experienced or why people left their countries of origin, because the trauma of past events, including the journeys taken to the country of asylum, was not the focus of this research. Chambon et al (1998) warn against undertaking 'trauma-exploration' or retraumatising participants in the zeal to exploit access to interviewees, which can feel like an arduous task for the researcher. Instead, the questions focused on experiences in the country of asylum, housing and the meaning of home, and participants were informed while scheduling the meetings and immediately before the interviews began, that they could skip any questions that made them uneasy, and they could ask about any question's relevance to the home/lessness theme of the research.

In terms of its own research, the Canadian Centre for Victims of Torture (CCVT) states: "The past must be addressed as filtered through the present" (CCVT, 2000). Following the CCVT's protocol for interview schedules, questions relating to refugees' background in the country of origin were asked as closed-response questions limited to the type of housing in which they had lived and with which they were familiar, their level of education, proficiency in English, and type of employment. It was presumed that open-response questions about the meaning of home and homelessness, especially related to country of origin and country of asylum, would capture information about the effects of persecution if directly related to interviewees' integration or settlement.

Another sensitive issue was smuggling. On this issue, the centrality of agency, control and choice of destination country is important. Within refugee studies, it is recognised that exit from the country of origin by smuggling is a matter of survival as well as being a migration and human rights issue (Koser, 2001), and it influences resettlement because it is exponentially more difficult for people to adapt to environments they did not choose in addition to having been forcibly displaced from their country of origin.

The chronological order of the interview schedule allowed participants to tell the story of their departure, arrival, and settlement in a linear narrative, which facilitated recall and made the flow of the interview predictable and comfortable. Smuggling is an issue related to departure and arrival, and therefore was to be raised within the first few questions of the interview. The question as it was finally posed read: "Because it is often very difficult and dangerous to escape one's country, some people need help. But sometimes agents or smugglers can be very expensive or they can be very bad people. If you used agents or smugglers to leave your country, can you tell me how they helped you or how they hurt you or caused problems?".

In response to this question, people either instantly described how agents or smugglers were used, or denied their use. This question is premised on the fact that the risk of persecution in the countries of origin necessitates the use of smugglers to save lives, which destigmatises the smuggler and smuggled (see Hynes, 2003). In 60 interviews, only two people refused to answer this question.

Using photographs

The meaning of home, which was central to each interview, was defined by participants to reflect their experiences, background, and ethno-cultural and linguistic specificities. The meaning of home – as a domestic residence, as a source of comfort arising from meeting basic needs, as routine and habit, as a region, nation, and community, as feelings of safety and protection, as family and kinship ties, and as one's spiritual and ancestral origins – was elicited through conversational probing, through soliciting metaphors, proverbs and similes from the country of origin as illustrative of the meaning of home, particularly important for cultures with a strong oral tradition, and through photography as an alternative medium to document and symbolise home and homelessness (Hurworth, 2003; Clark-Ibanez, 2004). In this way, the parameters of each of the interviews were situated in the culture of each of the interviewees. In particular, photography, which was used to concretise the role of the researcher as 'bearing witness' (Chambon et al, 1998), acted to:

- bridge psychological and physical realities;
- allow the combination of visual and verbal language;
- assist with building trust and rapport;
- produce unpredictable information;
- promote longer, more detailed interviews in comparison with verbal interviews;
- provide a component of multi-methods triangulation to improve rigour;
- form a core technique to enhance collaborative/participatory research and needs assessments; and
- be preferable to conventional interviews for many participants (Hurworth, 2003).

The photographs generated conversation about the emotional and physical aspects of home and housing, dwelling and nation, and were useful in sharing the subjectivity, loss, and privileges of refugees' lives. They were testimony to refugees' residential conditions, and additionally facilitated the communication of dimensions of home/lessness in relation to different scales and sites of dwelling, symbolic or literal (Clark-Ibanez, 2004), through non-verbal means.

When scheduling the interview, prospective participants were asked to think about what home meant to them and what not being at home or feeling homelessness meant to them and what I should photograph to represent each feeling. Nothing would be photographed without permission and no one would appear in the photos without consent. Refugees described what they had chosen and why into the tape recorder while I took the photos. The photographs allowed people to open up the subjective: quality and satisfaction; and just as in telling their stories and evaluating their housing, advice, and access to benefits, framing the photo was an act of agency. Refugees expressed satisfaction at documenting their substandard housing conditions. In addition, they were glad to receive copies of the photos taken to keep or send to their families, since many did not own cameras.

Not everyone felt comfortable with the camera, and some preferred simply to offer a description. Generally, people's homelessness photos reflected their housing problems, including pictures of mould, small rooms, filthy communal facilities, and general disrepair. People's photos of home included leisure and relaxation activities such as TV, Game Boy, music, instruments and football, which were also continuations of their usual activities in their country of origin. Home photos also reflected family and friends present in the UK and pictures brought from the country of origin.

The photographs were the final answer to the first question in the interview, and were taken on completion of the interview process. This was an effective complement to a long and language-intensive interview process, closing the discussion of what made people feel at home and what made people feel homeless in the UK.

Conclusion

For refugees who arrive to the UK without existing relationships or secure accommodation (Quilgars, 1993), NASS provides dispersal accommodation outside of London and the South East, except in special circumstances. Although accommodation may be provided by the state, the absence of material and social incentives to remain in the dispersal area on receipt of positive decisions results in housing loss and secondary migration. Without respect for the networks that constitute the social domain of 'home', refugees or asylum seekers may *feel* homeless even though they are housed, especially in dispersal cases, which often remove asylum seekers from family and friends who are crucial in the initial stages of arrival. Dispersal may leave asylum seekers socially excluded and isolated but so does the threat of destitution in London for those who refuse dispersal, and others who return to London on receipt of their decision. Asylum seekers who rely on their social or kinship networks for accommodation and support may create increased stress on already marginalised communities or households (Zetter and Pearl, 1999), tolerate overcrowded dwellings, and risk tension and abuse, especially during extended determinations. One way to understand home as an indicator of refugee integration is through qualitative research that acknowledges the human effects of structures that create dissonance and/or harmony among the social, legal and physical domains of home.

RCOs and NGOs as interviewees offered a viewpoint on integration that complemented refugees' stories. Ethno–cultural organisations had a high degree of involvement in the everyday lives of their clients, and were an efficient and effective recruitment resource for participants. They helped to recruit participants who could speak English well, or for whom an interpreter could be found. However, refugees themselves were the most enthusiastic about the research, and provided a number of referrals. Using both avenues to find people to take part in the research helped to broaden the sample base.

To strengthen communication, I appealed to an oral tradition in the interviews to evoke the symbolism and metaphor of 'home', and photography was used to document people's housing conditions and their multi-local, multi-scalar sense of home/lessness. The photography prompted discussion and creativity, and facilitated comparison with the housing experiences of refugees in Toronto by exposing and documenting housing quality.

An important tenet of this research was to maintain a distance from the trauma of refugees' pasts by focusing on the present and on refugees' agency. Issues informing the present would surface without interrogating refugees' histories. However, where sensitive questions were integral to the research, emphasising the structures that produced the experience or event was essential to guarding interviewees' self-esteem and recognising their survival and agency. Openness was imperative to a productive dialogue and honest narrative. It was necessary that interviewees felt confident and secure in the interview process and in the researcher's commitment to anonymity and confidentiality. This included having recourse to complain about unsatisfactory research practices.

Empathetic in-depth qualitative interviewing with 30 participants, key-informant interviews, and a foundation on previous research evidence provide testimony to the effect of refugees' accommodation histories and on feelings of disjuncture and attachment during their settlement trajectories. Because home is a concept of place and space, it allows analysis of a trajectory beyond the physicality of any particular dwelling. A key element of this discussion is that a sense of home can also influence refugees' evaluation of the quality of a residence, at one extreme making the material irrelevant to their settlement and belonging at the scale of nation, city or accommodation. Integration and belonging are metaphors for relationships practised at various geographical scales, and it is possible to pursue methodologically sound and innovative techniques that begin to unravel these complex ideas.

Note

[1] This research was funded in part by the University of London Central Research Fund.

References

Alexander, C., Edwards, R. and Temple, B. (2004) *Using interpreters to access services: user views*, York: Joseph Rowntree Foundation.

Anderson, I. (2003) *Migration and homelessness in the UK*, Report for the European Observatory on Homelessness, Brussels: FEANTSA.

Bardsley, M. and Storkey, M. (2000) 'Estimating the numbers of refugees in London', *Journal of Public Health Medicine*, vol 22, no 3, pp 406-12.

Black, R. (1994) 'Livelihoods under stress: a case study of refugee vulnerability in Greece', *Journal of Refugee Studies*, vol 7, no 4, pp 360-77.

Black, R. (2002) 'Conceptions of "home" and the political geography of refugee repatriation', *Applied Geography*, vol 22, no 2, pp 123-38.

Bloch, A. (1999) 'Carrying out a survey of refugees: some methodological considerations and guidelines', *Journal for Refugee Studies*, vol 12, no 4, pp 367-83.

Bloch, A. (2002) *The migration and settlement of refugees in Britain*, New York, NY: Palgrave Macmillan.

Carey-Wood, J. (1997) *Meeting refugees' needs in Britain: The role of refugee specific initiatives*, London: Home Office.

Carey-Wood, J., Duke, K., Karn, V. and Marshall, T. (1995) *The settlement of refugees in Britain*, Home Office Research Study no 141, London: HMSO.

CCVT (Canadian Centre for Victims of Torture) (2000) 'Befriending survivors of torture – building a web of community support', (www.ccvt.org/befriendingworkshop.html).

Chambon, A., Abai, M., Dremetsikas, T., McGrath, S. and Shapiro, B. (1998) 'Methodology in university–community research partnerships: the Link-By-Link project, a case study', (www.ccvt.org/research.html).

Clark-Ibanez, M. (2004) 'Framing the social world with photo-elicitation interviews', *American Behavioral Scientist*, vol 47, no 12, pp 1507-27.

Daly, G. (1996) *Homeless: Policies, strategies and lives on the street*, Toronto: Routledge.

Dench, S. (2004) *An EU code of ethics for socio-economic research*, RESPECT Project, Report 242, Brighton: Institute for Employment Studies.

Dummett, M. (2001) *On immigration and refugees*, London: Routledge.

Edgar, B., Doherty, J. and Meert, H. (2004) *Immigration and homelessness in Europe*, Bristol: The Policy Press.

Foley, P. and Beer, A. (2003) *Housing need and provision for recently arrived refugees in Australia*, Australia: Australian Housing and Urban Research Institute, Southern Research Centre.

Garvie, D. (2001) *Far from home: The housing of asylum seekers in private rented accommodation*, London: Shelter.

Goldberg, D.T. (1993) *Racist culture: Philosophy and the politics of meaning*, Malden: Blackwell Publishers Inc.

Home Office (2000) *Full and equal citizens: A strategy for the integration of refugees into the United Kingdom*, London: The Stationery Office.

Hurworth, R. (2003) *Photo-interviewing for research*, Social Research Update 40, Surrey: University of Surrey (www.soc.surrey.ac.uk/sru).

Hynes, T. (2003) *The issue of 'trust' or 'mistrust' in research with refugees: Choices, caveats and considerations for researchers*, New Issues in Refugee Research, Working Paper no 98, Geneva: Evaluation and Policy Analysis Unit (EPAU), United Nations High Commission for Refugees (UNHCR).

Korac, M. (2002) 'The role of the state in refugee integration and settlement: Italy and the Netherlands compared', *Forced Migration Review*, no 14, June, pp 30-2.

Korac, M. (2003) 'The lack of integration policy and experiences of settlement: a case study of refugees in Rome, *Journal of Refugee Studies*, vol 16, no 4, pp 398-421.

Koser, K. (2001) 'The smuggling of asylum seekers into Western Europe: contradictions, conundrums, and dilemmas', in D. Kyle and R. Koslowski (eds) *Global human smuggling: Comparative perspectives*, Baltimore, MD: Johns Hopkins Press, pp 58-74.

Mason, J. (2002) *Qualitative researching*, London: Sage Publications.

Mumford, L. (1961) *The city in history: Its origins, its transformations and its prospects*, New York, NY: Harcourt, Brace and World.

Murdie, R.A. and Teixeira, C. (2000) 'Towards a comfortable neighbourhood and appropriate housing: Immigrant experiences in Toronto', CERIS Working Paper no 10, (ceris.metropolis.net/frameset_e.html).

Palmer, D. (2001) *Far from a home: A report on suitability of temporary accommodation provided by London local authorities*, London: National Homelessness Advice Service.

Patton, M.Q. (2002) *Qualitative research and evaluation methods*, Thousand Oaks, CA: Sage Publications.

Pearl, M. and Zetter, R. (2002) 'From refuge to exclusion: housing as an instrument of social exclusion for refugees and asylum seekers', in P. Somerville and A. Steele (eds) (2002) *Race, housing and social exclusion*, London: Jessica Kingsley, pp 226-44.

Porteous, J.D. and Smith, S.E. (2001) *Domicide*, Montreal: McGill-Queen's University Press.

Quilgars, D. (1993) *Housing provision for refugees*, York: Centre for Housing Policy, University of York.

Ray, B. (2002) 'Immigrant integration: building to opportunity', Migration Fundamentals, Migration Policy Institute (www.migrationinformation.org).

Renaud, J. and Gingras, L. (1998) *Landed refuge claimants' first three years in Quebec*, Studies Research and Statistics Collection No 2, Quebec: Direction de la planification strategique.

Robinson, V. and Segrott, J. (2002) *Understanding the decision making of asylum seekers*, Home Office Study 243, London: The Stationery Office.

Ryan, L. and Woodill, J. (2000) *A search for home: Refugee voices in the Romero House community*, Toronto: The Maytree Foundation.

Sales, R. (2002) 'The deserving and the undeserving? Refugees, asylum seekers and welfare in Britain', *Critical Social Policy*, vol 22, no 3, pp 456-78.

Stenström, E. (2003) 'Best practices and key lessons learned for integration of resettled refugees following the integration conference in Sweden', in *Listening to the evidence: The future of UK resettlement*, Conference Proceedings, London: Home Office, pp 28-32.

Temple, B. (2005) 'Nice and tidy: translation and representation', *Sociological Research Online*, vol 10, no 2 (www.socresonline.org.uk/10/2/temple.html).

Thompson, S. (1996) 'Paying respondents and informants', Social Research Update 40, Surrey: University of Surrey (www.soc.surrey.ac.uk/sru).

van der Veer, R. (1992) *Counselling and therapy with refugees: Psychological problems of victims of war torture and repression*, Bognor Regis: John Wiley & Sons Ltd.

van Teijlingen, E.R. and Hundley, V. (2001) 'The importance of pilot studies', Social Research Update 35, Surrey: University of Surrey (www.soc.surrey.ac.uk/sru).

Yu, E.S.H. and Liu, W. (1986) 'Methodological problems and policy implications in Vietnamese refugee research', *International Migration Review*, vol 20, no 2, pp 483-501.

Zetter, R. and Pearl, M. (1999) *Managing to survive: Asylum seekers, refugees and access to social housing*, Bristol: The Policy Press.

Zetter, R. and Pearl, M. (2000) 'The minority within the minority: refugee community-based organisations in the UK and the impact of restrictionism on asylum-seekers', *Journal of Ethnic and Migration Studies*, vol 26, no 4, pp 675-98.

Zetter, R., Griffiths, D., Sigona, N. and Hauser, M. (2002) *A survey of policy and practice related to refugee integration*, European Commission (www. brookes.ac.uk/schools/planning/dfm/RefInt/).

SIX

The community leader, the politician and the policeman: a personal perspective

Manawar Jan-Khan

Introduction

This chapter considers some of the issues that arise in service development and research that limits itself exclusively to community representatives, often self-appointed but sometimes elected, as sources of information. It explores the dynamic between community representatives, and the potential for interdependence with other key actors within the community setting in representing race-related issues, from specific and, arguably exclusive, perspectives that preclude the opportunities for other members of communities to articulate their views about what is happening in the development of social policy concerned with minority ethnic populations. The author argues that service development and research projects must counterbalance the dominance of these influences. In this way they might ensure that the range of views and ideas about how to tackle the issue of racism, including asylum and immigration concerns, on the ground becomes much more inclusive.

The chapter draws on the personal experiences of the author using two ethnographic case studies, one based in a northern city and the other in a southern conurbation. They both illustrate similar patterns of what have been described not only as 'injustices of recognition' (Aspinal, 2002) but also, in more appropriate terms, as 'injustices of engagement' (Temple and Steel, 2004, p 542).

The debate centres on the role of individuals in socially fragmented and isolated communities who are placed at centre stage as 'spokespersons' and asked to comment, on behalf of a wider community, on key public policy initiatives of which they may have little understanding. Issues of legitimacy and validity are often ignored for short-term gain by institutions of the state and local government. This is more evident within established black and minority ethnic communities, including refugee communities. The inherent dangers of institutional engagement with a small, self-selecting, and often self-serving, group of individuals are now being repeated with new sub-populations recently arrived in the UK.

As other writers have explored the relationship between public service provision and stakeholders (that is, local people and communities) (Ahmad and Sheldon, 1993; Modood et al, 1997; Temple, 2002; Temple and Chahal, 2002), I would like to focus on the perspectives of three key actors on the community stage and, in particular, on what could be described as a 'relationship of interdependence'. This will become evident through the two case studies. Researchers have a duty to ensure that they do not reinforce a methodology of engagement that is narrowly focused on a few chosen 'insiders'. Furthermore, ethically, the researcher has a duty to challenge those institutionalised modi operandi that are damaging to local communities and can lead to questionable evidence and results. This in turn can result in communities being denied representation or being controlled through unwitting alliances that disguise the real voices, needs, aspirations and opinions of the wider community.

The real danger is when the needs of a narrowly defined community are articulated at the expense of the wider population. In this sense, researchers have a duty to ensure that their methodology avoids any adverse impact on socially excluded groups.

It is worth noting that this process has occurred, and continues to occur, with established African, Caribbean and South Asian communities, who are among the most disenfranchised and ignored; it is also happening with newly emerging communities of asylum seekers and refugees. In the case of the former, the diaspora is now seeking to articulate a more assertive viewpoint; the latter communities, however, still tend to be represented, if not by the 'white privileged', then at least by individuals or groups who speak on their behalf as the dominant 'cultural brokers' (Temple, 2002).

The author explores these issues through a personal perspective that draws on his contrasting experiences in two cities, one made famous by the book burning of the 'Satanic Verses' (Bradford), and the other renowned for its academic reputation and elitism (Oxford). Geographically, demographically, culturally and socially they are opposites of each other, but in the context of minority ethnic communities in this debate, they are united by a similar discourse on the issues of representation, albeit at different levels of development.

The chapter is based on the author's own experiences as a community researcher, both on the 'outside', as a community campaigner in Bradford, and on the 'inside', as a city councillor in Oxford.

Community setting

As this chapter focuses on Pakistani communities in the UK, it is important to place their origins in sociological context and to understand how, through a process of migration and settlement, they have tried to adapt traditions and patterns of living to the modern world.

The vast majority are from mainly rural backgrounds in what is known as Azad (free) Kashmir (although there are smaller Pathaan populations from the North West Frontier Province of Pakistan). The city of Mirpur is a major centre of attraction, with its numerous monuments and mausoleums to migration – large and opulent residences that have been built by the frequent traveller and rented to locals, signifying success and status even though such properties may originally have been built from the remittances of the first generation of migrants toiling in the northern mills in England, and further enhanced by the second and third generations, wishing to cater for their own sense of westernisation.

Other migrants have travelled from the numerous villages that lead from Mirpur to the capital of Azad Kashmir, Muzzafrabad, and dotted along the route are the villages that are reached by winding pot-holed roads, now lined with oddly placed billboards advertising limousine hire, jewellery and bakery businesses back in Bradford.

In the opposite direction one can travel to the small town of Dina, via the Mangla Dam and onto the Great Trunk road, leading to Lahore or Islamabad, the federal capital, 60 miles away. The dam was completed in 1967 and led to the displacement of 40,000 people (Pakistan Water Gateway, 2002). Many villages were destroyed and the demise of what was known as old Mirpur was the catalyst to the early migration of first-generation Pakistanis to England. In a twist of irony, a project to raise the dam by 2006 will lead to the forced resettlement of another 40,000 people, some of whom may be the descendants of those forced to leave their homes when the dam was originally built (Pakistan Water Gateway, 2001).

Many of these people arrived to work in the mills in the industrial north of England and settled there with their families. In time, with the closure of the mills and the subsequent loss of jobs and growing dependence on the welfare state, what was once seen as a temporary solution to an economic, and for some, displacement problem, became a permanent situation – one not of choice but of necessity. As the second and third generations came along, the original arrivals became further entrenched in life in Britain. They made periodic visits back to the 'homeland'. Even though urban Pakistan had moved on in its outlook, the rural communities had not.

The Pakistani diaspora is, in all senses, "a community with a distinct identity, isolated from many aspects of modernity, holding onto cultural and traditional norms, which have long been redefined within a modern era, in the country that many may still call home" (Jan-Khan, 2003, p 38). Despite the advent of multimedia Asian cable channelling, some remain entrenched in a more traditional way of life. This could be the result of a process of self-protection and mutual support in the face of the misplaced efforts of public services that are still debating the relative merits of culturally appropriate service delivery models and unwittingly referring to a non-existent 'Mirpuri' or 'Kashmiri' community, confusing linguistic and local cultural traits of a specific small area of Pakistan with the wider Pakistani communities. Clearly there is a correlation between the migration and cultural patterns of these two groups, both of which have their origins in predominantly poor rural areas with a tradition of little or no formal education and without a strong middle-class base.

Such difficulties of lack of education or the difficulties in accessing public services have translated into decades of neglect and exclusion in many areas, including education; for example, Pakistanis and Bangladeshis are second only to Black Caribbeans in being less likely to have degrees or equivalent qualifications (Social Exclusion Unit, 2000). Such exclusion can also be seen in the labour market, with Pakistanis, together with Chinese people, more likely to be self-employed than in employed work. Statistics for 2001/02 show that around a fifth of Pakistani men (22%) were self-employed, with one in six Pakistani men working as taxi drivers or chauffeurs compared with one in 100 in the white British male population (Office for National Statistics, 2001).

It is this social and economic impoverishment that brings these cultural groups to the attention of researchers who wish to understand the reasons for it. A failure to understand the make-up of the distinctive cultural traits and political and social interrelationships within these communities leaves academics and social sciences researchers with a core skills gap. Seeking out the 'usual suspects' to consult with only reinforces greater fragmentation within socially excluded groups, dividing communities and reinforcing the hegemony of the few against the many, as the following case studies demonstrate.

Bradford – the politics of community

One of the reasons for the lack of representation and subsequent politicisation of the Pakistani diaspora community in Bradford was the perceived political corruption of the local Labour Party that led to the riots in West Bradford in June 1995.Before these riots took place, much exposure was given to the abuse of power within the local Labour Party, although the author is careful to note that other parties are not immune from such antics. The following account is based on research undertaken by the author following the riots of 1995 and relates to perceptions and views of local community members living close to the areas in Bradford West where the riots had greatest impact.

The constituency of Bradford West is home to by far the largest concentration of Pakistanis in Bradford. When the then sitting MP, Max Madden, announced his retirement in 1994, potential candidates for his replacement jostled for position. The rivalry of two senior Asian politicians for nomination – Mohammed Ajeeb, Bradford's first Asian Lord Mayor, and Councillor Rangzeb, a former chair of housing – was reported widely in the regional and national press (*The Times*, 1994). The local elections in May 1995 placed the issue at the centre of Bradford's politics (*Yorkshire Post*, 2005). Surprisingly, however, the Conservative candidate, Arshad Hussain, took the seat from Labour with a small majority.With a national swing against the Conservatives, this was even more remarkable in a Labour stronghold such as Bradford.

The article in the *Yorkshire Post* had reported on the suspension of Toller and University and Bradford Moor wards, "amid allegations that a core of its own members worked to try to win seats for Tory candidates". It was also alleged that a sitting Labour councillor had spent council money fraudulently. This claim was being investigated by the local authority Chief Executive and the police. In relation to the suspended wards (Toller and University, and Bradford Moor) it is striking that 'biradri' (kinship) was a factor, as well as sectarianism. The local political scene had been transformed into a corrupt and ugly fight for power. In Bradford Moor, the police were also investigating allegations that leaflets had been circulated urging Muslims to support the Muslim Conservative candidate rather than a non-Muslim Labour candidate.

The local media reported other allegations of corruption (*Yorkshire Post*, 2005). It was alleged that in one ward home improvement grants were offered to Asian residents in return for votes and more alarmingly money. Another ward nearby was also implicated and an inquiry launched into grants given to benefit community groups.

According to newspaper reports, the ensuing investigation was to focus on the following points:

- misuse of council grants to take advantage of Asian residents' lack of English to secure money and votes (residents were told their grant application would be processed more quickly through an eight-year waiting list if they paid up to £500);
- allegations that Labour members canvassed for Tory candidates because they belonged to the same class; and
- the publication of a 'hate' manifesto claiming that Labour was anti-Muslim.

The close relationship between local politicians and so-called community leaders became clear in the process of seeking of votes from local people.

This relationship was questioned further in June 1995 following the riots, which highlighted more clearly the divide between the first-generation Pakistani-born commentators and the British-born diaspora (Jan-Khan, 1995). On the Friday evening one of the two most senior local Asian politicians was most prominent at the scene (outside the Police Station in Manningham). He apparently was of little help, said one eyewitness and local resident:

> He was stirring people up even more by inflaming the situation – people started challenging him 'what are you doing? – do you want your community to be beaten up?' (by the police) – he was okay; he was stood on the steps of the police station. (Jan-Khan, 1995, p 21)

It became clear from these events that many local people had an ambivalent attitude to their local politicians. One politician decided to take matters into his own hands and borrow a police loudspeaker to talk to the assembled crowd on a nearby grass verge. While he was speaking, some young members of the crowd began to walk away, commenting that his remarks were inflammatory.

The message that seemed to be coming from members of the community was that they were disillusioned with the politicians. That was clearly the case when some young people marched into the police station demanding that no politicians should be allowed at the meeting.

It later became apparent that it was the members of the community rather than the politicians who were instrumental in reducing tension both in the short term and long term.

The Bradford riots highlighted the correlation between political structure and community leadership and representation, not just in Bradford but in other parts of the country. As Malik (1995) has pointed out, Bradford, Birmingham, Manchester and East London can all lay claim to allegations of corruption and jostling for political power:

> After the riots (1980–1981), it was clear to politicians of all hues that if the disturbances were not to be repeated, black people had to be integrated into the political process. 'The parties went head-hunting', remembers Ali Hussein, a community activist from Bradford at the time. 'They pulled people off the streets and said, "Come and talk to us".' (Malik, 1995, p 33)

While some black people are now turning to the Conservative Party as the guardian of their interests, it is true to say that Labour has traditionally been the party of choice for many black voters and that over the years the Labour Party has acquired thousands of black members. Malik (1995) has argued that:

> In Bradford, observes Hussein, there developed a 'mutual relationship' between the community leaders, the council and the Labour party. The community leaders delivered the votes; the council delivered the money and the Labour party won a new layer of support. (Malik, 1995, p 33)

This perpetuates a system whereby it is in the interests of certain community gatekeepers to work with certain politicians to safeguard their own interests to the detriment of a wider community:

> In a study of black politics in Birmingham, sociologists Les Black and John Solomos recount the story of a black constituent who wanted to see the local (white) MP. Refused by a local 'community leader' (an aide to the MP), he went out and recruited nine party members – suddenly, the door opened to him. (Malik, 1995, p 33)

In such a system there are clearly problems of accountability and access, not only for the community but also for aspiring Asians wanting to climb the political ladder. Such problems are not confined to any one party, as events in Bradford Moor, described above, illustrate. Neither are they only a feature of black politics, as the Nolan Committee (1995) demonstrated. It may be true to say, however, that politicians have been quick to exploit black communities and that this situation has been tolerated in order to safeguard electoral success. It also seems somewhat hypocritical for the Labour Party to promote equality by forcing some female candidates on constituencies (a policy now abandoned) while not doing so for well-qualified, good calibre Black and Asian candidates – a somewhat bizarre equal opportunities stand.

In the most recent parliamentary elections in 2005, some of these problems have been further compounded by postal voting. In Bradford, it was alleged that community leaders illegally acquired postal votes from individuals in order to boost the number of votes for particular candidates. Two people were arrested and "held by Police as part of an inquiry launched last week following claims made against Conservative councillor Jamshed Khan" (Five, 2005).

The relationship between community leaders and those seeking political power is too close for comfort. In areas where parliamentary and local government seats can be changed by narrow margins, the votes of minority groups are much more valuable. As the experience of Bradford has shown, this interdependence can result in a system of patronage and unfair political advantage, and encourages the institutionalisation of selected community representatives.

City of spires

Oxford is renowned for its historic academic institutions, which have educated many great literary figures, politicians and world leaders. It conjures up images of tradition, heritage and excellence, which go hand in hand with privilege and elitism.

The black and minority ethnic population in Oxford city is around 12% of the total population, with the largest ethnic group being of Pakistani origin. As in Bradford, there are two distinct groups within this sub-population, in this case the Pushtoon community and Punjabi community. As Alison Shaw comments, "like other such communities in Britain, its members are drawn from just a few areas in Pakistan, mainly from Faisalabad and Jhelum districts in Punjab, Mirpur District, and Attock district in NWFP [North West Frontier Province]" (Shaw, 1994, p 37). The patterns of migration are similar here to those in other British cities, but with the added dimension that Oxford has become a point of internal, secondary, migration – an escape from the inner-city deprivation of the north. Placing a slightly different slant on Shaw's own terminology, this could be described as a modern form of internalised 'chain migration' (Shaw, 1994, p 39).

The author's personal experience has been shaped by growing up in Bradford and in particular by the circumstances surrounding the 1995 and 2001 riots. The Asian communities in Oxford are much less politicised. Not only is there a lack of representation, but also a lack of advocacy for the rights of black and minority ethnic communities. Relationships between the police and minority ethnic communities are of particular concern. Anecdotes circulate of random police stops of young African Caribbean and Asian men for no reason – one story goes that a white police officer stopped a Bangladeshi taxi driver and asked: "Where did you get the colour of your skin from?". Police community relations seem to centre round individual relationships with key figures from the Asian and minority ethnic population. These individuals are often seen as 'cultural brokers' (Temple, 2002, p 843) by predominantly white-led public service institutions attempting to tackle the problems of institutional racism while denying their existence.

The author was one of the first three Asian Muslim councillors, and the only second-generation Asian Muslim, to be appointed to office in the city council elections in 2002. There was no sizeable minority ethnic or Asian population in his ward, unlike those of his fellow councillors.

The author found that becoming a councillor immediately provided him with political legitimacy. He was automatically considered to be a 'community leader' by the media and by public institutions, although at one point his fellow Asian councillors were given an opportunity to join a formal police consultative committee that he was denied. The author, however, did not see himself as an Asian community leader and always took pains to make this clear – he had not been elected as such, and his electorate did not reflect his own racial, cultural and religious group. This is an important distinction and one that researchers often fail to make, perhaps unsurprisingly given that it is easy for elected leaders to become institutionalised and far removed from the people they have been elected to represent.

Such assumptions by public institutions about the role of community leaders reinforces the status quo and allows them to create a dialogue only with those they feel comfortable with, ignoring those they consider 'awkward' or critical of their services or policies, and regardless of whether these selected individuals represent the views of any local community.

The following example highlights the gulf that can exist between the views of the local community and their representatives. In 2003 Thames Valley Police were involved in a high-profile raid, where "doors were pounded down; men were arrested in their beds by helmeted, body-armour clad policemen and led away handcuffed in full view of the world" (*Oxford Times*, 2004, p 4). The men arrested were predominately Asian and their religious identity was also made public. The newspaper reported that "only four of the ten men arrested were charged and stood trial, and found not guilty". It added that "two councillors claim the incident reinforces the Muslim and black communities' lack of confidence in the police". The author was one of the two councillors, and he saw the raid as an example of the institutionalised racism that exists within the police service, highlighted by the MacPherson Inquiry into the murder of Stephen Lawrence (MacPherson Report, 1999, para 6.34).

An alternative view was expressed in the same editorial by another 'representative' of the Pakistani community: "Mumtaz Fareed, Chairman of the Oxford Independent (Police) Advisory Group, said many people in the community felt that the raids were justified and that relationships were stronger", although the newspaper also reinforced the view that "the police have ended up with a certain amount of egg on their faces" (*Oxford Times*, 2004, p 4).

It could be argued that the institutionalising effect of all this on members of the community is self-evident. Ironically, in the case of Bradford, the diaspora and community at large who complained about police harassment were all the while being supported by community spokespeople appointed to forums and consultative committees to keep the peace between local black and minority ethnic populations and the police force. Arguably, they were very institutionalised themselves. It is also ironic that in her Fabian paper, 'Communities in control – public services and local socialism' (Blears, 2003), a Home Office Minister argued for the need for active involvement of communities in shaping public service reform, a message somewhat lost in this public arena.

Conclusion

For any research to have credibility in describing or articulating the needs of particular disenfranchised and excluded groups, it must ensure that any dialogue is diverse and inclusive of all sections of those communities. Tight deadlines and lack of experience can lead to researchers seeking out key individuals as a way of gaining a synopsis of a community way of life. These opinions, for that is really all they are, may lack factual evidence but, once written up, become the accepted views of the broader cultural, religious or racial group. Public institutions, including the police force, have 'played it safe' by encouraging, if not conspiring with, key individuals to maintain a semblance of order.

The system of limited and controlled representation has served many public institutions well for decades and these relationships have been nurtured to provide mutual benefit, with community leaders reinforcing their status while acting as gatekeepers and unintentional collaborators with the forces of law and order to control potential rebellion or dissent from their own communities. By default, such individuals begin to 'police' their own cultural and religious communities and may unwittingly become 'agents' of intelligence gathering for public institutions such as the police. It is important for researchers to recognise that information can easily be manipulated for the glorification of the community leader at the expense of the community. Such information, like all data, needs critical analysis, including by white, middle-class, privileged academics. This is not a time for liberal rationalisation of an individual researcher's racial or cultural baggage, but a requirement for closer examination of the evidence, through more than one primary source.

Clearly, whether communities are well established and politicised, as in Bradford, or lack structural and political development, as in Oxford, the issue of legitimacy of representation remains the same. External researchers are at a disadvantage in the debate from the very beginning, starting as they do from a position of privilege combined with a lack of understanding of the racial, cultural and religious domains. The views of local communities they least understand, and have little or no connection with, remain rooted in a situation where "because someone speaks a particular language, he or she can speak for everyone else or their views can be unproblematically attributed to a particular culture" (Temple, 2002, p 853). This is an unsophisticated and amateurish approach to developing confidence in such groups.

It is also one where subjectivity replaces objectivity and it is taken for granted that the source of information about the community is a respected pillar of that community. This is where it is crucial for researchers to ensure not only the validity of the message but also the legitimacy of the messenger conveying the message. It is easy to ignore potential bias on the assumption that the messenger is best placed to relate to the community by virtue of being of the same cultural or religious groups. Such rationalisation may lead to misjudgements on the part of the researcher. This is not to say that such sources of information should not be used, but that it is dangerous to treat them as the only point of contact and ignore the voices of other members of the community.

The lack of interaction between public institutions and members of the wider community, whether they be activists, community campaigners, alienated young people, women and interest groups, only seeks to heighten community tensions that can lead to destructive consequences such as the Bradford riots. In examining cause and effect in their research studies, it is easy for academics to overlook their own processes of maintaining the 'status quo' and 'conservative' model of community engagement and involvement that further alienates such distrusting populations. Instead, researchers should strive to safeguard community integrity by challenging methodologies that exclude wider opinions or thought processes, and seeking a critical discourse on issues of social policy.

References

Ahmad, W. and Sheldon, T. (1993) '"Race" and statistics', in M. Hammersley (ed) *Social research: Philosophy, politics and practice*, London: Routledge, pp 124-30.

Aspinall, P. (2002) 'Collective terminology to describe the minority ethnic population: the persistence of confusion and ambiguity in usage', *Sociology*, vol 36, pp 803-16.

Blears, H. (2003*) Communities in control – public services and local socialism*, London: Fabian Society.

Five (2005) 'Postal vote fraud: Bradford Conservative arrested', 4 May, (www.five.org/blog/2005/05/postal-vote-fraud-bradford/html).

Jan-Khan, M. (1995) *The voices must be heard – a community response to the Manningham disturbances*, Bradford: Foundation 2000.

Jan-Khan, M. (2003) 'The right to riot?', *Community Development Journal*, vol 38, no 1, pp 32-42.

MacPherson Report (1999) *The Stephen Lawrence Inquiry*, London: The Stationery Office.

Malik, K. (1995) 'Party colours', *New Statesman & Society*, vol 8, no 361. pp 18-19.

Modood, T., Berthoud, R., Lakey, J., Nazoo, J., Smith, P., Virdee, S. and Beishon, S. (1997) *Ethnic minorities in Britain: Diversity and disadvantage*, London: Policy Studies Institute.

Nolan Committee (1995) *First Report of the Committee on Standards in Public Life*, (www.public-standards.gov.uk).

Office for National Statistics (2001) *Ethnicity and religion*, London: HMSO, (www.statistics.gov.uk).

Oxford Times (2004) 'Focus on the issue', Editorial, 16 February, p 4 (www.thisisoxfordshire.co.uk/oxfordshire/archive/2004/02/16/ TOPCOMMENT0ZM.html).

Pakistan Water Gateway (2001) 'Annual Report' (www.waterinfo.net).

Pakistan Water Gateway (2002) 'Increasing storage capacity of Mangla Dam' (www.waterinfo.net.pk/artisc.htm).

Shaw, A. (1994) 'The Pakistani community in Oxford', in R. Ballard (ed) *Desh Pardesh: the South Asian presence in Britain*, London: Hurst & Co, pp 35-57.

Social Exclusion Unit (2000) *Minority ethnic issues in social exclusion and neighbourhood renewal*, London: Cabinet Office.

Temple, B. (2002) 'Crossed wires: interpreters, translators and bi-lingual workers in cross-language research', *Qualitative Health Research*, vol 12, no 6, pp 844-54.

Temple, B. and Chahal, K. (2002) 'The science of terminology: housing research with older people from minority communities', *International Journal of Social Research Methodology: Theory and Practice*, vol 5, pp 353-69.

Temple, B. and Steele, A. (2004) 'Injustices of engagement: issues in housing needs assessments with minority ethnic communities', *Housing Studies*, vol 19, no 4, pp 541-56.

The Times (1994) 'Asians seize on fast route to Westminster', 30 September, p 9.

Yorkshire Post (2005) 'Inquiry into Labour "help" for the Tories', Editorial, 15 May, p 1.

SEVEN

Complexity and community empowerment in regeneration, 2002-04

Felicity Greenham with Rhetta Moran

Self-management for empowerment

This chapter draws on the recent experience of one of the authors who developed community-level engagement in an urban health regeneration programme. By engaging with people and exploring and documenting their experiences, she was able to help those who were seeking to acquire self-control and empowerment and, in the process, move away from feeling passive and unable to shape any aspects of their own lives.

The participatory action research (Reason, 1988; Stephen and McTaggart, 1988; Stringer, 1996) involved in this work and discussed in this chapter is best described through reference to Wadsworth's (1998) formulation that participatory action research is a new understanding of social science, because it is:

- more *conscious of 'problematising'* an existing action or practice, and more conscious of who is problematising it and why;
- more *explicit about 'naming' the problem*, and more self-conscious about raising an unanswered question and focusing on the answer;
- more *planned* and *deliberate* about commencing a process of inquiry and involving others who could or should be involved in that inquiry;
- more *systematic* and *rigorous* in our efforts to get answers;
- *more carefully documenting and recording action* and what people think about it, in more detail and in ways that are accessible to other relevant parties;
- more *intensive* and *comprehensive* in our study, waiting much longer before we 'jump' to a conclusion;

- more *self-sceptical* in checking our hunches;
- attempting to develop *deeper understandings* and *more useful and more powerful theory* about the matters we are researching, in order to produce new knowledge that can inform improved action or practice; and
- *changing our actions* as part of the research process, and then further researching these changed actions. (Wadsworth, 1988)

The chapter begins by discussing how individual awareness about needs can grow to the point where people become able to form groups, dedicated to identifying operational issues and practical tasks that can improve their situation. This process and its constituent parts are described in the first part of the chapter before moving on to an exploration of how the evidence bases that were developed in the first phase of the research were consciously moved into a second phase where the original groups discovered if and how they could influence or impact on policy through networks operating at meso- and even macro-strategic levels (Learmonth, 2005).

Felicity Greenham's role as the action researcher within this process was that of the intentional catalyst who openly and consistently invited, encouraged and supported people to become aware of their own actions, behaviours, needs and potential power, through conscious self- and group reflection and documentation, so that they could identify:

- whether and what they might want to act on in order to create constructive change processes; and
- how they might develop explanations for what they were doing that could become models for change processes within an urban health regeneration setting.

This approach accords with the overarching aim of Greenham's work to achieve a significant degree of health improvement in the population. Her philosophy is a relatively simple one: people need to have fundamental power and control over themselves and over the decisions that affect their lives. It is a philosophy that has held true since the 1980s when she worked with a range of individuals, from those who had spent part of their life in a long-stay institution and were being rehoused in the community, to those diagnosed with HIV seropositivity who took medical control of their condition.

In this chapter, we argue that this act of consciously documenting situations at the operational level, with the purpose of allowing people to see how they and others perceive these situations (through pictures and people's storytelling that is then written up for everyone to have as a record), can be used to engender change processes for the future. This conscious documentation, which is then used to identify the patterns of these processes and their relationships both to the tactical and strategic levels of public health delivery, and to ideas or theories about how to create change within the public's health, make this action research that can be distinguished from casework.

However, we go on to discuss how the research approach that was found to be highly productive and very effective for community development at an operational level failed to secure sustained change at the tactical and strategic levels. This failure, rather than being a reflection of the limits of current forms of participatory action research, is bound up in the absence of an equivalent commitment to learning from, and applying, the action research process on the part of people working at the tactical and strategic levels (Schön, 1983). This characteristic has been found to be prevalent within the management levels of the health service and was identified by the founder of action learning, Reg Revans, as an institutional form of 'parataxis' (Revans, 1966, p 266).

Emerging histories and the impact on health inequalities

When Maslow's (1968) hierarchy of need is met, individuals can begin to try to shape and control their own situations. The extent to which any individual may achieve this control is governed by conditional power, information, access, economics, opportunity and existing social systems (Baum, 2000). During the 1990s, the concept of 'community governance' emerged at the strategic level. This was a catch-all phrase for policy makers to use in their efforts to develop and operationalise forms of community-level control (Leat et al, 1999) and it epitomises the mainstream version of Greenham's philosophical view.

What people need

In this chapter we address situations that explore, and then expand on, individual notions of power and control and how they transform individual notions into collective action. However, the content and significance of the individual stories that initiated this research cannot be divorced from the impact of social systems that reinforce power imbalance. Indeed, understanding the interrelations between the individual and the social has been a central part of the research process:

collectivism is a key dynamic in communities taking charge for themselves and this is evidenced (Health Focus Group, 2003) when individuals share issues and develop common goals.

Refugee people in the 21st century first have to reconstruct Maslow's hierarchy of needs – striving to secure food, shelter and warmth in transit. On arrival in the host country, the need to secure these fundamentals continues. Once these basic needs have been satisfied (and for destitute people seeking asylum they are, by definition, not satisfied), the need for a sense of safety and then the psychological need for affection, belonging and acceptance by others, take precedence.

On the understanding that the determinants of health reflect socio-economic inequalities (Dahlgren and Whitehead, 1991), the research that Greenham has been involved in since 1999 has concerned both communities of people with histories of displacement and indigenous communities who are at a social disadvantage because of urban deprivation. Definitions of deprivation and disadvantage remain general, for example, Townsend's (1987) description of an observable and demonstrable state of disadvantage relative to the local community or the wider society or nation to which an individual, family or group belong.

Developments in legislation and policy

Over the past few years, since the introduction of forced dispersal, refugee people seeking asylum have been rehoused in areas in the UK identified as needing regeneration (Sheffield Hallam University et al, 2003). The 1999 Immigration and Asylum Act removed benefit entitlement from all asylum applicants and created the National Asylum Support Service (NASS) to support and disperse asylum seekers (Home Office, 1999) even with mounting opposition to its effects (Asylum Coalition, 2002).

Some of the interim findings of the health regeneration action research programme conducted in a regeneration area in the North of England with both indigenous people and refugee people seeking asylum are briefly presented here. After outlining developments over the past decade in community involvement within existing socially deprived areas, we describe the ways of working and researching that evolved between a social inclusion single regeneration budget (SRB) project with refugee people seeking asylum and local people involved in a Neighbourhood Renewal New Deal for Communities (NDC) regeneration area. This leads into a description and explanation of some of the communities' responses to the displaced people who were allocated to the area: a number of the themes, both for research and for development, that have been encountered to date, operationally, tactically and strategically, the research processes involved and the initial analysis of outcomes, including preliminary modelling.

In addition, because this work tried to impact on community structures across the tactical and strategic level, we would like to illustrate the chapter with models from the emergent Community Board (CHAP, 2001) that are aimed at integrating and empowering individuals and enhancing collective action and community governance. We conclude with some observations about the potential for this developing approach to help all partners to learn about and develop participatory action research processes through partnerships – now and in the future – for the benefit of all.

Developments in community involvement

There are 'people who have' and 'people who do not have' and there are the related impacts on people's health (Black et al, 1980; Wilkinson, 1996; Acheson, 1998). Over time, a raft of workers has tried to find ways of addressing communities' poor health outcomes through method and policy initiatives. Throughout the 1980s and 1990s, 'community development' was a key feature of statutory provision, research and the labour market. In the late 1990s and early 2000s, the intended outcomes of the concept of community development were redefined. In its efforts to develop joint mechanisms that address health inequalities, government has directed cities to include 'social inclusion' and 'community capacity' with 'community cohesion' as current targets (Office of the Deputy Prime Minister et al, 2002). 'Community empowerment' has superseded community development and a new paradigm has come to the fore that demands evidence of patient and public involvement in their own lives and in the services they use (Department of Health, 2002). The meaning that our project ascribed to the call for 'evidence' extended to include evidence about how and why we were doing what we were doing. We wanted this evidence to be sufficiently detailed so that we could later extrapolate some models that could be shared and adapted for use elsewhere, that is, offer some formative theory building (Wadsworth, 1998).

The key difference between this and the preceding model is that the old-style participation and consultation relied largely on community development workers delivering the agenda. Now, policy tells us (as discussed later) that enhanced local democracy needs to be developed over a period of time during which trust builds up (Learmonth, 2005, p 102) between local workers and local people, to the point where local people begin to deliver on their own agenda. The action research dimension of this work that instilled the discipline of making full accounts of what was happening, and making sure that those accounts were shared and discussed as a key component in the process of developing the next steps, was critical for self-delivery of the agenda.

Legislative change at the heart of government's thinking in the past decade (Department of Health, 1999; Department of Health, 2000) about neighbourhood renewal is based on the principle that it is local people who know best about the priorities and needs of their own neighbourhoods (Office of the Deputy Prime Minister, 2005). It also clearly indicates that they must have the opportunity and the tools to participate in their own regeneration. Directives such as the Department of Health Expert Patient Programme (EPP) have been operational in this country since 2002 (Department of Health, 2002). EPP demonstrates that self-empowerment for people with chronic long-term conditions has a significant effect on self-efficacy (Bandura, 1997) and, subsequently, on an individual's health status. Investment in prevention and secondary prevention that does not rely on the bio-medical model but develops social models, such as EPP, moves towards greater patient control.

Prior examples of engaging with communities contrast with these attempts to secure sustained health gain through local people and patients. The idea is that they develop and drive the agenda initiated with front-line workers, modifying its direction and gradually becoming involved in policy development as key and equal stakeholders. Within this model, the gaps between communities and the services they use are supposed to be narrowed and become seamless, as the vision of joined-up working turns into reality.

Overview of a New Deal for Communities and a social inclusion project

This research looks at work derived from two practical examples of the government's strategy for tackling social exclusion: an NDC area-based regeneration project that began in 1999, and an SRB 5 project with refugee people seeking asylum in 2002 that joined it.

NDC is a key programme in the government's strategy to address multiple deprivation in the most deprived neighbourhoods in the country, with the intention of giving some of our poorest communities the resources to tackle their problems in an intensive and coordinated way. The aim is to bridge the gap between these neighbourhoods and the rest of England. A major feature of successful bids for monies for NDC was that they demonstrated that local people in vital strategic positions had been instrumental in both the planning and the decision making around the bid and the subsequent action plans. While it is acknowledged that the problems of each area are unique, NDC partnerships must tackle five key issues: poor job prospects; high levels of crime; educational underachievement; poor health; and problems with housing and the physical environment. Key characteristics of NDC initiatives are:

- *long-term* commitment to deliver real change;
- communities at the heart of this, in *partnership* with key agencies;
- *community involvement* and ownership;
- *joined-up thinking* and solutions; and
- action based on evidence about '*what works*' and what doesn't.

SRB was introduced in 1994 to provide resources that support regeneration initiatives in England. Aimed at simplifying and streamlining the assistance available for regeneration, it brought together programmes from a number of different government departments. Its main concern was to enhance the quality of life of local people in areas of need by reducing the gap between deprived and other areas, and between different groups. The schemes that gain funding must be aimed at tackling the problems faced by communities in the most deprived neighbourhoods (Office of the Deputy Prime Minister, 2001).

This chapter is based on the work between an area-based neighbourhood renewal NDC initiative in Salford (Salford Neighbourhood Council, 2001) and the SRB 5 project with refugee people seeking asylum.

Real action

As part of the bid for NDC funding, communities worked alongside the city council to establish an NDC strategy for regenerating their area. Although the district in question stands out as an area that has many problems, it also has a well-defined community with strong links in terms of family, services, jobs and education. It was awarded

NDC status in 1999. In 2001, the second-round partnership bid succeeded in attracting £53 million of NDC funding to deliver the New Deal for Communities Delivery Plan 2001-2011.

The NDC team helped the project to develop and then worked with the local Community Health Action Partnership (CHAP) to establish a ten-year health action plan. CHAP was formed from a group of local residents in 1999. As part of the partnership, CHAP was actively involved in a dual process: empowering local people to become involved in the design and management of health services and in making services more accessible to the community.

The underlying principle within the NDC is working at the heart of the community. In the early days, before pathfinder status was awarded, the city was generating interest and awareness about the prospect of an NDC regeneration project. It was at one of these early events in 2000 that the first community members volunteered to become involved. They went on to play a key role in CHAP, influencing the health and social care agenda.

It is important to consider why people become involved in voluntary activities that take them out of their homes on cold winter nights into churches and community halls to work collectively. Greenham's observational analysis recognises that people volunteer for a number of different reasons and, for the purposes of this research, she worked with people's motives for volunteering, drawing on her previous experience. In this case she found that people volunteered because they were angry or annoyed about something; they wanted to learn a new skill or make new friends; the agenda was particularly pertinent to them; and/or they wanted to 'put something back' because of a life event that had affected them.

For one or all of these reasons the local community became energised and formed a new group that has subsequently and consistently driven the health agenda. Ninety-eight per cent of the group had a health-related problem themselves. Greenham made the observation that explained why they were volunteering and reflected it back to them, which reinforced their commitment to the process and their desire for better services.

CHAP became constituted in early 2000 and by September 2002 had an impressive record of partnership working. A high level of trust existed between members, and there was a subsequent increase in the levels of social reciprocity in the area. The first chair of CHAP was a local Salford man with great patience and understanding, who was passionately committed to improving the strength of the community. He ensured that every member of the group understood what was being discussed and reached decisions collectively. Consensus was achieved by ensuring that disagreements and debates were fully played out in meetings and any potential damage that could have resulted from divided power bases intelligently brokered. This reflective process evolved through the documentation of differing viewpoints, the acceptance of the differences within the group and then group analysis of what was shared and what was divisive before drawing out the tactics that would allow acknowledgement of the differences and development of consensus on how to move forward collectively.

Under the leadership of this Chair, backed by a dedicated secretary and treasurer, the CHAP Board acquired nine members and the membership increased to more than 50 people. The skills of the community members flourished. A classic moment in the group's development was when the NDC health plans had to be drafted (Salford New Deal for Communities, 2001). With the NDC health task group, CHAP undertook a joint public health/community needs assessment of the area (Salford New Deal for Communities, 2002). The partnership produced a theoretical set of ways of presenting health issues that were then worked up into project outlines for funding. A sub-group of CHAP members pored over statistics and epidemiological data in order to prioritise the population's health needs. At the following week's meeting, not only had they grasped and understood the complicated data, but one member of the group had drawn a graph of the Charlestown district's standard mortality rates against those of the City of Salford. Greenham arrived while they were having a broad discussion on the implications. Not only was there no skills gap here, but the research process ensured the high visibility of that skills base. In November 2001, local people in the NDC area became aware that, with no preparation by either central or local government, more than 50 young people seeking asylum had been rehoused into a single block of low-level flats in the area. Within 24 hours, the entrance to the block had been 'ram-raided' by a group wearing balaclavas that set fires in the doorways while the residents slept (*Manchester Evening News*, 2001). Senior figures within NDC tackled the issue by fostering debate within CHAP and NDC about how the local communities could and should respond and encouraging a ripple out of that debate into the wider NDC environment. This could only happen through exhaustive discussion within the group about how to respond until the core membership was very clear about the message it was going to take out into the wider community.

This marks the beginning of when CHAP and the fledgling charity Refugee Action Participatory Action Research (RAPAR) began tentatively to develop some tactical modelling for moving their perspectives into the policy setting. During the following months, conversations about racism and immigration issues involving CHAP members took place in shops and launderettes, gradually evolving into a welcome event for refugee people seeking asylum, hosted by NDC in a local church hall and supported by RAPAR. Structured conversation about the possibilities for people within the regeneration area took place against a backdrop of dancing and sharing food. One of the known outcomes of this event was that a newly arrived Muslim refugee family who had experienced harassment from their neighbours from day one found the confidence to post a Christmas card through the front door of every house on their street. Immediately, the harassment stopped and the refugee children found Salford playmates. This could only happen by capturing such outputs in documentary form, disseminating them and subsequently exploring new strategies for addressing the problems of social exclusion.

Shifting the balance

In the process of pursuing these mini-projects, NDC and CHAP came to understand that a key aspect for the future success of their work would be to ensure the creation of a practical and physical overlap – real space in real time – between the existing local NDC indigenous communities and the refugee people seeking asylum living in the area. Since this work was completed, the identification that actual physical spaces are needed in processes of bridging and bonding has reached the public domain (Temple et al, 2005). The gradual process outcome of this organic development was to shift the balance of power away from a strategic focus towards front-line workers and local people (Department of Health, 2001).

Another key process outcome of the work was the emergence of the philosophy of working at an operational, 'real' level with the issues that people presented and affirmed that they wanted to work with, rather than following a superimposed agenda. A handful of very involved and influential people, both community members and paid workers, validated the importance of ensuring that the communities drove the agenda and that local people identified and addressed issues that were pertinent to them. The maintenance of control over decision making about both the appropriate context and the timeframe for the work was secured through joint governance groups of local people and newly dispersed people living in the area. This movement between the process of identifying what people want to do and the process of describing it, doing it and capturing evidence of its impact lies at the heart of the participatory action research process.

By 2002, with national and international patterns indicating that refugee people seeking asylum would become an increasing part of the country's resident populations, the need for a partnership approach to all aspects of the work in the city had been clearly identified. Growing out of the RAPAR network, an SRB 5 bid developed by RAPAR with the Revans Institute at the University of Salford secured around two thirds of a million pounds for a Salford Community Development Team for three years. It was funded under the SRB guidelines of addressing social exclusion and improving opportunities for the disadvantaged (Moran and Sheikh, 2002). Within this project, the indigenous population and refugee people seeking asylum themselves would be supported to develop the evidence base and participate in constructing solutions with the local agencies charged with the responsibility of improving local practice.

Gradually, people involved in either the NDC or the SRB 5 projects began to act as catalysts. Greenham's original role as key researcher gradually cascaded into a wider grouping of people that are closer than she could ever be to the realities of their lives and needs, thus bringing other people from their respective projects together. Being, literally, physical neighbours, the partnership between NDC and Salford RAPAR workers and volunteers began immediately. This was influenced to a great extent by the welcoming behaviour and attitude of the NDC team, with strong leadership from its director at the time. In addition, delays in accommodating the Salford RAPAR team at its permanent base prompted NDC to offer its hospitality, through both accommodation and resources.

Developing a trust culture

The high trust culture models that emerged (Figure 7.1) were the result of individuals from the indigenous community and new residents seeking asylum working together. Within this research, the energy and outcomes emerged when both the subject areas that people were communicating about resonated with all parties and they also held common values and goals. A rich or 'high trust' culture flourished within and between real projects – 'real space in real time' – across the SRB and NDC. During this period, it became evident that NDC shared core values with the Salford RAPAR team. With the common purpose of striving to achieve successful relationships with local people and workers in order to tackle inequalities, the two groups began a

Figure 7.1: Culture-trust matrix

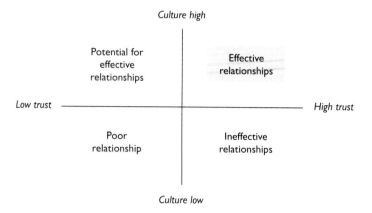

dialogue that quickly developed into an effective relationship best summed up by the phrase 'high trust culture'. The analytic process enabled us to recognise that in a high trust culture, background and ethnic origin are irrelevant because an effective relationship exists where:

- communication is clear;
- there is no hidden agenda; and
- there is a shared desire to achieve equality between all people.

This is an example of the way in which the action research process managed to evolve some tentative theoretical frameworks (see Figures 7.2 and 7.3 at p 126).

However, these examples were being realised through a complex set of highly interdependent and interconnected networks. These networks were the central planks of the NDC agenda of building communities. Salford's action research was seeking to find ways of taking forward the involvement of lay people in developing policy and services, and the development of partnership working (Salford Social Exclusion Unit, 2000). Working together, the NDC and SRB strategic partnership developed a high trust culture.

'Real space in real time' case studies

Between September 2002 and March 2004, the partnership began to develop operational responses to individual case presentations made to either Salford RAPAR or NDC. The chosen cases tended to fall within the areas of interest of both groups and presented complete and individual scenarios that could be analysed for their usefulness in demonstrating patterns of service response to a range of scenarios. The operational work covered issues relating to mental health, teenage pregnancies, domestic violence, TB, HIV seropositivity, homelessness, maternity, unemployment, inappropriate accommodation and children's needs. The partnerships' networks were engaged in a constant process of discussing, negotiating and developing plans for action on the basis of these presentations. They offered leading examples of how to define/describe the range of problems being experienced in Salford by both refugee people seeking asylum and the indigenous population. They also offered leading examples of how to respond to these problems so that productive models could begin to emerge that crossed complex boundaries between individuals and groups in the locality and between residents and practitioners.

Shifting communities

By late 2001, the predominately white working-class city of Salford was beginning to experience a shift in the make-up of its population. The regeneration area became the home of increasing numbers of refugee people seeking asylum and, over time, the composition of CHAP shifted to reflect these changes in order to represent those communities more accurately – another example of the action research process in action.

This operational work wove itself into communities' structures, thereby having an impact at the tactical and strategic levels. By way of illustration, we present below three 'real time in real space' case studies that relate to the CHAP community group and/or the CHAP Board and the Salford RAPAR project in different ways. They demonstrate the processes that empower individuals for enhanced collective action and community governance and offer new ways of thinking about how to develop this most complex and exciting agenda.

Case study 1: Mylin

A family moved into the NDC area in early 2003 with five children, and the mother pregnant with her sixth child. The eldest daughters attended the local college and the younger children went to the local junior school. All the children were fairly proficient in English, and were the main translators for their mother. Mylin, who wanted to pursue a career in nursing, had a series of disputes with her father and subsequently moved out of the family home to a local young persons' hostel. As a result of her growing independence, she integrated in her own right with the local community and was one of the first people to become a CHAP member. She worked with the Salford RAPAR project social work student to tackle her difficulties in accessing a female GP whom she could confide in. While she was in the process of accessing support and making friends, she was also breaking down myths associated with people seeking asylum. Her actions could be perceived as socially transformatory, although she was also just a teenager growing up.

Case study 2: Moshe

In mid–2003, a young man in his late twenties presented to the Salford RAPAR project. A qualified medical doctor, he had found himself isolated, unemployed and depressed since fleeing his home country. He had limited English and was not an immediate candidate for the General Medical Council retraining scheme. NDC devised a tailormade programme to help him reach the appropriate level of skill in English language and he undertook a six-month placement as a doctor from Salford RAPAR to the NDC health focus group. As he conducted community and professional consultations that informed the development of the successful Salford Personal Medical Services bid, his linguistic skills developed. He was supported through the partnership between the NDC health focus group, REACHE North West and Salford RAPAR.

In March 2003, as part of his NDC placement, he attended a CHAP business development residential workshop. In one session, where delegates were discussing crime and disorder, he talked about his reluctance to leave the house after 9 pm for fear of assault. This simple shared experience brought home to others the problems faced by people seeking asylum in a strange country, and helped forge friendships and reduce barriers of discrimination and xenophobia within the indigenous population.

Case study 3: Heather

The impact that front-line workers have had, as catalysts for both shifting the balance of power in policy terms and impacting on 'real time in real space' activities, should not be underestimated.

Heather is a member of the Salford RAPAR community

development team, who has worked tirelessly across NDC and CHAP and been instrumental in developing new structures for communication and improved relationships. She has achieved this by becoming a member of the CHAP board herself and introducing new people to the board. She was fully conversant with community development/ empowerment models in her home country and has guided the asylum seeking and indigenous Salford populations in building bridges across the gaps imposed by culture and language. She participated in an expert patient programme, sharing her own medical history and creating links between people with common conditions. She has encouraged a wide range of activities, from people cooking together, to students spending working vacations in Africa. Her work will impact on future generations through a Saturday school that started off as a children's summer activity.

Analysing complexity

A key feature of this research is its location deep within the community. It grew 'inside' communities. People who found themselves living in the same area consciously explored how they could form common bonds and generate friendships. These social exchanges developed within interpersonal interactions where small elements of communities connected and were seized by the researcher so that they could be examined for their potential contribution to building shared goals and visions that could be translated into practice. The common characteristic of the NDC and SRB projects was that they both worked alongside and within communities. Another common feature was start times: NDC started as a 10-year project to renew the neighbourhood and address inequalities one year before the SRB was funded, to identify the needs of refugee people and people seeking asylum, and develop action in services. While the neighbourhood renewal project was concentrated on a particular area with a population of 10,000 and the SRB was located across the city, it was the synergy in the NDC area that provided the catalyst for the activities documented.

This chapter has attempted to explain a series of complex situations where people meet, interact and are influenced by each other, by the environment they live in and the social systems that constrain them. Communicating and implementing the principles needed for sustained social change appear to have remained unheard and therefore ignored in practice for a long time (Figueroa et al, 2002). Occasionally, however, the combination of environment, individuals and serendipitous relationships allows partnerships to make research processes through which collective goals emerge and visions become achievable: the kinetic energy inside the research process generates more of its own energy and succeeds, at an operational level, in disrupting the traditional polarisation of energy between the relatively powerless and the relatively powerful.

As it stood, the NDC–Salford RAPAR partnership (Figure 7.2) was working very well at ground level.

Although the first phase of the research process was complete, it remained to be tested by observing whether and how this effective relationship (Figure 7.3) would continue to be accommodated at the tactical level and, thereby, impact and disseminate its successes – and its processes – at the strategic level in a sustainable way.

Figure 7.2: Location of the partnership work

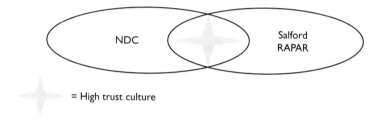

= High trust culture

Figure 7.3: Modelling regeneration partnership

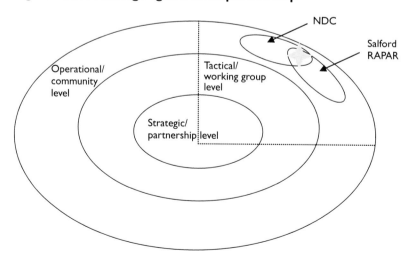

Developing action

A guiding principle of this research has been to invest in developing participatory partnerships at the operational, community level. These communities of people were the primary researchers and, as such, by organising their experiences into formats that could be disseminated and shared, they minimised the gap between real-world knowledge, analysis and potential public health solutions. The research focused on people's actual situations and attempted to develop health and social care responses at a tactical and strategic level. By ensuring that the operational power was located within the marginalised populations, it also offered the potential to enhance individuals' cultural competencies and increase social cohesion. However, this was not enough.

The key lesson to be learnt from this research is the recognition that, when sharing power across and within communities, it is not inevitable that close and trusting relationships will emerge that can subsequently enhance greater individual control and collective community governance. Indeed, such relationships will not begin at all unless all parties are empowered to articulate their perspectives in ways that are appropriate to them and that explore how breakdowns in relationships that span the operational, tactical and strategic can and do happen, however hard people try. Documenting the problems makes it possible for participants to reflect on why they have occurred.

If there is an alternative account for what has happened, based in the contemporaneous evidence base from the research process itself, and there is a site within which to place that account, then it becomes possible to challenge the prevailing account of what has occurred. This can be achieved by the people who originally created the evidence base revisiting the original intentions that underpinned the development of the evidence base in the first place. If they are confident that the change processes worked at the operational level, and were indeed directed towards achieving the original aims agreed at the beginning of the research process, they can move on to analyse why these processes failed to have an impact at the tactical and strategic level.

When partnerships do break down, and when there is a failure to redistribute any real power over operational community decisions at the strategic level, the failure is often mistakenly attributed to a skills gap in the community. By contrast, Greenham's experience in this action research is that communities have undiscovered and limitless skills, and any failure is more often the result of an inability at the tactical and strategic level to recognise these skills, or operational difficulties on the part of statutory sector to work effectively within communities.

Ultimately, the practice of retaining control and power over what to do and how to do it at the strategic level, irrespective of the implicit contradiction between this and the concept of 'community governance', is difficult to dislodge. It needs a publicly accountable arena where the protagonists can map out an infrastructure that will support the research process so that the consistently communicative process that characterises effective ground-level relationships can be reproduced and monitored at the meso and macro levels.

Finally, our action research processes identified operational synogen and self- and collective management processes. However, they also disrupted the unquestioning assumption held by the 'community governance' policy maker that it is sufficient to legislate for such policy at a strategic stakeholder level: as it stands, policy-level legislation is simply not securing community-level control of any duration, nor is it advancing that model within the hierarchy. If enhanced community capacity, social inclusion and community empowerment are really our goals, then all the energy that operational front-line workers and the community expends is in danger of being neutralised by the control mechanisms that interject both tactically and strategically. Quid pro quo.

Conclusion

The National Strategy for Neighbourhood Renewal and NDC partnerships are beginning to reveal valuable lessons that need wider translation. The keys to that change are pivotal to improving local services by increasing community capacity, that is, enabling people to do more for themselves, and adopting an evidence-based approach to delivering change, that is, getting proof of what works in practice (Salford Social Exclusion Unit, 2000).

Within this research, the gap between communities and the services they use are supposed to narrow and become seamless as the vision of joined-up working turns into reality. However, in practice, as our research has revealed, it appears that the gap between services and policy is widening.

More longitudinal research may reveal whether policy changes that direct actions from community development models to empowerment models are another form of reclaiming civil society. Are they in fact a means of reinventing ways of exerting strategic power at an operational level and increasing control over communities? Community-led schemes can have an energising impact on communities, as we have demonstrated in this chapter. If the evidence bases generated by these communities are accorded the respect they deserve at the strategic level and used to inform the construction of research evidence bases, they could help us understand how to create sustained community empowerment.

Where a breakdown in communication across boundaries occurs, it is sometimes attributed to lack of readiness and skills within the community. Some of the key community members and activists are still living in the area and it would take more longitudinal research analysis to measure any sustained, enhanced changes in community governance.

However, our action research analysis reveals either a gap in the organisations' cultural competencies at the strategic level, or an inability of services to transfer control and power to citizens. The complexity of our changing communities and the legislation pertaining to people seeking asylum compound inequalities. A successful strategy to combat inequalities and encourage self-empowerment must work both from above and below.

As demonstrated in this chapter, it is possible to create ground-level research partnerships across cultural boundaries within regeneration areas dedicated to self-improvement. However, if such partnerships are to become sustainable over timeframes that are commensurate with the length of regeneration strategies, there must be an acceptance of the authenticity of what they do, and what they demonstrate about what they do. This, together with an ability and preparedness to share decision-making power, underpins any tactical and strategic-level support for their development.

Without this, attempts to develop action research will falter and ultimately fail as people who become enabled within the research process become disabled when the traditional power relations reassert themselves. The consequences for research are bound up with the capacities for regeneration initiatives to devolve decision making and power. The problem seems to be that people with power never willingly give it up.

References

Acheson, D. (1998) *Independent inquiry into inequalities in health*, London: The Stationery Office.

Asylum Coalition (2002) 'Developing a positive agenda for asylum, immigration and citizenship. A joint statement on the White Paper on asylum, migration and citizenship' (www.refugeecouncil.org.uk/downloads/coalition_statement_april02.pdf).

Bandura, A. (1997) *Self-efficacy: The exercise of control*, New York, NY: Freeman.

Baum, F. (2000) 'Social capital, economic capital and power: further issues for a public health agenda', *Journal of Epidemiology and Community Health*, vol 54, pp 409-10.

Black, D., Morris, J., Smith, C. and Townsend, P. (1980) *Inequalities in health: Report of a research working group*, London: Department of Health and Social Security.

CHAP (Community Health Action Partnership) (2001) *CHAP vision*, Salford: New Deal for Communities.

Dahlgren, G. and Whitehead, M. (1991) *Policies and strategies to promote social equity in health*, Stockholm: Institute of Future Studies.

Department of Health (1999) *Saving lives – our healthier nation*, London: The Stationery Office.

Department of Health (2000) *The NHS Plan*, London: The Stationery Office.

Department of Health (2001) *Shifting the balance of power in the NHS*, London: The Stationery Office.

Department of Health (2002) 'Patient and public involvement' (www.dh.gov.uk/PolicyAndGuidance/PatientAndPublicInvolvement/fs/en).

Figueroa, M.E., Kinacaid, D.L., Rani, M. and Lewis, G. (2002) *Communication for social change: An integrated model for measuring the process and its outcomes*, New York, NY: The Rockefeller Foundation.

Health Focus Group (2003) *Lower Kersal and Charlestown New Deal for Communities Annual Health Report*, Salford: G.U. Design.

Home Office (1999) *Immigration & citizenship: A joint statement on the White Paper on Asylum, Immigration & Citizenship*, London: The Stationery Office.

Learmonth, A. (2005) 'Action learning as a tool for developing networks and building evidence based practice in public health', *Action Learning: Research and Practice*, vol 2, no 1, pp 97-104.

Leat, D., Seltzer, K. and Stoker, G. (1999) *Governing in the round: Strategies for holistic government*, London: Demos.

Manchester Evening News (2001) 'Gun gang in ram raid on refugees', 5 November, p 1.

Maslow, A.H. (1968) 'Towards a psychology of being', in V. Nostrand (ed) *The farther reaches of human nature*, London: Penguin Books, pp 25-42.

Moran, R.A. and Sheikh, N. (2002) *Salford RAPAR SRB5 Project Proposal: 'Developing evidence about needs and action in services with refugee and asylum seeking communities'*, Salford: RAPAR and The Revans Institute.

ODPM (Office of the Deputy Prime Minister) (2001) *SRB round 5 bidding guidance: A guide for ODPM*, London: The Stationery Office.

ODPM (2005) 'Regional Development Agency's single budget programme', Neighbourhood Renewal Unit (www.neighbourhood.gov.uk.page.asp?id=639).

ODPM, Home Office, Local Government Association, Inter-Faith Network and the Commission for Racial Equality (2002) 'Guidance on community cohesion' (www.neighbourhood.statistics.gov.uk).

Reason, P. (ed) (1988) *Human inquiry in action: Developments in new paradigm research*, London: Sage Publications.

Revans, R. (1966) *Origins and growth of action learning*, Bromley: Chartwell-Bratt, p 266.

Salford Neighbourhood Renewal (2001) *A New Deal for Everyone: The Salford New Deal for Communities Delivery Plan (2001-2011)*, Salford: New Deal for Communities.

Salford New Deal for Communities (2001) *D-Day community event report. February*, Salford: New Deal for Communities.

Salford New Deal for Communities (2002) *Public health and community health needs assessment*, Salford: New Deal for Communities.

Salford Social Exclusion Unit (2000) *A new commitment to neighbourhood renewal: 'Social Action Research Project (SARP) (1999-2202)'*, London: The Stationery Office.

Schön, D. (1983) *The reflective practitioner – how professionals think in practice*, New York, NY: Basic Books.

Sheffield Hallam University CUPS, University of Manchester CRESR, Liverpool John Moores University EIUA (2003) *Seeking asylum in NDC areas: A report on experiences, policies and practices*, Sheffield: Sheffield Hallam University.

Stephen, S. and McTaggart, R. (1988) *The action research planner* (3rd edn), Geelong: Deakin University.

Stringer, E.T. (1996) *Action research: A handbook for practitioners*, London: Sage Publications.

Temple, B. and Moran, R.A. with Fayas, N., Haboninana, S., McCabe, F., Mohamed, Z., Noori, A. and Rahman, N. (2005) *Learning to live together: Developing communities where there are dispersed refugee people seeking asylum,* York: Joseph Rowntree Foundation.

Townsend, P. (1987) 'Deprivation', *Journal of Social Policy*, vol 16, no 2, pp 125-46.

Wadsworth, Y. (1998) 'What is participatory action research?', Action Research International, Paper 2 (www.scu.edu.au/schools/gcm/ar/ari/p-ywadsworth98.html).

Wilkinson, R. (1996) *Unhealthy societies: The afflictions of inequalities,* London: Routledge.

EIGHT

Refugee voices as evidence in policy and practice

Kirsteen Tait

Introduction

Until recently, asylum seeking in the UK involved only a few high-profile individuals and there was no need for a national asylum policy, statutory forms of support for asylum seekers, or for a formal refugee integration policy. Refugees[1] had been persecuted dissidents from behind the Iron Curtain or individually tortured human rights activists: recognised fugitives from world-stage catastrophes. No complex legal process was required to decide whether claims for asylum were genuine. It was not until the 1993 Asylum and Immigration Appeals Act that asylum was dealt with in primary legislation. Before that, the UN Convention was incorporated into Immigration Rules that operated according to the discretion of the Home Office. Quota refugee resettlement projects in recent years – the Polish programme 1945-49, Ugandan Asian programme 1972-73, Chilean programme 1974-79, Vietnamese programme 1979-82, Bosnian programme 1992-95, and the Kosovan humanitarian programme in 1999 – were one-off responses to specific, recognised emergencies rather than statutory arrangements, each drawing only a little on the lessons of its predecessor. But this all changed in the late 1980s with the arrival of large numbers of spontaneous asylum applicants, from persecuted ethnic groups and from a wide range of countries of origin. It ushered in a decade of national asylum policy making, followed by national asylum support arrangements and, more recently, a national integration policy.

Policy and practice have been developed to meet the new challenges in the context of a government commitment to generate an evidence base to inform national policy making[2]. The research programme on asylum and refugees, introduced by the Labour government in 1997 to underpin asylum and immigration policy, can be seen as part of this. Robinson (1998) describes the ideal process:

> ... problems which are deemed worthy of resolution (and
> resourcing) now become subject of policy. In order to
> formulate policy, accurate factual information has to be
> generated on the nature, scale and location of the problem.
> Evaluative information is also needed on what policy
> responses might be available, whether they have been
> implemented elsewhere, and with what success.... Policy
> options need to be discussed widely with those who will
> implement them and those who will supposedly benefit
> from them.... (pp 148-9)

David Blunkett agrees: "We need to be able to rely on social science
and social scientists to tell us what works and why, and what types of
policy initiatives are likely to be the most effective" (Blunkett, 2000).

This chapter takes for granted the principle that user voices are an
essential strand in evidence in all areas of policy and practice, and that
"refugees are the experts of their own experience" (Hynes, 2003, p 1).
Indeed, much of the online list of published and ongoing Home Office
research commissioned since 1997 states that it involves interviews
with asylum seekers and refugees (for example, Home Office, 2002a,
2002b, 2003a, 2003b, 2003c, current a, current b, current c).

Other government departments have also commissioned policy and
practice related research involving interviews with refugees. Two recent
examples include *Refugees' opportunities and barriers in employment and
training* commissioned by the Department of Work and Pensions
(Bloch, 2002), which surveyed 400 refugees and asylum seekers from
Somali regions, Iraq, Kosova, Sri Lanka and Turkey, in five English
regions, using multiple approaches to data collection; and *Asylum seekers
in Scotland*, which was commissioned to assess the effect of the
implementation of the 1999 Immigration and Asylum Act on asylum
seekers and devolved services in Scotland, a piece of qualitative research
involving a range of interviews including "sixty-three interviews with
asylum seekers of varying ethnicity, gender, age, household composition
and residence in Glasgow" (Barclay et al, 2003, p 1).

In spite of these intentions, the overall evidence base about refugees
and asylum seekers, let alone their experiences and voices, is recent
and cannot draw on years of government-commissioned research, as
can many areas of public policy. There is no nationally representative
dataset on which to base new research. To access refugee voices and
experiences, researchers have had to create their own datasets (Carey-
Wood et al, 1995; Bloch, 1999), and recent government-commissioned
research suffers from the same limitations. This chapter argues that in

these circumstances the existing government evidence base needs to be complemented and supplemented by other sources. It shows how the work of the Information Centre about Asylum and Refugees (ICAR)[3] at Kings College London, in identifying and recording sources of refugee experiences and voices, could be used to contribute evidence to influence policy making. The sources include: independently funded exploratory university research; research and studies by local authorities; research by the voluntary sector in the form of non-governmental organisations (NGOs) and refugee organisations; and research commissioned by refugee community organisations (RCOs) using asylum seeker and refugee experiences. The potential of these sources is illustrated here with reference to NGO, local authority and university studies, and ICAR's projects and publications, in particular *Making better use of existing information and data about refugees and people seeking asylum* (ICAR, 2004) and *The Somali community in the UK:What we know and how we know it* (Harris, 2004).

In response to a vast increase in numbers of asylum seekers and refugees, destitution, contractual obligations to provide support services, and grant and contract requirements, refugee agencies and NGOs have increasingly recorded asylum seeker and refugee experiences and voices, both for the purposes of service development and to underpin lobbying and advocacy on behalf of their clients (see case study 1). Local authorities, learning and skills councils and regional and local health authorities have for some years researched and recorded refugee experiences as service users, producing valuable information and statistical data, examples of which are discussed in case study 2. Independently funded university research of potential value for policy development has been carried out by individual academics spread across the UK in a range of disciplines through geography, psychology, law, human rights, anthropology, social studies, urban studies and healthcare. Refugee experiences and voices contained in qualitative and exploratory academic research, and in postgraduate dissertations, can complement and supplement Home Office research.

Issues of validity and accessibility can be successfully overcome and disparate sources drawn into a recognised corpus of evidence. Government does not have an absolute standard for evidence that is eligible for policy making. Even a casual look at econometrics and statistics shows that serious and insuperable difficulties arise in specifying and carrying out research that produces irrefutable conclusions. Serious methodological issues apply to all research involving asylum seekers and refugees, whether commissioned by government or others, and some apply especially to research commissioned by government. The difficulties of collecting sufficient, representative evidence of refugee voices and experiences, discussed in greater detail in other chapters, include:

- the lack of a random sampling frame;
- the enormous range of factors that need to be taken into account in trying to be representative of all asylum seekers and refugees – age, sex, religion, country of origin, circumstances of flight;
- the range of circumstances affecting experiences in the UK that include area of dispersal, housing, access to healthcare, security and racial harassment, age, gender, language skills, educational and professional qualifications;
- problems of access to interviewees;
- problems inhibiting refugees' freedom to speak – fears and concerns about the use to which interview data may be put;
- relationship to interviewer or interpreter;
- gatekeepers who skew samples;
- cost of interpretation and problems of mistranslation;
- ethical considerations of researching an extremely vulnerable group;
- the loss of researcher neutrality when confronted with horrific experiences; and
- research fatigue among the asylum seekers and refugees themselves (Temple, 1997; Robinson, 1998; Bloch, 1999; Estherhuizen, 2004; Harris, 2004).

In the absence of a long-standing rich evidence base of refugee voices and experiences, this chapter argues for an inclusive approach to potential evidence, which nonetheless maintains rigorous methodological standards.

Among potential contributors to the evidence base, the voluntary sector and local authorities have unique opportunities to collect unassailable data. They work directly with asylum seeker and refugee clients and have fewer problems of accessing refugee interviewees than outsiders, although this relationship may unintentionally skew interview samples and the interpretation of data. Their funding increasingly requires them to keep client casework records of a kind that can provide a powerful starting point for research into experiences. Their research may have limitations for government purposes: it may be limited in timeframe, scope or client group, and it may not conform to government methodological preferences. But this does not mean that they have nothing to contribute. Past research can be examined for what it can offer and future research can be guided by Home Office requirements of evidence for policy making. 'Flexible templates' could be provided (Robinson, 1998, p 158).

A Home Office workshop was convened in 2004 to discuss methodological issues related to sampling and accessing refugees and asylum seekers for the purposes of research. It aimed specifically to identify innovative ways that circumvented the limitations of using NGOs and RCOs as gatekeepers where there were risks of research fatigue. Further workshops would be useful.

Guides such as *Doing case studies for the refugee sector: A DIY handbook for agencies and practitioners* (Estherhuizen, 2004) can help ensure that case studies and surveys meet standards required. The explosion of interest in asylum and refugee issues at postgraduate level in universities provides a rich resource of people, with taught research skills, keen to carry out research with policy implications for NGOs.

The following case studies show how a broader evidence base of refugee experiences and voices might be built up using past research by NGOs.

Case study 1: understanding why asylum seekers come to the UK

This case study examines a recent piece of Home Office-commissioned, policy-oriented research and recognises its methodological rigour, but suggests that the validity of its findings are limited by its provenance and purpose. Examples of research commissioned by NGOs with different strengths and limitations are used to show how the evidence base can be boosted without reducing its rigour, provided that questions are asked about its provenance and purpose, design and methodology. ICAR's online digests of recent reports provide an example of how a process of applying systematic questions to non-governmental research might be organised.

Dramatically increased numbers of asylum applications, and backlogs and appeals against initial decisions on these applications, meant that the Home Office urgently needed to know why so many people came to the UK; an example of a problem "deemed worthy of resolution" (Robinson, 1998, p 148). Realising that little is known about how asylum seekers choose their destination, the Home Office commissioned a research series to address the knowledge gap. Several of these projects involved interviews with asylum seekers and refugees. *Understanding the decision-making of asylum seekers* (Home Office, 2002a) had the clear, and clearly stated, purpose of *examining factors influencing decision making of asylum seekers and reasons for choosing the* UK (emphasis added). The methodology involved a review of the research literature and "in-depth qualitative interviews with 65 asylum seekers" (Home Office, 2002a, p 1). The authors explained that every effort was made to generate a sample of respondents with different countries of origin, gender, age, length of residence in the UK, legal status, place of residence and household type, but not all groups could be included, and the authors do not claim that the results are representative of all asylum seekers. Issues of representativeness are addressed with particular care, pointing out that those genuinely in need of safe haven may have been more inclined than others to come forward to be interviewed. On the other hand, many of the interviewees had nothing to lose. Having received final decisions on their cases, whether positive or negative, some reported freely that they had been advised to lie to protect entry routes and human smugglers, and many volunteered highly sensitive information – about illegal routes of entry, for example – and were honest to the point of damaging their claim to asylum if the information was passed on.

A major issue for the researchers was the difficulty of accessing interviewees, which was overcome only by the researchers' prior contacts and known credibility and reputation. Cold calling did not produce results; there was a reluctance to participate in a Home Office research project and much suspicion about the uses to which the results might be put. Time and effort was expended on calming fears, putting out explanatory flyers distributed by third parties and gaining trust by fully disclosing the details and provenance of the research.

This research is discussed in detail here because it is a model of clarity about purpose and provenance, methodology and scope. By doing so, it pinpoints the issues that matter and therefore the tests that need to be applied to non-governmental sources of refugee voices that might supplement and complement the corpus of evidence. Taking a cue from the researchers' methodological awareness and rigour (see in particular Robinson, 1998), we have to question whether the findings are sufficiently representative as a basis for policy making.

It is not so much the size of the sample but the manner in which the interviewees were selected. Obtaining interviewees through RCOs and refugee agencies can skew results. Many asylum seekers and refugees do not use RCOs, and RCOs cannot necessarily represent all shades of opinion within a community, especially where inter-tribal and inter-clan rivalries have been the cause of flight. Nor do they necessarily represent women's points of view.

The fact that research is policy-oriented may also limit its validity. Some people will not participate in research commissioned by the Home Office, while others may tailor their responses accordingly. Serious issues of trust arise: "barriers arising out of a general mistrust of strangers and people perceived to be in authority" (Refugee Women's Association and Greater London Authority, 2002, p 7). Research with other purposes – awareness raising or even advocacy – conducted by non-government bodies may therefore be more genuinely representative. This chapter argues that almost any research involving interviews with asylum seekers can contribute to the evidence base on why people come to the UK, provided its purpose and provenance, methodology and scope are stated clearly and so can be taken into consideration.

Asylum voices: Experiences of people seeking asylum in the United Kingdom (Bradstock and Trotman, 2003) is an interesting example. It contains 146 case studies of asylum seekers' experiences of the process of seeking asylum and their individual stories of why they came to the UK. The research states its aim unambiguously as being the recording of the voices of asylum seekers in the interests of justice and compassion and to right the balance in a debate dominated by the tabloid press. The authentic voice heard in this report is to make sure that in all future debate, the views of people seeking asylum and refugees themselves cannot be ignored. Along the way it seeks to nail some misconceptions (Bradstock and Trotman, 2003). While the aim did not pretend to be open-ended, the methodology is exploratory in being designed to allow individuals the opportunity to emphasise what they consider significant, and enable researchers to listen to and record the circumstances of flight. The necessary details are provided that allow the readers to reach their own conclusions about its representativeness: interviewees came from 37 countries of origin, 108 male and 38 female, 7% under 20, 49% aged between 20 and 30. The research includes interviews with legal representatives, caseworkers and GPs, all of whom have had "regular first hand contact with people seeking asylum, many of whom were refugees themselves so offering a double perspective" (Bradstock and Trotman, 2003, p 65). Confidentiality was assured and interviewees suffered from none of the suspicions experienced in the Home Office-commissioned research about the purpose to which the findings might be put. In fact, they were delighted to have a chance to express themselves freely. A fraction of each story is contained in the report, and the raw data could contribute significantly to an evidence base about why people come.

Evidence about why people come can also emerge indirectly from research on other subjects with other purposes. Research with apparently limited scope, for example into a specific refugee group, can also be a source of evidence. *A gap in their hearts* (Hannan, 2003) looked at the personal experiences and vulnerabilities of Somali children who were smuggled into the UK, Sweden and North America without parental or guardian support. Its purpose was "that the plight of such children may in the future be better addressed in the homeland and in the host countries" (Hannan, 2003, p 3). It contains interviews with "Somali separated children, parents and families; state authorities, immigration and police officials, and professionals working in the support and welfare services of the host countries; as well as Somali smugglers and 'fixers' who arrange the transportation of the children out of Somali territories" (Hannan, 2003, p 10).

It uses a composite story line based on interviews and actual experiences. *The Somali community in the UK* comments:

> Some of the richest material we have of this kind dispenses with the attempt to find a statistical base and relies on qualitative material. A recent example is Lucy Hannan's outstanding report: *A gap in their hearts* (2003). The depth of both background research and interviews with young people, including extensive personal accounts, inspires confidence that her findings are representative, even if this cannot be statistically proven. The impossibility of obtaining a random sample is irrelevant. (Harris, 2004, p 17)

These examples meet the requirements of clarity about purpose and provenance, methodology and scope proposed in this chapter, and so they can contribute to a growing evidence base from asylum seekers themselves about why people come. However, in order to transform individual studies from various sources into a coherent evidence base, a simple method for applying these tests is needed. One possibility is provided by ICAR's digests of recent reports, which contain entries in a standard format about author, commissioner and funder (that is, 'provenance'), subject, geographical and other coverage ('scope'), research objective/stated aim ('purpose'), methodology, as well as summaries of findings and conclusions (www.icar.org.uk/res/drp/drpindex.html). These digests could be used to select studies that involve refugee interviews and voices, meet the clarity requirements about provenance and purpose, scope and methodology, and therefore have the potential to complement and supplement the evidence base.

This is best illustrated by quoting a digest entry, for example, that for *Right first time? Home Office interviewing and reasons for refusal letters*, which was commissioned and published by the Medical Foundation for the Care of Victims of Torture (Smith, 2004) and which ICAR describes as follows:

Research objective/stated aim

To assess to what extent Home Office Reasons for Refusal Letters [RFRLs] present evidence of full, reasoned decisions on asylum claims, and to examine the asylum interview as an effective means of obtaining the necessary information to determine an asylum claim, particularly in relation to applicants' experience of torture. Impetus for this research was the poor quality of many interview records and RFRLs in the files of Medical Foundation clients.

Methodology

Research is based on analysis of 46 files of Cameroonian clients who sought the services of the Medical Foundation in 2001 and 2002. These were compared with the RFRLs and Statement of Evidence Form (SEF) interview records of Cameroonian clients in 2003, to assess whether there had been improvements in procedures. Evidence is quoted from Asylum Policy Instructions [APIs], RFRLs and SEFs. Interview records of clients in the sample were read by an expert to assess the efficacy of the process of obtaining information about experience of torture. Footnotes mainly refer to instruments concerned with the definition of torture. A bibliography is provided.

(www.icar.org.uk/res/drp/drps/drp121.html)

If such tests of eligibility as evidence for policy making are to be applied to research into refugee experiences from non-governmental sources, the research must first be known to exist and be easily accessible. Action may be needed to unearth scattered research from different sources. Less recent research reports get lost or are no longer available (especially those published before online copies were routine). This is well illustrated by ICAR's examination of the state of knowledge about Somalis in the UK discussed below. Much of the research examined there is in the form of time-limited, small-scale studies by local authorities and voluntary sector organisations and:

> Many of these remain in duplicated form, are not widely distributed, and ... are extraordinarily hard to obtain. All too often, local authorities, NGOs and RCOs who have produced the report have no knowledge of it a few years later, let alone spare copies. In general, information is fragmented, poorly catalogued, and badly circulated. (Harris, 2004, p 13)

Accumulating evidence that might otherwise be lost is a principal purpose of ICAR's *Making better use of existing information and data about refugees and asylum seeking people project* (ICAR, 2004). It has built a matrix to record existing data about data across the sector (not the data themselves, which may often be confidential). It catalogues datasets from organisations with refugee clients and records on which organisation holds which data, and makes access to the matrix available on a password-protected section of ICAR's website (www.icar.org.uk/ ICAR-DM-Search-Basic.jsp). It identifies research results, client casework databases, questionnaire results and case studies, and the existence of data that involve refugee voices and experiences can easily be identified. Recorded fields include type of dataset, scope, geographical coverage and content summary.

Datasets have so far been contributed by a range of different sorts of organisations having only in common that they have asylum seeker and refugee clients: Refugee Council, Refugee Action, Shelter, Bail for Immigration Detainees, East Midlands Consortium for Asylum Seeker and Refugee Support, the Northern Refugee Service, the Refugee Legal Service, a GP practice dealing with a large number of asylum seeker and refugee clients, and several RCOs. In the interests of constructing a corpus of evidence, this has two advantages. The organisations have audited their complete range of information and research to date, some of which might otherwise have been forgotten or lost, and smaller participating organisations have been helped to develop client casework databases capable of recording in the future what they want to know for the development of policy, advocacy and services for their own purposes, in addition to what may be required of them to fulfil contracts. This could be expanded in a number of ways.

Case study 2: a national refugee integration policy

The development of a national refugee integration policy is neither as time-sensitive nor as politically fraught as finding out why people come to the UK for the purposes of asylum policy. The Home Office's public commitment to using evidence as a key component in its development (Home Office, 2002c) has a greater chance of success. This case study welcomes the extent of government commitment but suggests that, even so, the existing evidence base of the refugee voices and experiences needs to be complemented and supplemented in order to create a realistic picture of the effects of policies.

Several recent Home Office-commissioned studies on integration are intended to explore and record refugee voices as evidence:

- A literature review, *Integration: Mapping the field*, examined research and expertise that might be used to inform policy making, and identified gaps in knowledge and policy relevant research (Home Office, 2003d).
- A critical appraisal of integration literature examined the applicability of systematic review methodology to research on the integration of refugees (Home Office, 2002c).
- *Indicators of refugee integration framework* showed how levels of refugee integration in the UK might be measured, the relationship between these and current policy and the views of refugees and host communities themselves (Home Office, 2004).
- A longitudinal study has been commissioned to track 5,000 refugees and other immigrants over three years to measure how successfully they are integrating, and to assess the value of policy initiatives to support them (Home Office, current c).

The authors of *Integration: Mapping the field* (Home Office, 2003d) noted that: "It is striking that we were not able to identify any UK-based research that focuses specifically on asylum seekers/refugees' attitudes towards integration and/or their vision about what constitutes 'successful' integration". The feasibility study *Refugee integration: Can research synthesis inform policy?* (Home Office, 2002c) had nothing to contribute in terms of refugee voices. The *Indicators of refugee integration framework* (Home Office, 2004) exercise identifies aspects of integration such as employment, housing, health and education and groups them under four themes: 'means and markers' that are key areas for refugee engagement; social relationships and networks; skills and knowledge required to be active and secure; and the responses that refugees have a right to expect from the other members of their communities and vice versa. Although the exercise to identify indicators is based on research with refugees (and others), the resulting framework and the tests by which progress towards integration are to be measured are inevitably broad and cannot record what is happening to groups of refugees from different countries of origin, religion, age, gender, circumstances of flight, languages spoken, education and qualifications. To be a useful instrument for the development of policy and practice, the indicators will need to be regularly reviewed against real experiences and voices. And until the longitudinal study (Home Office, current c) starts to provide material, more evidence about refugee experiences will need to be obtained from non-government sources.

ICAR's research into the Somali community (Harris, 2004) illustrates with reference to one refugee group that a considerable corpus of non-governmental research into refugee experiences and voices exists; and that it has the potential to contribute to an evidence base of refugee voices about integration. Subject to the tests of purpose and provenance, scope and methodology described above, a number of studies could contribute to an emerging picture to be used to measure outcomes against the Home Office's indicators of integration framework (Home Office, 2004). *The Somali community in the UK* (Harris, 2004) identified the existence of 139 sources concerned with Somalis in the UK without claiming to be comprehensive. Sixty per cent of the sources (84 items) were reports by voluntary and statutory bodies, such as local authorities, health authorities and learning and skills councils. The report shows that both the size of the Somali population in the UK and the evidence that many Somalis suffer from complex problems suggests that, if deprivation and marginalisation is to be avoided, policy making and practice needs to become aware of their experiences. There is no one Somali voice and a corpus of knowledge needs to be constructed that gives appropriate weight and value to a range of sources. The point is made in respect of the Somali community but applies to other refugee populations.

The Somali community in the UK (Harris, 2004) summarises the evidence about the experiences of a single refugee group. Somalis' experiences in the UK differ according to a range of factors: when they arrived in the UK, the circumstances of their flight and arrival, which area of Somalia they came from, their clan affiliations and social class, their knowledge of English, and previous education and qualifications, the areas of the UK in which they have settled, the services available and the level and frequency of racial harassment and abuse. None of these subtleties are currently part of the evidence base for integration policy but many Somalis will not settle successfully in the UK unless the evidence is taken into consideration in policy making.

The Home Office national refugee integration policy is not at present supported by data about the numbers and whereabouts of refugees. For example, it is confidently alleged that Somalis in the UK represent the single biggest Somali community outside Somalia and the region, but there are no national figures. The 2001 Census for the first time collected figures for those Somalis not born in the UK, one section only of the UK Somali population. Harris (2004) has collected examples of estimates made by Somalis and Somali researchers (Granby Toxteth Community Project, 1993; Smythe and Mohamed, 1997; Berns McGown, 1999; Stokes, 2000; Green, 2001; Cox, 2002; Thomas and Abebow, 2002; Holman and Holman, 2003). Estimates vary considerably in these studies. The usual questions need to be asked about the data and there is a powerful case for a government-commissioned survey, but, in the meantime, estimates made by Somali refugees themselves constitute the best available evidence.

The Somali community is often described as an 'invisible community'. On the contrary, Harris finds that there is a good deal of research, much of it undertaken recently, that is potentially useful as evidence for policy making. Most recent research involves Somalis in some capacity, whether as researchers or interviewers, or in the design. Somali voices bestow authenticity and Somali researchers can overcome the problems associated with government-commissioned research: distrust of researchers; desire for privacy for reasons of culture and caution; and respondents who are unlikely to give accurate information to unknown investigators. On the other hand, despite assurances of confidentiality, interviewees may not wish to disclose information to members of their community. Harris (2004) argues that open-ended ethnographic research such as *Somali and Kurdish refugees in London* (Griffiths, 2002) is needed to provide an accurate and representative picture.

A survey of the Somali community in Liverpool: An indepth analysis (Granby Toxteth Community Project, 1993), which is mentioned but not quoted in Harris (2004), perfectly illustrates the potential of non-governmental research to provide answers to tests of provenance and purpose, methodology and coverage, and to add to the corpus of knowledge and evidence, although it is some years out of date:

Granby Toxteth Community Project: The study questions

The study aimed to answer the following questions:

- What is the demographic profile of the Somali community in Liverpool?
- What are the thoughts and opinions of the Somali community on current services? and
- What are the situations and conditions of Somalis in terms of immigration status, use of English language, education, employment, housing and welfare benefits?

Type of study

The study was descriptive cross-sectional.

Study population

The study's objective was intended to survey as completely as possible all the Somali households in Liverpool. Therefore the study population was "all the households and all the members of the Somali community". The study took a member of the community to be "any person who considers him/herself to be a Somali". In order to cover the whole community, prior to the survey, compilers put together a list of all known Somali households, and extensive publicity was distributed. Leaflets and posters were sited in Somali centres and organisations; each household to be surveyed was sent information relating to the survey and was given information on why it was taking place. All information relating to the survey was published in both Somali and English. It was found to be impossible to obtain the addresses of all Somali families resident in Liverpool. The study covered 1,067 individuals in 546 households. The Somali population was estimated in 1989 to be in the region of 1,200. However, this was felt by many members of the community to be an underestimation at that time. The continuous arrival of Somali refugees has considerably enlarged their community. However, the 1,067 people covered in the survey obviously represent a very significant proportion of the total population.

Data required

The study required a mix of both quantitative and qualitative data on:

- demography: age, gender, country of birth, period of stay in the UK and pre-school provision;
- immigration matters: immigration status, extended family reunion, deportation and travelling problems; and
- use of the English language etc.

Method of data collection

> Data was collected in the form of interviews. The questionnaire consisted of 40 questions.... The questions were formulated in discussion with Somalis over a series of meetings. Eleven interviewers (both male and female) from the Somali community were recruited and given a series of training sessions to enable them to complete the questionnaire. They were provided with identification cards, and the Police were informed that a survey was taking place in the area.
>
> The fieldwork was carried out ... resulting in the successful completion of 546 questionnaires, which contained data, about 1,067 individuals. For the fieldwork aspect of the survey, networks of support systems were established for the interviewers and their work was monitored to ensure that respondents were correctly interpreting questions. The Somali communities and organisations have fully participated in the implementation of all phases of the survey.
>
> *Limitations*
>
> Non-response bias ....
>
> (Granby Toxteth Community Project, 1993, pp 5-7)

While the conclusions of the Granby Toxteth Community Project cannot automatically be applied to all Somali groups in all areas of the UK, its findings about the problems suffered by many of them provide rich evidence which could be set against the indicators of integration targets, and contribute to an evidence base for the development of policies and services that are needed to support them. A small, specific study with no pretensions to being representative research can contribute to the evidence base in a different way. Somali Women's Association (1987) expresses its purpose clearly:

> *The first reason we wrote this book was for ourselves – to remember our lives and our history....* [Other reasons included to practise talking, reading and writing in English and to tell young Somalis about their experiences] *Lastly, we wrote the book for all people who want to learn about other cultures – to let them know who we are.* We tried to keep the voice of the story-teller.... Although we wanted to write in clear English, ... we didn't want to write as if we were English people. (Somali Women's Association, 1987, p 1) (emphasis added)

Its limitations in scope and methodology are compensated for by the authenticity of the stories about Somali women's identities and experiences in the UK.

However, Cole and Robinson (2003) present a different case again:

> A key inadequacy in current awareness and understanding of the housing needs of black and minority ethnic groups is the failure to appreciate their unique circumstances and aspirations. The Somali population in Britain is one ethnic group whose needs seem to have been largely ignored. In response, this report sets out to cast light on the neglected experiences of Somali households, focusing in particular on their housing situations, aspirations and needs. (Cole and Robinson, 2003, p i)

They go on to state that the only way to *"get funding agencies to listen to their requests for assistance and secure a share of resources was if there was solid evidence of the problems faced by the Somali people"* (Cole and Robinson, 2003, foreword) (emphasis added).

Because of its overt intention to influence perceptions and practice, its purpose is not open-ended and exploratory in the sense of the Granby Toxteth Community Project (1993). The research approach involved group discussions with Somali community group leaders in five areas to explore housing and related issues and focus group sessions with particular demographic groups – young people, women, and so on – that were conducted by members of the research team skilled in the Somali language. In such a case, the allocation of the research to an appropriate place in the corpus of evidence about refugee experiences might require further information about the research approach. It would be important, for example, to find out whether working through community leaders reduced the representativeness of the sample, how the members of focus groups were contacted and how many people attended each focus group – information not given in the report. The cluster areas were selected "to give a regional spread, to cover both high demand and low demand local housing markets and to include long-standing and more recent areas of settlement" (Cole and Robinson, 2003, p 11), but further questions might need to be asked to judge its representativeness as evidence for policy making.

In spite of the prevailing impression of the Somalis as a 'hidden' or 'invisible' community, there is in fact no lack of material. What is missing is the allocation of existing research and data, based on Somali experiences and voices, to a suitable place in the evidence base used for integration policy. As Harris (2004, p 13) comments: "The repetition of findings and duplication of recommendations have not resulted in consistent practice based on a shared corpus of research". There is research fatigue among Somalis, a sense that they have given evidence again and again but nothing has changed. Similarly, there is no lack of data and research about refugee experiences in the UK generally, although it is customary to refer to an information black hole. It is vitally important to recognise that the evidence base is richer than government research recently commissioned on either asylum or integration policy would suggest. What is needed is:

- information about who refugees are, what their needs are, and where they live;
- information about what policies have been tried and found to be successful here in the UK and elsewhere; and
- information to educate the public, change the climate of public opinion, and alter the climate in which policy must be devised, resourced and implemented. (Robinson, 1998, p 159)

The main obstacle to a richer evidence base, as shown in this case study like the previous one, is finding practical ways of accessing and using what is already available. The case has been made for spreading the evidence net widely while applying rigorous tests of provenance and purpose, methodology and scope. The remaining obstacle is availability:

> Many documents are hard to track down, and some have disappeared without trace.... With few exceptions, research is contained in brief, small-scale studies, often undertaken by local NGOs. Many of these remain in duplicated form, are not widely distributed and ... are extraordinarily hard

to obtain. All too often, local authorities, NGOs and RCOs who have produced the report have no knowledge of it a few years later, let alone spare copies. (Harris, 2004, p 10)

By cataloguing grey literature containing refugee voices and experiences, by recording on 'refdata' online sources that might otherwise be lost, by providing standardised information on provenance and purpose, methodology and scope of recent reports in a 'digest' series, and by summarising existing states of knowledge, ICAR can facilitate the process of supplementing and complementing the evidence base for policy making.

Notes

[1] The word 'refugee' is used in this chapter to include people who have received refugee status and other forms of temporary protection in the UK in recent years but does also include other immigrants. 'Refugee voices and experiences' includes asylum seekers where there is no need to distinguish between the two groups. 'Asylum seeker voices' applies to asylum seekers only.

[2] For the kind of evidence used to support the choice of policies, see www.addingitup.gov.uk/epc/epc_overview1.cfm.

[3] ICAR was set up by the author in 2001 to raise the level of public debate and understanding about asylum and refugees in the UK through the collection and dissemination of high-quality information and data.

References

Barclay, A., Bowes, A., Ferguson, I., Sim, D. and Valenti, M. (2003) *Asylum seekers in Scotland*, Edinburgh: Scottish Executive.

Berns McGown, R. (1999) *Muslims in the diaspora: The Somali communities of London and Toronto*, Toronto: University of Toronto Press.

Bloch, A. (1999) 'Carrying out a survey of refugees: some methodological considerations and guidelines', *Journal of Refugee Studies*, vol 12, no 4, pp 367-83.

Bloch, A. (2002) *Refugees' opportunities and barriers in employment and training*, Research Report 179, Leeds: Department of Work and Pensions.

Blunkett, D. (2000) *Influence or irrelevance: Can social sciences improve government?*, London: Economic and Social Research Council (www.bera.ac.uk/ri/no71/ri71blunkett.html).

Bradstock, A. and Trotman, A. (eds) (2003) *Asylum voices: Experiences of people seeking asylum in the United Kingdom*, London: Churches Together in Britain and Ireland.

Carey-Wood, J., Duke, K., Karn, V. and Marshall, T. (1995) *The settlement of refugees in Britain*, Research Study 141, London: Home Office.

Cole, I. and Robinson, D. (2003) *Somali housing experiences in England*, Sheffield: Sheffield Hallam University.

Cox, S. (2002) 'Hooyo: A study of Somali children and their mothers based in two nurseries in Brent', Unpublished MSc dissertation, Brunel University.

Estherhuizen, L. (2004) *Doing case studies for the refugee sector: A DIY handbook for agencies and practitioners*, London: Information Centre about Asylum and Refugees, Kings College London.

Granby Toxteth Community Project (1993) *A survey of the Somali Community in Liverpool: An indepth analysis*, Liverpool: Granby Toxteth Community Project.

Green, M. (2001) 'Profiling refugees in Tower Hamlets to deduce their particular health needs and how to meet them', Unpublished dissertation funded by Tower Hamlets Primary Care Trust, London School of Economics.

Griffiths, D. (2002) *Somali and Kurdish refugees in London*, Aldershot: Ashgate Publishing.

Hannan, L. (2003) *A gap in their hearts: The experience of separated Somali children*, Geneva: Integrated Regional Information Network, United Nations Office for the Co-ordination of Humanitarian Affairs.

Harris, H. (2004) *The Somali community in the UK: What we know and how we know it*, London: ICAR (www.icar.org.uk/content/proj/prs.html).

Holman, C. and Holman, N. (2003) *First steps in a new country: Baseline indicators for the Somali community in London Borough of Hackney, London*. London: Sahil Housing Association.

Home Office (2002a) *Understanding the decision-making of asylum seekers*, Findings 172, London: Home Office (www.homeoffice.gov.uk/rds.pdfs2/r172.pdf).

Home Office (2002b) 'Asylum seekers' experience of the voucher scheme in the UK – fieldwork report', Research Development and Statistics (RDS) Online Report, London: Home Office (www.homeoffice.gov.uk/rds/immigration1.html).

Home Office (2002c) 'Refugee integration: can research synthesis inform policy?', RDS Feasibility Study Report, London: Home Office (www.homeoffice.gov.uk/rds/immigration1.html).

Home Office (2003a) 'English language training for refugees in London and the regions', RDS Online Report 14/03, London: Home Office (www.homeoffice.gov.uk/rds/immigration1.html).

Home Office (2003b) 'Asylum seekers in dispersal areas – healthcare issues', RDS Online Report 13/03, London: Home Office (www.homeoffice.gov.uk/rds/immigration1.html).

Home Office (2003c) 'Listening to the evidence: the future of refugee resettlement', Online Conference Report, London: Home Office (www.homeoffice.gov.uk/rds/immigration1.html).

Home Office (2003d) 'Integration: mapping the field', RDS Online Report 28/03, London: Home Office (www.homeoffice.gov.uk/rds/immigration1.html).

Home Office (2004) *Indicators of refugee integration framework. IRSS guide to government funded research*, London: Home Office.

Home Office (current a) 'An exploration of the factors affecting the successful dispersal of asylum seekers' (listed as 'ongoing research' in government-funded and other relevant research on refugee integration, immigration and asylum issues, Home Office paper, undated, acquired in 2004).

Home Office (current b) 'Skills audit of people granted refugee status and exceptional leave to remain (listed as 'ongoing research' in government-funded and other relevant research on refugee integration, immigration and asylum issues, Home Office paper, undated, acquired in 2004).

Home Office (current c) 'Longitudinal research into the integration of resettled refugees on the UK Gateway Protection Programme' (listed as 'ongoing research' in government-funded and other relevant research on refugee integration, immigration and asylum issues, Home Office paper, undated, acquired in 2004).

Hynes, T. (2003) 'The issue of "trust" or "mistrust" in research with refugees: choices, caveats and considerations for researchers', *New issues in refugee research*, Working Paper no 98, Geneva: UNHCR Evaluation and Policy Analysis Unit.

ICAR (Information Centre about Asylum and Refugees) (2004) 'Making better use of existing information and data about refugees and asylum seeking people', (www.icar.org.uk/proj/mbu/making.html).

Robinson,V. (1998) 'The importance of information in the resettlement of refugees in the UK', *Journal of Refugee Studies*, vol 11, no 2, pp 146-60.

Smith, E. (2004) *Right first time? Home Office interviewing and reasons for refusal letters*, London: Medical Foundation for the Care of Victims of Torture.

Smythe, K. and Mohamed, A. (1997) *Refugees in the North West of England*, Manchester: Refugee Action.

Somali Women's Association (1987) *Our strength comes with us*, London: Somali Women's Voices.

Stokes, P. (2000) *The Somali community in Liverpool*, Birmingham: Foundation for Civil Society.

Temple, B. (1997) 'Issues in translation and cross-cultural research', *Sociology*, vol 31, no 3, pp 607-18.

Thomas, F. and Abebow, M. (2002) *Refugees and asylum seekers in the Learning and Skills Council North London area*, London: Africa Educational Trust.

NINE

Challenging barriers to participation in qualitative research: involving disabled refugees

Jennifer Harris and Keri Roberts

Introduction

Qualitative research involving interviews and focus groups has become a popular means of collecting data in the social sciences (Mason, 1996). Yet literature that discusses the practical aspects of arranging and conducting qualitative research is still relatively rare. With the exception of articles in specialist methodology journals (such as the *International Journal of Qualitative Methods* and the *International Journal of Social Research Methodology: Theory and Practice*), few authors write in detail about how they did their research. Rarer yet is any acknowledgement of the difficulties or barriers that need to be overcome to enable both potential interviewer and potential respondent to participate in the qualitative research process; this is despite Croft and Beresford's (1992) call for researchers to explicitly consider the support needs of research participants. Where such discussions are found, they tend to be within specialist publications relating to population groups who are perceived to be 'hard to reach', for example disabled people (Barnes and Mercer, 1997) or minority ethnic groups (Edwards, 1998); and may or may not go so far as to include strategies for overcoming the identified barriers.

The lack of detailed discussions about the practicalities of conducting qualitative research within the 'methods' sections of most mainstream qualitative literature means there is little guidance available for researchers who wish to inform their own methodological practices. Readers are left thinking that arranging and conducting qualitative interviews and focus groups is a straightforward process, and the lack of evidence to the contrary encourages funding bodies to question requests for the resources and time that may be necessary to facilitate participation. Similarly, a lack of consideration of the barriers faced by those who wish to participate in qualitative research does little to encourage the involvement of those who are least likely to have their voices heard.

Building on the history of addressing these issues within disability studies and minority ethnic studies, this chapter[1] is specifically concerned with the practicalities of involving disabled refugees and asylum seekers in qualitative research. While methodological literature in the minority ethnic field frequently addresses issues related to overcoming linguistic barriers in research contexts (for example, Jentsch, 1998; Temple and Edwards, 2002), literature in the disability studies field tends to focus on overcoming barriers associated with impairments and developing research practices based on social and political perspectives of disability (for example, Zarb, 1997; Humphrey, 2000). The strength of this chapter is that by focusing on experiences of engaging disabled refugees and asylum seekers in qualitative research, it transcends the traditional disciplinary boundaries of disability or minority ethnic studies. Considering disability-related barriers alongside linguistic and cultural barriers to participation in research enables a focus on "the polarities, the extreme challenges, the range of diversity and provides the opportunity to get to the essence of the problem" (Stubbs, 1997, pp 257-8).

Specifically, we address the need for clarity about how qualitative research is carried out in the field, the barriers and challenges that researchers face, and the measures required to overcome them. Moreover, we hope that by demonstrating that extreme barriers to participation can be overcome, we will encourage researchers in less challenging research settings to adopt measures designed to facilitate access to the research process.

Background to the research

As part of the 'Disabled refugees in Britain' research project, we arranged and supervised the completion of 38 semi-structured qualitative interviews with disabled refugees and asylum seekers. These interviews were conducted by a team of seven first-language interviewers, who themselves experienced barriers to their participation in the research. None of the interviewers spoke English as a first language, all but one had claimed asylum in Britain and three had personal experience of impairment. Thus in order for the interviews to be successfully completed, many barriers, faced by both interviewees and interviewers, had to be overcome, particularly in relation to the health, impairment and linguistic needs of all the participants.

The 'Disabled refugees in Britain' research project was carried out on behalf of the Refugee Council, the leading campaign organisation promoting the rights of refugees and asylum seekers in the UK. It has long been recognised that disabled refugees are "the most invisible ... among the uprooted populations who have fled violence in their own countries" (Boylan, 1991, p 4). Yet, there is still no official source of data on the prevalence of impairments and chronic ill health among refugees and asylum seekers in Britain. Apart from material written by the authors (Roberts and Harris, 2001, 2002a, 2002b; Harris and Roberts, 2003), there is little evidence to suggest that academics engaged in either the disability studies or refugee studies fields have considered the situation and particular experiences of disabled people in refugee and asylum-seeking communities. Similarly, disabled people rarely feature in so-called 'grey' literature relating to refugees and asylum seekers. This is, in part, because of the multiple barriers disabled refugees and asylum seekers experience in having their voices heard.

Within a multi-faceted methodology, the qualitative interview phase of the project was carried out with disabled people from four refugee communities – the Tamil, Somali, Vietnamese and Sorani-speaking Kurdish communities. The barriers to participation in the qualitative interview process, and the measures needed to enable all those participating (interviewees, interviewers, researchers) to take part, form the basis for the discussion below.

Identifying and challenging barriers

Conceptual framework

The 'Disabled refugees in Britain' research project was informed by the social model of disability – a conceptual framework that stresses that people who have impairments are disabled by the way in which society is organised. The social model of disability argues that individuals are not disabled by their impairments, but rather by the physical, social, political and economic barriers, and inadequate support services they encounter within a society that fails to appreciate difference (Oliver, 1990; Barnes, 1991). The concept of barriers to participation in society is central to the social model of disability and provides a practical starting point from which to challenge the discrimination and disadvantage experienced by disabled people. Rather than expecting disabled people to adapt, the social model of disability calls for society to accommodate difference by identifying and challenging the barriers to participation in society as experienced by individuals who have impairments. For example, this might involve removing physical barriers that prevent people with mobility impairments entering buildings or providing support services to enable people with learning difficulties to participate fully in employment, education and leisure pursuits.

Using the social model of disability as a guiding principle, it is clear that as barriers to participation exist within society, we should also expect them to operate within the context of a qualitative research interview. Thus, with a research design that involved interviewing disabled people from refugee and asylum-seeking communities, it was immediately evident that people wishing to participate in the research were likely to experience linguistic, health and impairment-related barriers, unless measures were taken to specifically address difference in experiences. Given our commitment to involve disabled refugees and asylum seekers in all aspects of the project (including as interviewers), we knew we were likely to face similar problems to those that threatened the completion of Zarb's (1997) research when he employed disabled interviewers; notably, staffing problems and shortfalls in meeting the additional costs associated with disability. Forewarned, our research proposal incorporated measures to counter as many barriers as possible, most notably by allowing an extended time for fieldwork, and a budget that incorporated funds for meeting impairment-related and linguistic-related requirements.

Practical measures

We begin with a detailed discussion of the practical steps and measures taken within this research project to challenging the barriers to participation experienced by interviewees, interviewers and the researchers. Following a discussion of the general measures, we present a case study that illustrates the importance of addressing barriers faced by all participants in the interview process.

The interviewees

The aim of the qualitative study was to conduct semi-structured interviews with disabled people (people who had physical, sensory or multiple impairments) and who had arrived in the UK as refugees or asylum seekers.

At project recruitment stage, it was clear that material advertising the project and calling for respondents would need to be produced in a variety of languages and formats to alert people who may find printed English material inaccessible. Thus leaflets in English, Tamil, Sorani, Vietnamese, Somali and Braille were prepared and distributed to relevant refugee community groups across Britain. Translated advertisements were also placed in minority ethnic newspapers and audiovisual advertisements were played on minority ethnic radio and TV stations. Care was taken in all these advertisements to stress that the interviews would be carried out by interviewers from minority ethnic communities, and that respondents would be able to specify whether they wished to talk to a man or a woman. In addition to these measures, the lead researcher and a number of the first-language interviewers attended various cultural and disability events to promote awareness of the project and encourage people to participate. In these ways, measures to challenge barriers to participation were integral to the recruitment process and 38 people fulfilling the recruitment criteria were successfully recruited.

Barriers to participation in research are not, however, limited to the recruitment stage. During any qualitative interview, further barriers exist and must be challenged if the interview is to be successfully completed. Many venues traditionally used for qualitative interviews can be inaccessible and choosing a venue needs to include a consideration of potential social and physical barriers to participation. All the respondents were offered a choice regarding an interview venue, including their own home, or alternatively a local community centre or refugee community group. We ensured that these alternative venues were culturally appropriate and physically accessible for people with impairments, and we covered transport costs incurred by the interviewee (and a carer or personal assistant as required). While the majority of respondents chose to be interviewed in their own homes, interviews were also carried out at two disabled refugee organisations. Linguistic barriers to participation in the interviews were minimised by the use of first-language interviewers and the provision of sign-language interpreters for deaf interviewees. As failing to consider the health- and impairment-related circumstances of interviewees during an interview can also act as a barrier to its successful completion, the interviewers took particular care to be flexible during the interviews themselves. Thus, interviews were sometimes cancelled or curtailed due to ill health, and multiple breaks were offered to interviewees who fatigued easily. When requested to do so, interviewers assisted with the preparation of refreshments during breaks. All the interviewees received a small gift in recognition of their participation in the research, and requests for assistance in comprehension of official letters received by the interviewees were often met at the end of the interviews. Information about entitlement to welfare services was also provided to the interviewees.

In view of the extent of the barriers to participation in society experienced by some of the interviewees, time-limited support was offered after the completion of the interviews. Notably, the researcher and interviewers responded positively to requests to write letters, for instance requesting that service providers correspond with the interviewee in accessible formats. They also frequently provided details of local organisations able to provide ongoing support to the interviewees. Finally, following the completion of the research, arrangements were made for each interviewee to receive a summary of the research findings in an individually appropriate format.

The interviewers

Central to the recruitment of the first-language interviewers was the requirement that they should be fluent in the language in question (Tamil, Vietnamese, Somali or Sorani); have an understanding of the experiences of disabled people; and be familiar with refugee experiences (for example, persecution, flight from country of origin, the process of claiming asylum). In view of the guiding theoretical framework of the project – the social model of disability – barriers that could prevent suitable candidates from applying for these posts, or subsequently working as first-language interviewers needed to be identified and actively challenged.

The first-language interviewer posts were advertised via refugee community groups, minority ethnic newspapers and university-based job centres. Additionally, individuals already known to the research team were alerted and encouraged to apply for the posts. Further particulars were available in alternative formats (for example, in Braille, on disk, and so on) and the particulars stressed that the researchers would welcome applications from men and women, disabled people and refugees and asylum seekers. Informal discussions with the researchers were encouraged and individuals selected for interview were contacted to ascertain their particular access requirements at interview. Candidates who required assistance with making travel arrangements were offered support, and in one case a candidate was interviewed by telephone after his travel arrangements broke down. The recruitment process was successfully completed and a total of

Figure 9.1: The interviewers

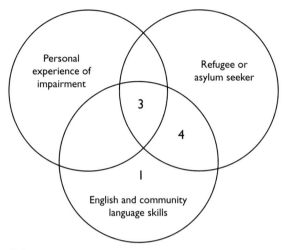

Source: Harris and Roberts

eight first-language interviewers were appointed, seven of whom had arrived in the UK as refugees or asylum seekers and three of whom had personal experience of impairment (see Figure 9.1).

All those appointed as first-language interviewers were invited to attend a two-day training course at York University. Materials used during this course were provided in Braille and on disk as required and the equipment training session (with tape recorders, microphones, and so on) was designed to take account of visual impairment and variations in dexterity. The training venue and the hotel in which the interviewers were accommodated were both physically accessible and the researchers joined the interviewers for an evening meal at a restaurant that could cater for both halal and other dietary requirements.

As it was recognised that the interviewers were also likely to encounter difficulties when arranging, conducting and transcribing interviews, support in overcoming potential barriers was offered throughout their period of employment. Notably, interviewers were encouraged to request assistance in making travel arrangements, and the cost of taxis rather than buses was met for those who found public transport inaccessible. The researcher accompanied each interviewer (with one exception) on at least one of their interviews for training/ support purposes and provided telephone support before and immediately after each interview. This was vital because of the frequently distressing nature of the stories told by the interviewees, and the interviewers' sometimes shared experience of torture.

Regular contact with the interviewers was also maintained between interviews and workloads were adjusted to take account of changes in both the physical and mental health status of individual interviewers or members of their families. Similarly, requests for extended holidays, needed to visit family who had been scattered across the globe following their flight from persecution, were accommodated.

The researchers

The two authors of this chapter provided each other with mutual support during the course of this research project. Given the distressing stories told by many of the interviewees (often including detailed accounts of torture and consequent permanent impairments), it was crucial that the tasks of supporting the interviewers and analysing the transcripts be shared, particularly as one of the researchers experienced an extended period of ill health during the research. This sharing of the support role and subsequent analysis ensured that both authors were able to step back periodically from the material and thus minimise the threat to their own well-being.

Case study

Interviewer A has a visual impairment and contacted the researchers to let them know that he had recruited a number of deaf refugees and asylum seekers to the project. He requested assistance in arranging appropriate sign-language interpretation and in preparing for these interviews. A Tamil Sign Language (TSL) interpreter was booked and arrangements made to meet the interviewee at a refugee community centre. However, the TSL interpreter was unable to attend at short notice, and an alternative British Sign Language (BSL) interpreter was provided on the day of the interview. On arrival at the community centre, it was noted that the interviewee used a combination of gestures, basic TSL, family-specific signs and lip reading of spoken Tamil to communicate. Her formal language skills were limited due to the barriers she had experienced in accessing education. The interviewee requested that her father be present during the interview; in addition, the BSL interpreter requested access to the project contact who was fluent in both BSL and TSL and the researcher was present to verbally relay visual cues to interviewer A.

Interviewer A conducted the interview with the assistance of the

Figure 9.2: Forms of communication used by each person present at the interview

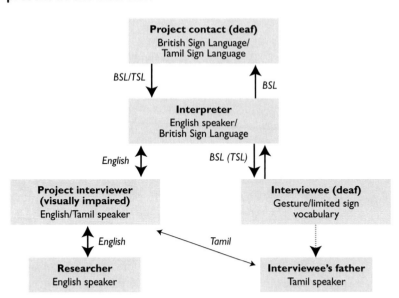

BSL interpreter and the lead researcher who provided verbal cues to indicate the progress of the sign-language conversations. The BSL interpreter consulted with the project contact for advice about alternative signs for use with the interviewee. Despite the measures taken, the interviewee continued to experience communication barriers and at times she indicated that questions should be addressed to her father. When this occurred, interviewer A spoke to him in Tamil. Information gained in this way was then translated into English so that the BSL interpreter could use signs to confirm that the interviewee agreed with her father's statements. Thus the interview was conducted in a combination of English, Tamil, gesture, BSL and TSL (see Figure 9.2). The progress of the interview was extremely slow and discussions with the interviewee were limited to facts rather than abstract concepts. Nevertheless, the interview was successfully completed. This interview provided compelling evidence of the extreme isolation and communication barriers experienced by many disabled refugees and asylum seekers, but also demonstrated the value in attempting to challenge such barriers.

Discussion and conclusions

With the social model of disability as a guiding theory, this research was always going to be conducted in a manner that challenged barriers to participation. Yet, even with awareness of potential barriers, issues arose which had not be foreseen. Certainly, at the outset of the project it was not anticipated that a visually impaired interviewer would interview a deaf person. Nevertheless, a flexible and inventive approach, alongside a commitment to challenging barriers and adequate funding, allowed the research to be successfully completed.

While the circumstances faced in this research were extreme, a willingness to challenge barriers to participation should be incorporated into all qualitative research. Barriers exist throughout society and affect people in different ways. Research staff can become ill; people on low incomes cannot afford to travel to research venues; parents can encounter childcare difficulties; and employees can face problems getting time off work. Without an awareness of these and other barriers to participation, qualitative research is unlikely to incorporate the voices of those who find it difficult to take part and the voices of 'hard to reach groups' will remain ghettoised in specialist literature.

Utilisation of the social model of disability sensitised the researchers to consider the following accommodations. When preparing research proposals and budgets researchers need to take account of barriers to participation and the measures required to overcome them. Specifically, researchers should allow extra time to recruit respondents such as those in this study. Contacting people who face barriers to participation takes time and energy as well as determination but is clearly possible and adds to the range of experiences highlighted by qualitative research.

The research timetable should allow extra time to cover periods of illness among research staff. During longer research projects covering two years or more, it is almost certain that someone in the research team will experience an illness, accident or bereavement that requires them to take time off work. Researchers should budget for interviewees' travel costs, including for a proportion of journeys that will not be made using public transport. Many people, including both disabled people and parents with young children, find public transport in Britain inaccessible. Additionally, people with care responsibilities (for children or disabled or sick relatives) can have extreme pressures on their time that means public transport is unsuitable.

Recognising barriers to participation in qualitative research involves acknowledging and pre-empting the specific challenges and taking steps to overcome them. A 'can-do' attitude is important here.

With more and more research being conducted by researchers on short-term contracts, the pressure to present a succinct and sanitised view of how qualitative research is conducted is great. Yet an openness about the realities of arranging and conducting qualitative research is vital if funders are to agree to cover the true costs incurred. Moreover, it should be acknowledged that the process of collecting qualitative data can be as instructive as the data itself. As such, researchers have an obligation to share this knowledge with fellow members of the research community.

Note
[1] The authors would like to thank the *International Journal of Qualitative Methods* for permission to reproduce a version of the paper from Harris and Roberts (2003).

References

Barnes, C. (1991) *Disabled people in Britain and discrimination*, London: Hurst & Co/BCODP.

Barnes, C. and Mercer, G. (1997) (eds) *Doing disability research*, Leeds: The Disability Press.

Boylan, E. (1991) *Women and disability*, London: Zed Books.

Croft, S. and Beresford, P. (1992). 'The politics of participation', *Critical Social Policy*, vol 35, pp 20-44.

Edwards, R. (1998). 'A critical examination of the use of interpreters in the qualitative research process', *Journal of Ethnic and Migration Studies*, vol 24, no 2, pp 197-208.

Harris, J. (2003) 'All doors are closed to us: a social model analysis of the experiences of disabled refugees and asylum seekers in Britain', *Disability & Society*, vol 18, no 4, pp 393-408.

Harris, J. and Roberts, K. (2003) 'Challenging barriers to participation in qualitative research: involving disabled refugees', *International Journal of Qualitative Methods*, vol 2, no 2 (www.ualberta.ca/~ijqm/backissues/2_2/pdf/harrisetal.pdf).

Humphrey, J. (2000) 'Researching disability politics, or, some problems with the social model in practice', *Disability & Society*, vol 15, no 1, pp 63-85.

Jentsch, B. (1998) 'The "interpreter effect": rendering interpreters visible in cross-cultural research methodology', *Journal of European Social Policy*, vol 8, no 4, pp 275-89.

Mason, J. (1996) *Qualitative researching*, London: Sage Publications.

Oliver, M. (1990) *The politics of disablement*, Basingstoke: MacMillan.

Roberts, K. and Harris, J. (2001) 'Disabled refugees and asylum seekers in Britain: Numbers and social characteristics', Report (in-house) NLCB1816.05.01KR/Jha, York: Social Policy Research Unit (SPRU), University of York.

Roberts, K. and Harris, J. (2002a) *Disabled people in refugee and asylum seeking communities in Britain*, York/Bristol: The Policy Press/Joseph Rowntree Foundation.

Roberts, K. and Harris, J. (2002b) *Disabled refugees in Britain*, Final report for the Refugee Council and National Lotteries Charities Board, York: SPRU, University of York.

Stubbs, S. (1997) 'Engaging with difference: soul searching for a methodology in disability and development research', in E. Stone (ed) *Disability and development: Learning from action and research on disability in the majority world*, Leeds: The Disability Press, pp 257-79.

Temple, B. and Edwards, R. (2002) 'Interpreters/translators and cross-language research: reflexivity and border crossings', *International Journal of Qualitative Methodology*, vol 1, no 2, Article 1, (www.ualberta.ca/~ijqm).

Zarb, G. (1997) 'Researching disabling barriers', in C. Barnes. and G. Mercer (eds) *Doing disability research*, Leeds: The Disability Press, pp 49-69.

TEN

Why religion matters

M. Louise Pirouet

Introduction

Religion matters when researching refugees and those fleeing
persecution or intolerable situations for two main reasons: first, because
it is very important to so many of these people themselves, and second,
because support groups for asylum seekers and refugees often have a
large input from faith communities. Yet Gozdziak and Shandy (2002)
found that this was a neglected area of research:

> Despite the fact that religious persecution figures
> prominently in the UN definition of a refugee and faith-
> based organisations provide emergency relief to refugees,
> facilitate the settlement of refugees and provide them with
> a wide range of social services, public debates about
> migration and displacement on the international and
> national levels have tended to ignore religious issues. (p 129)

Religious adherence and practice is far more common in many of the
countries from which people come to seek refuge than in the highly
secularised West. In many non-Western countries, most people still
have a religious outlook and religion is not separated from ethnicity
and culture. To fail to pay attention to religious identity is, then, to fail
to pay attention to an important personal identifier, as well as an
important means of understanding and dealing with trauma (Gozdziak
and Shandy, 2002, p 130).

When researching this topic, one needs to consider various stages
in the career of people seeking and finding asylum. First, whereas
many asylum seekers are given 'temporary admission' (TA), others are
detained from the start. All detention centres (now redesignated removal
centres) have a statutory obligation to appoint a manager of religious

affairs and must call in appropriate ministers of religion to minister to the different religious groups detained there.

Second, most newly arrived asylum seekers are placed initially in emergency accommodation and attend an induction course before being allocated to more permanent accommodation by the National Asylum Support Service (NASS). They may, however, remain in emergency accommodation for some time before NASS is able to place them. There is no religious provision during the induction process, or when a person is placed in NASS accommodation, unless it is provided by a voluntary organisation.

A third group of people to be considered are refused asylum seekers who cannot be removed back to their home countries because it would not be safe to do so or because the Home Office cannot obtain documentation necessary for their removal. Those who have attracted most attention are asylum seekers from Zimbabwe, but there are substantial numbers of others (Scottish Green Party, 2004).

Those who are recognised as refugees and given indefinite leave to remain must next be considered. How are they integrated into the host community – or do they fail to become integrated – and what role, if any, does religion play in this process?

It is also important to consider a further, special group – those seeking refuge from religious persecution.

Detention/removal centres

There are currently nine detention centres in the UK: Campsfield House near Oxford; Colnbrook at Heathrow (the most recently opened); Dover; Dungavel, near Glasgow; Harmondsworth (temporarily closed after an arson attack and riot by the detainees); Haslar near Portsmouth; Lindhome, near Doncaster, a section of a prison; Oakington Immigration Reception Centre, a designated place of detention in spite of its name; and Yarl's Wood, near Bedford, part of which has now been reopened after it was burnt down by former detainees in a riot.

It is, oddly enough, in detention centres that the religious adherence of the detainees is paid most attention. The detainees may include those awaiting a first decision on their asylum claim, failed asylum seekers and other immigration detainees awaiting removal. The *Detention Centre Rules* (Crown, 2001) which came into force in April 2001, follow the prison service model in laying down that each centre must have a manager of religious affairs, usually a minister of religion though not necessarily of the Christian religion, and must call in ministers of religion to meet the needs of the different religious groups represented in the centre. Two detention centres have Muslim managers of religious affairs. The Church of England has recently appointed the Right Reverend Colin Fletcher, Bishop of Dorchester, to have a responsibility for Anglican chaplains in detention centres, and chaplains of other denominations have been happy to talk with him. Detention centre chaplains, however, do not receive anything like the level of support provided by the Prison Chaplaincy Service, although, arguably, they have a far more difficult job.

The majority of people held in immigration detention centres declare a religious allegiance. Very few state that they have no religion or are atheists, or simply fail to fill in the question about religious adherence. A recent 'snapshot' of religious affiliation at Oakington Immigration Reception Centre showed that just nine per cent fell into this category. Nearly seventy-five per cent gave their religion as Christian or Muslim, equally divided between the two faiths. The remainder were mainly Hindu or Sikh, with just one person identifying as Falun Gong, another as Buddhist and two as Alevi. The Christians ranged from Orthodox and Catholic to Pentecostal, or simply defined themselves as 'Christian'. A minority of Muslims gave their religious adherence as Shi'a. Attendance at religious observances held at this centre is also high, and some groups (Muslims and Evangelical and Pentecostal Christians) will attend prayers or gather to sing hymns and pray whether there is anyone there to lead them or not. This spontaneity by the Christian groups is not always welcomed by the staff of detention centres.

The chaplain of one immigration detention/removal centre noted:

> Generally speaking (and not specific to Christians alone) there is at any point a *minimum* of between 30%–40% of the population [of the removal centre] who actively subscribe to some form of religious observance. At times this figure has been as high as 65% and it is probable that even higher figures may have been experienced. (Lundberg, 2004)

This chaplain noted that detention centres hold all kinds of immigration detainees as well as asylum seekers. He noted: "Many in detention will recommit themselves to their faith, while existing adherents often draw considerable strength from the right kind of spiritual care". However, this chaplain also noted that they were very vulnerable when in detention and that "assertive religious influence" needed to be avoided. In other words, detainees, like secularised westerners, may fall back on religion when in difficulties: one only has to think of how Soham parish church became a focus of strength for the villagers after the murder of two young girls from the village in 2002, or how the churches and mosques in Liverpool held candlelight vigils for the Briton, Ken Bigley, held hostage in Iraq in late 2004.

Chaplains are sometimes able to make links for an asylum seeker who is given temporary admission and leaves a detention centre. Using the networks to be discussed below, as well as personal contacts, chaplains have sometimes been able to find people in faith communities in the area to which released detainees are sent, or in organisations working with asylum seekers, who will meet and welcome those just released and given temporary admission. Something of the same sort has occasionally happened when a person is being removed. Arrangements have been made for deportees or refused asylum seekers to be met, or to have an address and phone number they can use on arrival in the home country. Chaplains have occasionally been able to find small sums to help a penniless deportee on arrival.

Newly arrived asylum seekers and those awaiting a decision on their asylum claim

Newly arrived asylum seekers and those in NASS accommodation awaiting a first decision on their asylum claim are a very vulnerable group. Placement in emergency housing while they attend an induction course is meant to be a temporary expedient prior to being allocated accommodation by NASS, but it often lasts for weeks, even months. The process of allocation to NASS accommodation is now recognised to have been a disaster. Local communities were not prepared, as the Home Office promised they would be, and the arrival of asylum seekers in an area, and their placement in scarce housing, guaranteed that they would be met with hostility. The Metropolitan Borough of Oldham produced a leaflet to try to dispel 'myths' current in the area about asylum seekers, for example, that 'asylum seekers are taking our housing,' and 'asylum seekers are allowed to go to furnishing stores to buy furniture and carpets for their homes, paid for by the council'. These stories were refuted by real-life stories (Oldham Metropolitan Borough, 2003).

Asylum seekers finding themselves in these circumstances may experience hostility and racism if they venture out. Those who step in to help often include members of local churches and other faith communities, and there is some evidence to show that asylum seekers who have temporary admission and those who have been recognised as refugees (or have some other form of leave to remain or humanitarian protection) are helped to settle if they can find a faith community where they are accepted. *Understanding the stranger* (D'Onofrio and Munk, 2004) has little to say about religion, but does recognise that: "The majority of asylum seekers, as well as some local people and key players, said that religious organisations can be effective in promoting understanding, as religion and faith can provide meeting opportunities for people which are based on common interests and beliefs, regardless of ethnic background"(p 43).

This report went on to quote a Rwandan woman asylum seeker:

> In church people are friendly. ... One of my friends told me about church and meeting in church every Sunday, because I want to meet English people for friendship. Because sometimes they say "you can give one another peace" and they shake your hands without a problem. (D'Onofrio and Munk, 2004)[1]

Faith communities assisting asylum seekers and refugees

This brings us to the second reason for researching religion: the involvement of religiously based organisations and church groups in many ventures to assist refugees and asylum seekers. D'Onofrio and Munk (2004) noted that: "Community initiatives based on religious conviction were identified in most of the dispersal areas studied" (p 43).

An unpublished micro-study of church-related community projects in Leicester (Scott, 2003) focused on the response of these groups to asylum seekers and refugees who had recently arrived in the city. Leicester already had well-established Asian communities whose membership had been greatly increased in 1972 by British Asians expelled from Uganda by Idi Amin. The response of the churches to recently arrived asylum seekers was studied through small 'focus' groups and was, perhaps, surprisingly positive. Although church-based, these groups assisted all who needed help, regardless of religion. The arrival of these newcomers had been a challenge that the groups studied had risen to meet.

There is some evidence that, as the vilification of asylum seekers has increased in sections of the press, so some Christian groups have responded by recognising that their religion calls them to love the stranger as they love themselves, and that to refuse hospitality to the stranger is to refuse hospitality to Christ (Leviticus 19:33 and

Matthew 25:31-46 are among the Biblical passages these Christian groups cite). The emergence of the network Enabling Christians in Serving Refugees in 2002 is one important example of this. This network is backed by the Evangelical Alliance, but is not limited to evangelical churches and it welcomes and works with refugees of all faiths and none. It is based at The Welcome Centre in Maple Road, London SE20 8LP and has a useful, up-to-date website (www.ecsr.org.uk) that gives country-wide links and information.

The Catholic Bishops' Conference gives one of its members a special responsibility for refugees and migrants, and has an Office for Refugee Policy as well as a National Council of Migration. Each year the Catholic Church celebrates Migration Day. There is a network of chaplaincies to foreign immigrants based in London and some other large cities that are listed in the Catholic Directory (Vaughan, 2004). By no means are all of these relevant to refugees, but a number are. The National Catholic Refugee Forum (NCRF) was established in 2000 when it was launched at St Chad's Cathedral, Birmingham. Catholic churches host a variety of community projects designed to help refugees and those seeking asylum, whatever faith (or no faith) they profess. The volunteers often include members of other faith communities as well as Catholics. Among the groups affiliated to the NCRF are the Jesuit Refugee Service, an international agency with a branch in London, which concentrates on visiting detained asylum seekers, and 'Revive', a joint initiative of the Holy Ghost Fathers, another international religious order, and Salford Diocese. It offers advice, counselling and practical support to asylum seekers and refugees based on St Boniface Church in Lower Broughton, Salford. Its manager and outreach coordinator are assisted by volunteers. The National Forum runs training programmes, provides advice to those who work with refugees, and publishes a contact list enabling people to network.

On 9 November 2004, BBC One's local evening news coverage for the East of England broadcast an appeal from the Anglican Diocese of St Albans. It asked for hospitality to be given to asylum seekers who had been made destitute under section 55 of the 2002 Nationality, Immigration and Asylum Act, or who been refused after exhausting the appeals process and who had therefore been evicted from their accommodation, lost financial support, were not allowed to work, and were denied primary health care. They could not be returned to their home countries, however, because these were not considered to be safe (for example, Zimbabwe) or the home country refused to readmit them because they were without documentation. The previous Sunday a Catholic priest in Bristol Diocese told the Sunday programme on

Radio 4 that he was giving sanctuary in his church to a survivor of the Rwandan genocide whom the Home Office wished to deport. He would not allow the police or the Immigration Service into his church to arrest the young woman. These seem to be further signs that some churches believe that government harshness to asylum seekers has gone too far.

J-CORE, the Jewish Council for Racial Equality, has long been concerned for refugees and asylum seekers and campaigns on their behalf, motivated by its members' own experience of persecution and exile. Jewish people are involved in many of the secular groups assisting refugees, including the Medical Foundation for the Care of Victims of Torture. Helen Bamber, its founder, is a Jew who went to assist Holocaust survivors immediately after the end of the Second World War (Belton, 1998), and it is out of this experience and her work with Amnesty International and torture victims that the Medical Foundation sprang.

When so much work is done under the auspices of faith communities, one must ask whether those they assist are protected from proselytisation. Asylum seekers and refugees are very vulnerable and might easily feel pressured. The networks mentioned above state that they offer assistance to those of all faiths and none, and are careful not to exert pressure. This perhaps needs testing. Many of the church-based groups use volunteers from other faiths and people who profess no faith at all, which should help to ensure that no pressure is put on people.

If one asks why churches are so often the venue for refugee and asylum work, it is partly because they are some of the few property owners in city centres that might be able to make space available for centres to be opened up. In Newcastle-upon-Tyne, the West End Refugee Service is based in a vicarage that was no longer needed and that the church was able to release. The upstairs flat is let, but the ground floor provides office space, counselling rooms, rooms where clothes and household utensils are stored for use by asylum seekers and refugees, and a space for socialising and drinking coffee.

In detention centres, as in the prison service, chaplains are very aware that they are there to support, not to proselytise. In one instance, two men from a former eastern bloc communist country approached the Orthodox chaplain and asked for baptism: they had never before had the chance of being baptised, though Orthodoxy was in their cultural tradition before the imposition of a communist state. This raised major questions, and all kinds of permissions had to be obtained, not least from the church authorities.

All these groups and others have a wealth of information about asylum seekers and their needs, including religious needs, providing a potentially rich field for research.

Defining 'faith communities'

The much-used term 'faith community' needs definition. A study into how 'faith communities' might become engaged in urban regeneration quoted a member of the Churches Regional Commission as saying: "We do not know what this [term] means and are awaiting further guidance, but we assume it means people from black and ethnic minorities" (Farnell et al, 2003, p 5). The authors of the report interpreted the term to include all 'faith communities', the parish church as well as the Sikh Gurdwara, and were surely correct to do so.

The manner in which a mosque, paid for and built by a group of Muslims who came to Britain from Pakistan, relates to that ethno-religious community is, however, different from the relationship of the Anglican parish church or the Baptist chapel to the community. An appropriate Christian parallel to the former might be the churches built by white immigrants in New Zealand or Australia in the early days of settlement. Like Pakistanis in Britain, the immigrants clubbed together to build a symbol of their homeland, often in an architectural style resembling that of the churches of their home areas. People who might have abandoned church attendance 'at home' in Britain, resumed it in their new home, as they tried to reinforce their English or Scottish or Welsh identity in their new circumstances.

D'Onofrio and Munk (2004) are not altogether correct in assuming that ethnicity is overcome in faith communities. Among Christian communities in Cambridge, one notes that Greek and Russian Orthodox have separate places of worship; Welsh language services have been held for many years; the main Roman Catholic Church, Our Lady and the English Martyrs, holds masses in Polish and Italian as well as English; Chinese services are held in Eden Baptist Chapel and Korean language services in Regent Street Baptist Church.

Several different 'faith sub-communities' may worship within one overarching community – theoretically a Muslim can pray in any mosque – but different ethnic groups will often establish their own places of worship and others may not feel entirely welcome. Lewis (1994) gives an account of Muslim communities in Bradford. These are based on ethnicity, reflecting the different Pakistani and Indian Muslim communities from which people came, each of which had reached a different cultural synthesis with the pre-existing Indian culture of the area. Immigrants with a common heritage of language and culture naturally tended to band together. There are some highly divisive religious practices as well as ethnic and cultural divisions, for instance the celebration by some groups of the Prophet Muhammad's birthday (milad an nabi), which is strongly disapproved of by other groups (Lewis, 1994).

Among the Muslims of Asian origin in Britain are some from East Africa, mainly from Kenya and Uganda. A study by Salvadori (1983) of Asian communities in Kenya, which also largely holds true for Ugandan Muslims of Asian origin, gives an insight into the extreme complexity of Muslim groupings there, some of which has reappeared in Britain. The British Asians expelled from Uganda included a number of Ismailis, Shi'ia Muslims whose leader is the Aga Khan. He has encouraged his followers to modernise and adapt to local cultures wherever possible. The mosques, temples and gurdwaras established by Asian groups in Leicester are not merely used for prayer and worship at prescribed times, but are important community centres, and ethnicity and language are important to the coherence of such a 'community'. This does not necessarily indicate exclusiveness. In Britain there are examples of Muslims of different national origins banding together to build a mosque and continuing to attend prayers together, but the importance of language, food preferences and dress styles cannot be ignored, and it may not be easy for someone of the same faith but from a different cultural ambience to be fully accepted. Moreover, Muslims seeking asylum may be reluctant to pray in their own community mosque lest those who pray there have connections with the group in their home area who have been responsible for persecuting them. It may not be easy for them to fit in elsewhere. Is this problem less acute for Hindus and Sikhs?

Then how does one classify a Methodist church in North London led by a charismatic black African Methodist minister in which many black African Christians have found a home? Should it be simply considered as part of the Methodist church in the area, or has it become a special case by reason of its large black African congregation? Most Ugandans who have settled in Britain (and are now mostly British citizens) came here originally as refugees from oppression of different groups by different regimes. A Luganda-speaking congregation, Okusinza mu Luganda, meets regularly at St John's Church, Waterloo Road in London. Acholi speakers from northern Uganda, driven into exile from persecution at a later period, have formed the Acholi London Fellowship and meet at St John's Church, Stratford (Uganda Church

Association Newsletter, 2000, p 52). Could either of these groups incorporate newer refugees?

There must be many such exiled Christian groups waiting to be researched: how able are they to accept newer asylum seekers and refugees whose experience has been entirely different and who may come from different ethnic groups?

None of this, however, fleshes out the contention of D'Onofrio and Munk (2004) that acceptance into a faith community assists the settlement of refugees. There seems to have been little research into this at a time when asylum seekers have become vilified and branded as 'bogus'. Can established faith communities accept them and assist them to settle? It is a general complaint that British congregations do not always find it easy to welcome even fellow British newcomers at the best of times. African Christians are among those who have felt alienated:

> African peoples are very warm, friendly and hospitable. Against this backdrop, some Nigerian Christians feel rather disappointed when they get to England to find that no one cares about them. The best that happens to them is the discussion over coffee at the end of the service, where they are subjected to all kinds of questioning and inquiries about themselves and their families. It is more disappointing when such chats don't lead to friendship; they go through another week without anyone following up on them. (Fagbemi, 2002)

If the mainstream Christian churches fail to follow up foreigners and incorporate them (Fagbemi was writing about Anglicans in particular and suggested that the Pentecostals were warmer-hearted), then other faith communities may even feel threatened by asylum seekers. One wonders if this problem is particularly acute for Muslims, beleaguered as they are at the moment by the current outbreak of Islamophobia. Groups that feel themselves threatened may be very reluctant to accept asylum seekers, as demonstrated in the outbreaks of trouble in Peterborough between local residents of Pakistani origin and asylum seekers. Research is urgently needed here.

Many further lines of research suggest themselves. For instance, do faith communities respond by engaging in political action as a result of seeing how asylum seekers and refugees are treated under current legislation? What particular events drive them to take political action, and what form does the political action take? Is it effective? To what extent were faith communities involved in the action to get rid of the system of giving asylum seekers vouchers instead of cash? These had to be spent in designated supermarkets that were not allowed to give change if there was an under-spend. Which faith communities involved themselves in this campaign? One might ask further, why were bodies such as the Churches Commission on Racial Justice so slow to protest at the 2004 Asylum and Immigration (Treatment of Claimants etc) Act even though it was so blatantly unjust? Public protests, as distinct from quiet lobbying, by national religious leaders such as the Archbishop of Canterbury, the Cardinal Archbishop of Westminster and the Chief Rabbi, have sometimes been effective (*The Times*, 1991)[2], so why have public protests been so few and far between? Is it that they cannot rely on the members of their communities supporting them if they go public?

More is known about the Christian churches' efforts to work with refugees and asylum seekers than is known about other faith communities and their response to those who share their faith but who are still in the process of applying for asylum, and therefore on the more precarious edges of British society than longer-established, 'immigrant' faith communities. Again, research possibilities open up here.

Those recognised as refugees or given leave to remain

Even less is known about newly recognised refugees than about asylum seekers. Is there a carry-over from the assistance given through faith communities to these people while they were still seeking asylum, and what happens to them once they have been recognised as refugees under the 1951 Refugees Convention, or have been given some other form of humanitarian leave to remain?

Once recognition is granted, NASS support quickly ceases, but it may take weeks or sometimes months before documentation arrives enabling the newly recognised refugee to access social security benefits or find work. Where do refugees turn in these emergencies? Do refugees who are members of faith communities find that these communities help them through this temporary destitution? Under current legislation, social security benefits are only available to someone recognised as a Convention refugee in the area to which they were dispersed by NASS as an asylum seeker, that is, where they may have already experienced discrimination and hostility.

Do attitudes towards people change when they are granted refugee status? Will faith communities who may have been reluctant to incorporate asylum seekers into their fellowship be more accepting once that person has been recognised as a refugee under the Convention? If a faith community has supported someone through the asylum-seeking process, then they will presumably rejoice with that person that their claim has been successful. But will it make someone more acceptable when they have previously been cold-shouldered and when they are able to bring their family to join them? How will members of the Christian community respond to those of other faiths when their claims succeed and they are able to bring their family to Britain?

Refused asylum seekers who cannot be removed to their home country

The plight of refused asylum seekers and others who cannot be removed back to the countries from which they have fled is highlighted in *Welcome*, a film by Camcorder Guerrillas of Glasgow that comes with an action pack. It shows the plight of three refused asylum seekers in Glasgow: two men and a woman who cannot be returned to their home country because it would not be safe to send them back. Why have they not been granted any form of asylum, a Glasgow City Councillor pertinently asks. Others cannot be returned because their countries refuse to readmit them, or refuse to provide documentation without which no airline will carry them. Those who had been refused asylum and had reached the end of the road with no more possibility of appeal against refusal were no longer eligible for any support and were evicted from their housing on to the streets – except that some Glaswegians of goodwill took a few of them into their homes until until some longer-term solution could be found. Other refused asylum seekers exist up and down the country, with little known about their plight. Although legal action on human rights grounds is pending, this will take many months to be concluded. In the meantime, these refused asylum seekers become totally dependent on the people's goodwill to prevent them from destitution and rough sleeping. Or they may, of course, be driven by poverty and desperation into illegal working and crime. The role of faith communities in helping such people is another area requiring research. Are they being reached at all, or is their plight virtually unnoticed?

Asylum from religious persecution

Some people who seek asylum do so on the grounds of religious persecution, as Godziak and Shandy (2002) noted. These include Christians from China, Pakistan, India, the Near and Middle East, and some other Muslim countries (including northern Nigeria, where campaigns for the introduction of Shar'ia law are being used to promote the extension of tribal domination); members of the Ahmadiyya movement from Pakistan (Ahmadiyya claims to be a reforming sect of Islam but is not accepted by other Muslims); Falun Gong from China[3]; Buddhists from Tibet; and some Iranians who have converted to Christianity since arriving in Britain to seek asylum for some other reason[4].

The Home Office has sometimes seemed especially reluctant to grant asylum to those who flee religious persecution, though a Buddhist monk who had fled Tibet was recently quickly recognised as a refugee under the Convention. Chinese people claiming to be Falun Gong are often suspected of making spurious claims (and sometimes they are). Baha'i have been fiercely persecuted in Iran, and refugees from Iran form the core of Baha'i communities throughout the West. More precise information about the treatment of religious minorities in certain countries is needed.

Iranians who claim to have converted to Christianity after being refused asylum unsurprisingly find it difficult to persuade the Home Office of the genuineness of their conversion (Refugee Council, 2004), and the Home Office does not know how to test their sincerity. Trying to do so by asking questions about Biblical or creedal knowledge would seem to be useless. A better test would perhaps be continuing church attendance and identification with the Christian community over a long period of time, but the need to reach a decision about granting leave to remain may not permit this. A desire to change religion may indicate a weak allegiance to Islam in the first place, or else a deep disgust with oppression done in the name of Islam. The cultural and religious move required of those who convert to Christianity, however, is great: consider the move from Muslim prayers to Christian Eucharistic worship. There have been reports of Muslim asylum seekers becoming Christians because it was Christian groups who helped them on arrival when they could not get support from the mosque. As we have seen, many Muslims currently feel embattled, and may fight shy of assisting asylum seekers who are vilified in the press and often labelled 'bogus' and even, mistakenly, accused of being terrorists.

This raises questions about religion providing protection. When the Shah of Iran was overthrown, some Iranians converted to Christianity, possibly because they thought this might save them from being sent back to Iran. Some Jews in Nazi Germany obtained baptism certificates in the hope that these might afford them some sort of protection. Such conversion and use of religion for protection opens up a theological minefield.

There are, then, plenty of issues regarding religion that await research. Such research might best be carried out alongside other research. For instance, the group Bail for Immigration Detainees together with the Refugee Women's Research Project based at Asylum Aid recently carried out research into women's experience of detention (Cutler and Ceneda, 2004). It would have been relatively easy to ask each of the women interviewed if they had ever met a chaplain in the centres where they were held, or made use of the chapel or prayer room, and to expand on this.

In detention centres where women and children are held, the chaplains make a point of visiting the unit very frequently, though obviously they are unable to talk with everyone there. In the course of research in general, a question about religious affiliation in the countries from which people have fled and their expectation of religion in the host country would probably not be thought intrusive. One suspects that the researchers might be more diffident when asking questions about religion than the asylum seekers and refugees when answering them. The differences between faith communities mean that no simple answers can be expected. Even a question about how religion might help people to overcome their trauma is likely to have complex responses. For example, might religious and cultural norms and expectations make the shame of rape more, not less, difficult to overcome? Nevertheless, are the possibilities of religion being a valuable means of assistance to people trying to overcome trauma and to settle into a new life being underused and overlooked?

The challenge thrown down by Gozdziak and Shandy (2002) and referred to at the beginning of this chapter has not yet been sufficiently taken up.

Acknowledgements

This chapter could not have been written without the help of Mary Horbury, Sally Richmond, Shirley and Basil Scott, Gareth Wallace and Louise Zanre, to whom the writer wishes to express her gratitude.

Notes

[1] She was referring to the point in the Catholic mass and the Anglican Eucharist where the ancient practice of giving the kiss of peace has been restored. The celebrant addresses the congregation with the words "The peace of the Lord be with you", to which the congregation responds before being invited to share the peace, usually by shaking hands with those around them. One wonders how the church in question followed this up.

[2] Statement by the Archbishop of Canterbury, the Cardinal Archbishop of Westminster and the Chief Rabbi in a letter to *The Times* (1991), protesting about the absurdly short time limits for lodging an appeal against refusal of asylum. The time limits were lengthened as a result.

[3] Some people would dispute the inclusion of Falun Gong here, as it is not, strictly speaking, a religion, but its adherents usually declare it as such.

[4] There has been a recent influx of Iraqi Christians into Jordan and Syria following attacks on churches and on Christian-run businesses dealing in fashions, liquor and music, disapproved of by some strict Muslims (www.catholic-pages.com/forum.asp), but few, if any, are coming to the UK so far as is known. There is some evidence that the situation for Christians in the Near and Middle East is beginning to stabilise, but it is still too early to try to return Christians to these countries.

References

Belton, N. (1998) *The good listener, Helen Bamber: a life against cruelty*, London: Weidenfield and Nicolson.

Crown (2001) *The Detention Centre Rules 2001*, Statutory Instrument No 2001/238, London: The Stationery Office (www.legislation.hmso.goc.uk/cgi-bin/htm_hl.pl?DB=hmso-new&STEMMER=).

Cutler, S. and Ceneda, S. (2004) *They took me away: Women's experiences of immigration detention in the UK*, London: Bail for Immigration Detainees and Refugee Women's Research Project.

D'Onofrio, L. and Munk, K. (2004) *Understanding the stranger, final report*, London: Information Centre about Asylum and Refugees in the UK.

Fagbemi, S. (2002) 'A Nigerian reflects on the Church of England', in A. Wheeler (ed) *Voices from Africa: Transforming mission*, London: Church House Press.

Farnell, R., Furbey, R., Shams, S., Hills, A.H., Macey, M. and Smith, G. (2003) *'Faith' in urban regeneration? Engaging faith communities in urban regeneration*, Bristol: The Policy Press.

Gozdziak, E.M. and Shandy, D.J. (2002) 'Editorial introduction: the role of religion and spirituality in forced migration', *Journal of Refugee Studies*, vol 15, no 2, pp 129-35.

Lewis, P. (1994) *Islamic Britain: Religion, politics and identity among British Muslims*, London: I.B. Tauris.

Lundberg, E. (2004) Detention Workshop Paper presented at Enabling Christians in Serving Refugees (ECSR) Conference, Leicester University, 11-12 September.

Oldham Metropolitan Borough (2003) *Tackling the myths about asylum seekers*, Oldham: Oldham Metropolitan Borough.

Refugee Council (2004) *Inexile*, no 30 (www.refugeecouncil.org.uk/publications).

Salvadori, C. (1983) *Through open doors: A view of Asian cultures in Kenya*, Nairobi: Kenway Publications.

Scott, S.F. (2003) 'Welcoming refugees? A study of host community attitudes as seen in church-related projects in Leicester', unpublished MA Thesis, University of East London.

Scottish Green Party (2004) 'Glasgow's MSPs unite to condemn destitution of city's asylum seekers', Press release, 20 January.

The Times (1991) Letter to *The Times* from the Archbishop of Canterbury, the Cardinal Archbishop of Westminster and the Chief Rabbi, 12 November.

Uganda Church Association Newsletter (2000) *Ugandans in London*, London: Uganda Church Association.

Vaughan, R. (2004) *The Catholic directory*, pp 659-60 (www.cartes.freeuk.com/history).

ELEVEN

Action learning: a research approach that helped me to rediscover my integrity

Anna Maria Miwanda Bagenda

Introduction

By 2001, policies regarding refugee people seeking asylum were changing at great speed, with 'forced dispersal' being one such policy, introduced in 1999. Without the introduction of this policy, it is highly probable that most of the residents of the city where the project discussed in this chapter happened would rarely, if ever, have met a single refugee person seeking asylum. In response to the impact of that policy, in September 2002, the Salford RAPAR (Refugee and Asylum Seeker Participatory Action Research) project began. It offered an innovative research approach to tackling issues that were, themselves, new to the agencies and the communities in the city.

This research project was designed to involve and empower refugee people seeking asylum, the local community and local service deliverers, being most fundamentally distinguishable from casework by the fact that the process consciously sought to understand the nature of the presenting problems, and reactions to them in relation to the wider social context and surrounding networks (Wright Mills, 1963, p 440). It considered the processes at work at the level of society, rather than confining the approach to a consideration of the problems at the level of the individual. I understand the method used in the context of the work discussed in this chapter to be a participatory action research approach (Wadsworth, 1998) that has been conducted inside an action learning framework (Revans, 1982). The reasons for my decision to identify the methods in this way are rooted in the direct involvement of people who presented to our project in an evidence-base development process that included sharing information with service providers about such evidence as it was emerging: it is the actions that we took during this process that created opportunities for people to engage in a continuous learning process for effecting constructive change.

Further, the giving and receiving of support was not excluded from the project, as might be expected with casework. Rather, offering support was an integral part of the activities that combined to effectively engage with presenting issues, complementing the whole process by enabling trust and confidence to grow within and between the refugee people seeking asylum and the wider community. This was achieved through a participatory action research approach that invited people, including the research project team, to reflect on their own roles in the emergence of evidence bases (Lincoln and Guba, 1985) using the principles of action learning and, in this way, create opportunities for people to learn about how to ensure the necessary interactions for promoting social inclusion and community cohesion.

To many people, 'research' is a threatening word that only relates to higher institutions of learning. The word also carries fear for those who have had experience of researchers who ask questions but appear never to give feedback. If the participants are literate, they only read what was said about them. By contrast, as a refugee woman seeking asylum with work permission and employed on this project, I found that it contributed greatly to my process of rebuilding my life. It also shaped my thinking as I struggled to regain my integrity.

How it all started

The Salford RAPAR project stemmed from the investigation of a group of concerned front-line workers and academic researchers into the experiences of people seeking asylum who had been forcibly dispersed to the city. The original group consisted of four women: two health professionals, a health community worker and a researcher. Soon, with other academics and some representatives from the statutory sector and voluntary sector agencies across the conurbation, they formed a participatory action research forum, RAPAR[1], for networking about refugee and asylum issues. The forum set the trend in the area for developing a culture of using people's experiences in relation to asylum in order to solve asylum-related problems.

Through the RAPAR network, the first group of refugee people seeking asylum who had arrived in the city in 2001 managed to set up small community groups that highlighted their plight and their feelings. One example of this early work was the awareness raising they achieved around one failed asylum applicant who had emerged as a natural leader within the Afghan community, only to be deported to Austria (Cranna, 2003) through the third-country agreement (Leibaut, 2000).

The project is born

The founders of RAPAR were invited by the Local Strategic Partnership for the city to put together a bid for funding from a national social inclusion funding stream. The bid was successful and a substantial amount was allocated to the project. Its mission statement explained:

> The project aims at using the evidence gathered through participatory action research and community interaction between refugee people seeking asylum, local people and services to bring about awareness and action that will address: imbalances that exist between services; gaps that exist within services; and the need to include communities, as they develop their sense of belonging to the City. (RAPAR, 2002, p 1)

The project begins

In September 2002, a group of enthusiastic individuals who had been appointed to the project met to begin their work. The period September 2002 to January 2003 had been set aside for the induction as the group tried to find its feet and define the way forward.

The group soon realised that it was going to be a real bed of roses[2]: avoiding thorns was not going to be easy. Issues we were about to tackle were very emotive: on several occasions, I had heard statements from workers in mainstream organisations like "this whole thing is too new to the city" or "this city has always been predominantly white". The city may not have been ready for 'these people', but forced dispersal meant that issues of poor housing, eviction and assault had come to the fore.

The first test for the team was the organisation of the launch of the project. Difficult as this was, the team kept the focus on planning meetings, producing a video about the lives of the clients and setting up the office. This was not an exceptional project; it had its teething problems, but the 'forming and norming' stages (Palmer, 1988) passed without serious hitches.

The project was launched in January 2003 at the city's council chamber. The team took this opportunity to inform those present that this was not just like any other project – the intention was for evidence to be gathered and learning shared. It all happened at the seat of power in the city, in the presence of the 'City Fathers'. I thought we had won the first battle, only to be proved wrong two years down the line.

The learning begins

Many of the people who presented to the project had compounded problems, many of which arose from the forced dispersal programme. Although there were other, smaller, support groups for people seeking asylum in the city, the RAPAR project was the first to operate at a city-wide level and in a very different way: by including refugee people seeking asylum in the development of the project from the outset and by seeking to understand, document and communicate how the individual issues that presented related to the wider social context and networks within which they were located.

Time is the best teacher. I soon learned that as long as I did my business without disturbing the status quo, I was the centre of attraction. But my own understanding of what it meant to be a refugee or a person seeking asylum, twinned with my previous experience of working with uprooted people in Africa, enabled me to push harder, sometimes stepping on toes and upsetting the status quo.

How the project enabled

The team gathered evidence through its interaction with clients and language was not a barrier. Their stories and experiences formed part of the team's learning. The actions taken by the team, using the information from clients and with their full knowledge, determined the culture of the project: trust developed between the team and the people who presented to the project, which, in turn, led to the team enabling people to identify their own development processes. Talents and skills were identified and isolation began to become a thing of the past. Lives began to be rebuilt as a strong 'family' began to unite the scattered, isolated individuals who had previously had no connection with one another.

Developing project volunteers

There were many good reasons for involving volunteers in the project activities, not least that it would help to create well-defined and rooted opportunities for the mutual benefit of clients, volunteers, paid staff and city agencies. This shared understanding led to a formidable relationship between the project and its volunteers through the following principles.

• *Best practice:* Proper support and training was considered to be vital to any role that volunteers would be asked to perform.
• *Links with the community:* The plights of refugee people seeking asylum are many and varied. Coming to a different country, adjusting to a new way of life in a different cultural environment, and thinking about family members and relatives left behind all combine to prevent people from organising themselves and integrating in their new environment. The project aimed to enable refugee people seeking asylum living in the city to build new lives. This could be achieved by actively making links with the local community through working closely with the volunteers.
• *Links with clients:* The project worked with a wide range of refugee people seeking asylum in the city. This underpinned its motivation to welcome and work with volunteers from all backgrounds so that the clients felt at home and acknowledged the special way of responding to their needs that was different: doing things not for them but with them, in the understanding that "participation is the child, not of power, but of communal need" (Revans, 1980, p 238).
• *Diversity:* The project promoted the variety of skills, interests, life experiences and cultural backgrounds that volunteers came with. This diversity of background enabled them to work with refugee people seeking asylum who congregated in the city from all over the world.
• *Added value:* The project believed that involving volunteers presented a unique opportunity to extend support and assistance to refugee people seeking asylum. The volunteers could improve the efficiency and effectiveness of the project as a whole. By their contribution, volunteers could add value to the services provided by the project.
• *Different path:* Volunteers were able to get involved in activities that paid staff did not have time to do. They visited and interacted with clients and got to know, at first hand, the problems that would need the attention of the project staff. The project believed that volunteers could spread the message to other communities in the city about the situation that refugee people seeking asylum faced in the community. This helped to dispel myths and misconceptions about refugee people seeking asylum, as well as helping to improve public perceptions of them.

Each development worker had responsibility for developing a pool of volunteers. Between January 2003 and April 2004, volunteers organised a range of activities such as a Saturday school, a women's catering group, an arts group, summer activities and football team trips.

My good time with the project

When I first joined the project, the words 'action learning' were very new to me. I had taken part in participatory research projects in Africa and concluded that they only worked well and became a useful and valued exercise if all concerned had time to understand and agree about what participation meant. As a single refugee woman seeking asylum, I was given the job of community development worker on the RAPAR project, but I was also part of this research because of my current status in the UK: as a refugee person seeking asylum with permission to work. For almost a month, I struggled to understand my new job within this research that involved actions and learning. I studied the project mission statement and decided to break the words down and apply them to each case I handled, asking myself:

- What action(s) am I taking?
- Who else is taking or failing to take the action(s)?
- What learning is there for me as a researcher, for the agencies and the client(s)?
- How best to take action and for what results.

It became clear that it was not my job as a researcher to come up with solutions, but rather to find ways of sharing information about the nature of presenting problems and stimulating exploration about how they related to the policy frameworks operating and the wider social setting. In this way, the process of creating solutions could become a shared activity between the people directly affected, the research team and the service deliverers who had to put the policy context into practice. The process meant digging deeper through the problems, and asking difficult questions that many people working with refugee people seeking asylum may not have tackled in the past for a number of reasons, mainly stemming from lack of knowledge about the needs of refugee people seeking asylum[3].

Soon I learned that the participatory action research process we were creating, while dealing with clients within an action learning framework, involved much more than holding the hand of the client: it demanded that we offer them opportunities to take some responsibility for themselves, and then, when the time was right, letting go of their hands with care. I also learned that, through this process, the clients became empowered as the actions taken, and their learning through those actions, balanced one another. I also understood that the learning could only be realised through the actions taken by clients, researchers and agencies to solve the problems together. It therefore became a community action, where issues were analysed and solutions found together, rather than attempting to fix problems on an individual, case-by-case basis. I learned that this process provoked discussions where all could participate and that this could lead to a two-tier process: the communities came with a clearly defined problem and some ideas about solutions and the agencies might have provided more answers but did not assume that they could. This opened up the dialogue between them and the relationship began to deepen, creating bridges between communities and agencies.

I looked carefully at different, often difficult, issues such as housing, poverty and unemployment. These problems often gave rise to tensions between refugee people and the indigenous population living in the same area, but, gradually, the ways in which the project showed similarities between the two communities helped to bridge the gap between them[4].

Examples of presentations to the project

One morning in October 2002, Rehema (not her real name) came to the project and described her experiences of living in the city: "I come Somalia, my English no good, boy come throw stone, window break, he say to me asylum bad go away. My sister I am tired, I want new house please tell Home Office and NASS now".

While trying to flee Somalia with her children, a series of disasters had befallen her, including the disappearance of the agent who was engineering her escape, assault and rape that led to pregnancy, and betrayal by her cousins whom she had relied on for help. She felt stigmatised because she was pregnant and a widow in a strong Moslem community. She finally arrived in the UK in May 2002 with her children and with an untreated wound from the attack, and the culture shock added to her problems.

"I am here, you my sister help, stomach too big, pain", she burst into tears. I made her a cup of tea and tried some small talk; deep down I knew it was not the last time to see Rehema. She then asked me, "You like me?" meaning if I was also a single woman. I said "yes", she smiled and hugged me. "Children?" she asked. "Yes, three, but not with me" I replied. "No, I pray Allah children be safe".

As we worked through her problems, treating them not just as her individual concerns but with the understanding that such experiences were part of a wider pattern of experience, she located other Somali refugee women seeking asylum and brought them to the project. She soon registered for her first English lessons at a church drop-in centre, the same place that was used for single, local mothers with childcare problems. Volunteers organised play groups for the children for three hours each week to give the mothers some free time.

On the first day, I escorted Rehema to the drop-in centre and stayed to see how she settled in. The following week she appeared at the project with six Somali women who, as they introduced themselves, apologised for not speaking good English. Rehema was the interpreter. I escorted the group to the drop-in centre and left Rehema to take charge, though I kept eye contact with her throughout as support and encouragement.

The nuns who ran the drop-in centre also distributed clothes and tinned food. Rehema and her friends brought up the issue of halal food (meat from animals slaughtered according to Muslim holy law), which I explained to the nuns. The following week the nuns provided a wider selection of food that was suitable for the Muslim women, including packed rice, baking and brown flour, tinned beans and chick/green peas and spinach.

The nuns appreciated Rehema's leadership role and my presence – they, too, were learning. This is a very important aspect in the integration process, whereby all parties learn something – it is not just a one-way relationship. The nuns consulted Rehema on what food was appropriate and on other issues. If unsure, Rehema turned to me for support. She continued to bring more women to the project and offered to interpret where necessary.

Through our approach, Rehema came to understand that her struggle as a refugee woman seeking asylum was similar to the experience of other women. She formed relationships with other refugee women, not just Somalis, acting as an aunt, a big sister, a friend, a marriage counsellor or a mentor. Her English improved along with her confidence. She only came to the project for help when she was unable to help the women herself. The 'letting go' of the hand with care had worked. She was empowered and she was grateful to the project. In turn, she did the same for other women.

Cultures that can never be discarded

In the context of African culture, it is an accepted principle that women are either protected by their religion, through the church, or by their culture, through the tribe. The NASS dispersal programme never considered this and as a result many refugee women seeking asylum have found themselves in situations where they have nobody to turn to for help.

Alone and confused, Halima (not her real name) had had to venture out to look for a supermarket to buy food for her hungry children. She came face to face with racial abuse that ended in physical assault:

> This angry man run towards me and demanded for the mobile phone and money. He was too close and he smelt badly. "If you refuse to give me the money and the phone, you and your dogs will never live peacefully in your house. I will come with my friends tonight; we will rape you and burn that house. Your dogs will die tonight," he said. He meant my children. I had no phone so he took the money and promised to come back.

I visited Halima two days after the attack. She was in tears; her children were scared and very restless. There was no food in the house, although the police had been there twice to take statements. "I know why I am suffering, I have nobody to protect me, and I need a man to escort me around or an older woman," she said.

Through the group discussions that had taken place in the community room at the project, we knew that many single refugee women from the Islamic culture lacked the confidence to move around on their own; some had sons who had taken on the role of protector of the women in their families. Rehema had told me that this made her feel irresponsible: "My son is only 14, he has taken over the role of an adult. This whole situation has robbed his childhood."

The NASS dispersal programme had no formula; women were dispersed on the assumption that there would be established communities from their countries of origin in the places of dispersal, but this was usually not the case. Refugee communities were far flung and single women often found themselves isolated. The project's work in helping to relocate them, even just to another part of the city, involved relating the various reasons for the need, including racial harassment, which had to be proved beyond reasonable doubt. It took time to document these experiences, to communicate how and why they were a part of wider social problems and to try to engender the appropriate responses from the housing authorities.

In response to the lack of a coherent strategy to tackle such problems, women in the same situation tried to keep in touch with each other and go out in groups, although this did not prevent incidents of verbal and physical attacks, especially on public transport. They had to adapt to the new culture of being on their own and being there for each other whenever possible.

Doing things and involving people

The research approach in the RAPAR project enabled us to understand the difference between treating people in isolation by doing things for them on an individual basis, and involving, assisting and supporting them while giving them a chance to stand on their feet and to explore how the social environment and the policy frameworks were implicated in what was happening to them. Doing things like organising trips, making appointments for GPs or schools, both for themselves and with their new-found friends, empowered them. Even when they failed to get positive responses it was not in vain; it was seen as the beginning of their empowerment, an introduction to the integration process.

There are numerous examples of single refugee women seeking asylum who have regained their dignity and rebuilt their lives through the approach of the RAPAR project. They have been an integral part of my work because I can relate to their experiences, challenges and struggles to relearn the meaning of living without fear or blame for what we are, by understanding the commonality of our experiences and the role of wider policy frameworks within it. Together, we have discussed isolation, being away from the normal life, our culture, food and way of life. I have chatted to them on buses and laughed loudly only to see heads turn in disbelief. We have had to block the thought of "Who is staring at me?" if we dressed in our traditional dresses. They have all said to me that I am different because I can speak English; I wish they knew that it has not been an automatic entry into 'society' as it were. That it has often closed doors, especially during the course of this research where my asking and probing has caused me pain.

More learning through different actions

The action learning approach enabled the project to do both research and development work (Chivers, 2005). Issues that were tackled were not met with 'direct' answers from the team; rather, many of the people concerned, including front-line service deliverers and volunteers supporting clients, debated and explored the social problems that the individual situations highlighted and contributed to decision making about how best to proceed. During this process, individuals developed as they became directly involved and learned how to do things not only for themselves but for others as well. The development process continued in tandem with the research. This was a two-way process; the project team members were learning and the target groups (refugee people seeking asylum, local community, practitioners) were also learning, albeit at different rates, as the following example shows.

The project progressed and the number of volunteers increased. This came about due to the interaction encouraged by the project objectives. The local people had learnt about asylum issues and how best to support those in need.

The first piece of advice often given to a refugee person seeking asylum is to 'go to college and learn English'. It is true that without a common language, communication is limited. However, it took the project a whole year to find out why some of the African women did not want to go to college.

An African woman is regarded as the custodian of knowledge; this is what I was told as a Muganda girl from the Ganda of Uganda during my initiation: "Once a woman, you have all the answers". It is the same elsewhere in Africa. In addition, some refugee women seeking asylum come from a culture where men make the major decisions and the women are accompanied everywhere they go. The concept of going to college is alien to these women. For the refugee women seeking asylum it was not very easy, and some needed extra support in order to get into school.

In September 2003, extra lessons were organised by the project for the children of refugee people seeking asylum to improve their maths and English. The women escorted their children and sat in the next room and talked about their challenges: from marital problems to childcare and teenagers and how they found it hard to guide their children in this new culture. The eldest in the group chipped in with advice until they came to Nema's (not her real name) story. "You can't take your husband to the police," the women screamed. "They will take your children away."

From what I heard, I decided to visit Nema at home: the visit revealed bruises on her back and legs. Her daughter said: "You must help my mother, my father is so cruel, he blames her for everything, most fights arise from my mother asking for money to buy food." I asked if the daughter had reported this to the police or informed NASS and she said no, as the family was afraid of being returned to Somalia. She had talked to the landlord, who laughed it off and said, "If NASS gets wind of this you are done". The daughter didn't understand what this meant and the family kept quiet.

I contacted the Somali elders, who provided support to Nema and disciplined the husband. At the same time, I talked to NASS about giving Nema the right to handle the family allowance and also arranged for her to move to another house with the children, a small example of how our research was succeeding in securing adjustments in how policy was being interpreted by practitioners. Nema rejoined her husband after some months. She also became the main applicant of the family asylum process. I was left wondering what would have happened to this family if I had overlooked their culture.

Changes that affected my work

A house is not built in a day but can be destroyed in a second and there are different houses and various styles; while some take a few months to construct, others take years. However, there is no house built without a plan; even a simple hut in rural Africa has a plan. The tallest man who stands in the centre of the circle to hold the central pillar takes the measurements and he determines the height of the structure. Some houses are built in phases, with a clear vision as each floor is properly finished and put to use while construction continues to progress. In RAPAR, we thought we had built our house for this project with care and we started living in it as a happy family – until one day when a 'land grabber' descended on us like a proverbial thief in the night.

It began when an external partner representative joined the steerage meetings and asserted that, in their view, the project was not doing research, but rather casework that involved only support. Maybe, at that time, all they understood about research was of a positivist, deductive, hypothesis–testing nature, and the participation inside the action learning framework where we constantly sought to understand our relationship, as researchers, to what we were doing, was too different from their experience for them to recognise how the research process was being conducted.

However, not convinced by the arguments about the action learning approach to conducting participatory action research, they decided that they wanted to visit the project and talk to the team on a one-to-one basis. We were surprised and unsettled by their behaviour during this visit and, because we had established an open culture of sharing our thoughts, questions and feelings about what was happening at any given time, and without fear of reprimand for questioning, we raised our concerns. The management listened to our concerns and then discussed them as a group. They decided to explain the project's concerns about this individual's approach to the organisation that the individual represented, and to ask for an alternative organisational representative to participate in future meetings about the direction of the work.

Individual workers received letters of apology from the person at the heart of the difficulty, but the different partner organisations that had been involved in deciding to ask for alternative representation to the project received verbal complaints from the individual involved. All but one of the organisations responded by inviting the individual to come and talk with them further or put their concerns in writing – which they insisted that they did not want to do – but one of the partner organisations, representing a health organisation, decided to carry out an investigation into the verbal complaint.

Indications that the equilibrium of our project was becoming disturbed surfaced through the emergence of uncorroborated reports that one member of the project team was talking in negative ways about the project, outside the project and without bringing their concerns to the team collective. This sense of being disturbed became more acute when another member of the team told us all that they had been informally approached about taking up an alternative job with one of the main statutory organisations in the city.

By the end of 2003, there were several other indications that appeared to suggest that the project was being informally – and rather disconcertingly – disrupted, as specific, individual partner organisations began a series of actions that could be interpreted as by-passing the communication procedures and processes that the project had evolved.

These actions came to a head in the first part of 2004 and that led to one of the statutory sector partners from within the health sector demanding changes to the composition of the group with responsibility for developing the direction of the project's work and, finally, taking the project away from RAPAR and imposing a new line management arrangement upon the team.

Things fall apart

Unlike in Chinua Achebe's (1958) *Things fall apart* where he describes the bravery of Okonkwo who tried to fight colonialism without the support of his community, our centre could hold because, almost all the time, no single individual took action without involving the others: the collective deliberation and shared ownership over decision making about the challenges that presented to the project was a part of our participatory methodology. However, as individuals we had our doubts and fears. Our monthly Action Learning Set (Revans, 1998) ensured that we had the space to explore our concerns about the perceived threat to our jobs and our related abilities to secure our daily bread. I remembered and compared our situation to what was happening in Charles Dickens' (1949) *A tale of two cities* when Queen Antoinette of France did not realise that cakes and bread are made from the same ingredient and that if there is no bread, cakes cannot be found either.

The clouds were gathering and I feared that the storm could rip us apart. As I had done in the past, when I had faced real threats in other parts of the world, I found myself re-visiting and re-affirming to myself the personal principles that I hold and that have always guided me so far. With a crisis all around me, I had one consolation: the centre of the project, that is the people who had been the engines that had made it become a real project in the first place, still appeared to be holding firm, both to their original vision and to the view that because the project was developing from the bottom up and setting its research agendas according to the kinds of issues that people presented with to the project, the ways in which it had developed thus far were healthy and basically right. Whenever I heard the words from some of the people connected to the project who would say, "they are powerful, there is nothing else we can do", or "it [changing the project] has been decided, what are we going to do about it?" I would locate my own sense of being that needed to remain strong and still so that, with the centre visibly intact, more people could gradually give their support to the actions that were being taken to defend and protect our work so far.

When confronted with an unexpected problem, people react differently and – when it is a matter of survival – the pressure upon collectives and the mutual trust that they have created becomes tested: there is a tendency towards becoming individuals again. My view is that, as a team, we started to blame each other; we started to believe that we must be doing something wrong. This was in spite of our previous understanding that we had built up during our regular Action Learning Sets where we had discussed the competing demands on our project. In our Set we had identified that method as, first of all, accepting people's own evidence about what was happening to them and their families, or groups with whom they identified (for example, the Somali women's group). Thereafter, exploring how those experiences were affected by, and interrelated with, the wider social networks and prevailing policy contexts helped us to open up dialogues with the different service delivery sectors about how to improve their responses to these people's problems. This process cultivated a real trust between us and our clients such that the clients could feel free to be honest with us. This had led us to the view that the people with the really meaningful authority and experience to say that we were – or were not – doing what we were supposed to do, were our clients.

Lessons learned

Various lessons have been learned. We had criticised others when we felt that we needed to, and then the time came when we had to criticise ourselves. It created an opportunity for me to really experience, and thereby really understand, the saying, 'Taking your own medicine', and it was indeed a bitter pill for the team. It helped me to develop a deeper appreciation of the reality that no one inside a research process can stand outside what they do (Geertz, 1975; Delphy, 1984, p 157) and that, if you can enhance your reflexive capacity, you can become much clearer about the ways in which your actions inside of the research process affect it. One of the aspects of our research approach was that, in order to develop our individual and collective consciousness about the impact of our emotions upon our work, we had often shared our feelings about what was happening to each of us emotionally as we tried to develop our research (Vince, 2004).

It is true that some members of the project team had no previous working experience, as this was their first job in the UK. However, I also was acutely aware about the pressure put on all of us from the 'new managers' who were uncompromising in their view that the project should only be doing support and individual casework, rather than engaging in a research process where the act of determining how to collectivise understanding about the sources of individual problems so as to foster and enable socially based responses was inherently political (see Jan Khan, Chapter Six in this volume).

Was it a matter of forgetting our experiences and our history together so soon? If so, I would say that this 'forgetting' had come too fast. I began to doubt the concerns about my health; it seemed to me to be one way of telling me to shut up. I decided to keep my ears to the ground and listen to all the different vibes. It was the only way to keep track of what was happening and become able to record this experience.

Failing the refugee people seeking asylum

Putting my thoughts on paper is helping me to conquer my fears. I wanted to tell my own story as a person who, in the process of carrying out this research, witnessed an attempt to undo what had been done and remove the basis upon which it had been done. The ascending perspective within the group that had taken over control of our project was that our action learning model did not constitute a valid research enterprise: that the project should only be about community development for asylum seekers, where the term 'community development' is used to mean entertainment through taking a 'saris and curry' approach to cultural differences and social inequalities. The new management were determined that any 'research' activity should be taken up elsewhere and confined to that which is pursued using traditional frameworks where data is collected and the decisions about how to use it are taken out of the control of the people whose experiences make up the data in the first place. For me, that removal of control from the people directly affected became a part of the process whereby people seeking asylum began to be failed by their city.

Things cannot fall apart if the centre is intact

A house can only fall if the centre is not holding. At this time, the originators of the project and some concerned citizens who had taken it upon themselves to find out what was happening opened up a process of questioning the relevant authorities and asking them to explain what had happened and why (*Private Eye*, 2005). This exercise has taken me back so many years to when I enjoyed sitting under the trees and discussing issues affecting the students and members of staff. This was in Africa and it was my first encounter with Action Learning (Revans, 1980).

The learning continues

There are many different aspects to the process whereby we began to develop evidence about needs and action in services with refugee people seeking asylum, local people and practitioners.

The trust that evolved between the project team and the clients grew out of the team's ability to recognise the importance of listening to and respecting the emotions, as well as the actual experiences, of the people presenting to us, and was fundamental to our creation of authentic evidence bases about what was happening on the ground (see, for example, Moran et al, 2003). For me personally, the ability to achieve this was bound up in being a woman seeking asylum myself and being encouraged through the action learning set to become more aware that how I reacted emotionally to clients impacted upon how they felt about sharing their information with me, and how service providers felt when I approached them. I had to devise a way that protected clients, yet gained the trust and confidence of service providers.

Neither those responsive practitioners nor the people who had come to me to share their problems in the first place would necessarily be concerned about what label should be attached to this process: whether it was research, community development or casework. What mattered for them was that something concrete could change because of the ways we found to communicate with and help one another. Here, the research informed both the learning through action that we all experienced as project staff and volunteers, clients and, sometimes, service providers, and the community development processes that we nurtured.

The research has continued but at a different level and with a new team. The emphasis has been on understanding what happened to the original project – and why – and on finding a way of communicating that understanding to responsible bodies that can take positive action. Fortunately, the learning continues.

Notes

[1] Registered Charity 1095961 and Company Limited by Guarantee Number 04387010.

[2] The language used here offers a most interesting example of how differences in people's cultural frameworks can create very different meanings for exactly the same phrases (Temple and Edwards, 2002).

[3] Before forced dispersals were introduced in 2000, the city had had a very tiny population of refugee people seeking asylum.

[4] Olson (forthcoming) gives a clear picture of the most deprived areas in the city. Broughton is one of them and there are more than 400 refugee people seeking asylum living in the area.

References

Achebe, C. (1958) *Things fall apart*, London: Heinemann.

Chivers, M. (2005) 'Ordinary magic: developing services for children with severe communication difficulties by engaging multiple voices', *Action Learning: Research and Practice*, vol 2, no 1, pp 7-26.

Cranna, A. (2003) 'Appeal bid hopes for asylum seeker', *Salford Advertiser*, 14 December, p 16.

Delphy, C. (1984) *A materialist analysis of women's oppression*, MA: University of Massachusetts.

Dickens, C. (1949) *A tale of two cities*, Oxford: Oxford University Press.

Geertz, C. (1975) *The interpretation of cultures*, London: Hutchinson and Company.

Leibaut, F. (ed) (2001) *The Dublin Convention. Study on its implementation in the 15 member states of the European Union*, Copenhagen: The European Commission and the Danish Refugee Council.

Lincoln, M. and Guba, Y. (1985) *Naturalistic inquiry*, Newbury Park, CA: Sage Publications.

Moran, R.A., Saeed, M., Golmakani, Z., Abdi, M., Stitakova, M. and Ndjuimot (2003) *People seeking asylum and their experiences of personal safety in Salford*, Salford: Revans Institute for Action Learning and Research, University of Salford.

Olsen, W. (forthcoming) *Poverty and problems in Salford: An independent study*, Salford: Salford Community Network.

Palmer, J.D. (1988) 'For the manager who must build a team', in W. Reddy with K. Jamison (eds) *Team building*, Charleston, VA and San Diego, CA: Institute for Applied Behavioral Science/University Associates, Inc., pp 137-49.

Private Eye (2005) 'Educashun newz', no 1124, p 11.

RAPAR (Refugee and Asylum Seeker Participatory Action Research) (2002) *Developing evidence about needs and action in services with refugees and asylum seeking communities*, Information leaflet, Salford: RAPAR.

Revans, R.W. (1980) *Action learning: New techniques for managers*, London: Blond and Briggs.

Revans, R.W. (1982) *The origins and growth of action learning*, Bromley: Chartwell Bratt.

Revans, R.W. (1998) *ABC of action learning*, London: Lemos and Crane.

Temple, B. and Edwards, R. (2002) 'Interpreters/translators and cross language research: reflexivity and border crossings', *International Journal of Qualitative Methods*, vol 1, no 2, Article 1 (www.ualberta.ca/~ijqm).

Vince, R. (2004) 'Action learning and organizational learning: power, politics and emotion in organizations', *Action Learning: Research and Practice*, vol 1, no 1, pp 63-78.

Wadsworth, Y. (1998) 'What is participatory action research?', *Action Research International*, Paper 2 (www.scu.edu.au/schools/gmc/ar/ari/p.-ywadsworth98.html).

Wright Mills, C. (1963) 'Situated actions and vocabularies of motive', in I.L. Horowitz (ed) *Power, politics and people: Collected essays by Clifford Geertz*, Oxford: Oxford University Press, pp 439-68.

Appendix: Guidelines funded through the Economic and Social Research Council Seminar Series 'Eliciting the views of refugee people seeking asylum'

Introductory statement

We are operating within a context of ever changing policy which can be very difficult for refugee people seeking asylum. These guidelines have been produced because, despite an explosion of research *on* refugee people seeking asylum, research approaches are in our view very often inappropriate and unethical for a highly vulnerable and ever-changing population.

As a whole, these guidelines attempt to present an 'ideal' research methodology. However, in practice, we recognise that researchers are faced with limitations (often financial) which mean that it is not always possible for them to adhere to all the points that follow. In such circumstances, it would be helpful and ethical for researchers to specify the constraints under which they are working and the consequences those constraints have on the research. Research should be conducted within the professional ethics code of the appropriate professional body, e.g., the Social Research Association, the British Sociological Association, the British Anthropological Association or the British Medical Association.

Approach

In general and from the outset, good practice in research:

- recognises that people may see the social world differently. The research need to be open to different ways of seeing, interpreting and acting in the world so that these different ways of seeing the social world are able to be articulated and demonstrated;
- identifies existing research and justifies the usefulness of the new research in terms of benefits to refugee people seeking asylum;

- states clearly the researchers' aims and what they want to try and do with the research findings;
- sets up procedures ensuring adherence to confidentiality agreements reached with participating refugee people seeking asylum;
- aims to address issues affecting refugee people seeking asylum and therefore allows input from refugee people seeking asylum;
- acknowledges that refugee people seeking asylum have very valuable knowledge about the British system gained from their own experience;
- is open and honest with potential participants about the extent to which the researchers on the project intend to allow participants to become involved in shaping and directing the project;
- reports findings using non-discriminatory language. This involves recognising that certain words or phrases that may cause offence should be avoided. Most professional guidelines will offer advice;
- recognises that, whilst researchers cannot control what is done with their research once it is in the public domain, they need to be aware of the wider political context concerning refugee people seeking asylum and responsibly think through the implications and impact of their findings;
- is transparent and pro-active in consultation;
- that intends to consult with, rather than actively engage the participation of, refugee people seeking asylum, is made transparent from the outset.

Specifically, research that intends actively to engage the participation of refugee people seeking asylum, rather than merely consult with them:

- specifies how it is going to ensure the meaningful participation of refugee people seeking asylum in collecting, analysing, reporting and disseminating research data and findings;
- specifies which sections of communities/groups are being involved (e.g., self-appointed leaders, accountable leaders, voluntary organisation representatives, women);
- generates individual and community/group-level capacity building, e.g., helping the development of skills for creating and implementing action plans and/or initiating research themselves and/or advocacy capacity;
- recognises that the refugee people seeking asylum communities/ groups are heterogeneous (i.e. there is no one community/group

or voice) so that empowering one section of the community/group may cut across the position of another section;

- describes how to include the involvement of refugee people seeking asylum in developing the research plans for feedback to communities/groups or groups who are the focus of the research;
- enables researchers to inform participants of their funding sources, and any conditions associated with acceptance of the funding, and enables participants to give truly informed consent;
- ensures that the project has adequate resources to achieve its aims. This is especially relevant when researching with/about a population group such as refugee people seeking asylum, who may have many reasons to be wary of becoming involved in research/sharing their stories/describing how they feel, and therefore require a large investment in the early stages of the project for them to become involved. In this way, the 'hard-to-reach' label ceases to function as a catch-all excuse for not involving refugee people seeking asylum;
- describes how to include the involvement of refugee people seeking asylum in developing the research plans for dissemination, and who refugee people seeking asylum want to disseminate to, from the outset;
- conforms to data protection legislation (Data Protection Act 1998);

Methods

Good practice in research projects:

- prepares and supports community/group researchers adequately by creating regular opportunities for them to reflect on their own research activity with experienced and trustworthy colleagues and by integrating opportunities for the development of themselves and their communities/groups through the research;
- uses appropriate methods as determined by participants' preferences;
- is open to exploring different channels for contacting people for their involvement, i.e., beyond the local community/group/centre;
- recognises that words/concepts can have different meanings across languages and that these differences need to be recognised as effecting the research findings;
- articulates researchers' understanding that the use of different methods can position those involved in power relationships with one another, e.g. relying exclusively on unnecessarily technical or complicated jargon to present quantitative/qualitative data;

- uses methods that draw out the differences in ways of seeing, interpreting and acting on the world, i.e., techniques that make it possible for people to define their world in their own terms and do not assume that the researcher is the only/an expert;
- specifies the consequences that methodologies can have on who it is from refugee people seeking asylum communities/groups who do - or do not - have a voice in the research;
- recognises that descriptions of personal experiences are valid in their own right, even if this does not build on prior established knowledge, e.g., eviction into destitution is a new experience for refugee people seeking asylum in Britain and the methods selected for use should be chosen for their capacity to release new knowledge.

Index

A

Acholi London Fellowship 175-6
action learning methods 8, 9
  RAPAR project
    Action Learning Sets 196-7
    criticism of methods 197, 198
  see also participatory action research;
    RAPAR project
advertising for interviewees 83-4, 159
affective indicators of integration 75-6
African culture 32, 191, 193
  see also Somali refugees
age and integration 28
Ajeeb, Mohammed 101
Alexander, C. 86
anonymity of interviewees 26, 30-1, 84
Arab Women's Group 85-6
Asian Muslims in Britain 175-6
Asylum Aid 180
asylum claims
  research on reasons for refusal 141
  see also detention centres; failed asylum
    seekers; newly arrived asylum seekers
Asylum and Immigration Appeals Act
  (1993)(UK) 133
Asylum and Immigration (Treatment of
  Claimants etc) Act (2004)(UK) 177

B

Baha'i refugees 179
Bail for Immigration Detainees 180
Bamber, Helen 173
Beresford, P. 155
bias in research 9, 10
  community representation 107-8, 138-9
biographical research methods 8
  'intellectual autobiography' 46
  Task Force on Integration 24-5
Black, Les 103
Blears, Hazel 106
Blunkett, David 134
Bowes, A. 14
Bradford
  community representatives 98-9, 101-4,
    106, 107, 108
  Muslim faith communities 174-5
Bradstock, A. 139

British Refugee Council 3
British Sign Language (BSL) interpreters
  162-3
Butler, D.S. 57-8

C

Camcorder Guerrillas of Glasgow 178
Campbell, J. 7
Canadian Centre for Victims of Torture
  (CCVT) 89
capacity development research 10-11, 128
Carey-Wood, J. 86
Castles, S. 1
Catholic Bishops' Conference 172
'chain migration' 105
Chambon, A. 80-1, 88-9
CHAP in Salford 118-120, 123-6
chaplaincies in detention centres 169-70,
  173, 180
children
  and domestic violence 193-4
  lack of social space for Somali refugees
    62
  people smuggling 140
Christian communities
  assistance to asylum seekers 171-4,
    176-7, 178, 179
  defining faith communities 174
Church of England chaplaincies in
  detention centres 169-70, 173, 180
Churches Commission on Racial Justice
  177
Churches Regional Commission 174
citizenship: policy and integration 29
Cole, I. 148
collectivism 114
  of RAPAR project 196
communication *see* language issues
community
  deficit model of 10
  diversity in 12
  empowerment in regeneration areas
    111-29
    Salford RAPAR project 117-29,
      183-99
  lack of community space for Somali
    refugees 61-4, 71
  and participatory research 6, 7, 10-11